Strategy through people

Resource-based approaches to strategy have begun to attract a wii
following. This volume takes the ultimate resource: the human resource
and places it centre-stage in a challenging new analysis of business policy
and business growth.

By analysing the ways in which people drive business, the book shifts
the strategic debate beyond the traditional arena of the large corporation
and draws together three previously separate strands of research: entrepreneurship and small/medium-size business studies; human resource
management; and the mainstream debates on corporate strategy. The
result is a powerful new synthesis that shows how internal resourcing
issues shape strategic change.

The book gives a clearer picture of the dynamics of growth and survival
in the small–medium firm sector, recognized as the driving force behind
successful economies such as Germany and Japan. It illuminates the role
played in the strategy process by entrepreneurial individuals, management teams and 'the human resource' as a shaper of strategic options.
Finally, it emphasizes the need for a dynamic 'strategy through people'
rather than the more traditional systems approach typical of large corporations.

Chris Hendry is Centenary Professor in Organizational Behaviour at
City University Business School and Director of the MBA in HRM.
Michael B. Arthur is Professor of Management at Suffolk University,
Boston. **Alan M. Jones** is an Associate Research Fellow in the Centre for
Corporate Strategy and Change, Warwick Business School.

Strategy through people

Adaptation and learning in the
small–medium enterprise

Chris Hendry, Michael B. Arthur and
Alan M. Jones

London and New York

First published 1995
by Routledge
11 New Fetter Lane, London EC4P 4EE

Simultaneously published in the USA and Canada
by Routledge
29 West 35th Street, New York, NY 10001

Typeset in Palatino by
Ponting–Green Publishing Services, Chesham, Bucks
Printed and bound in Great Britain by
Biddles Ltd, Guildford and Kings Lynn

British Library Cataloguing in Publication Data

A catalogue record for this book is available from the
British Library.

Library of Congress Cataloguing in Publication Data
Hendry, Chris, 1947–
    Strategy through people : adaptation and learning in
the small–medium enterprise / Chris Hendry, Michael
B. Arthur, and Alan M. Jones.
        p.   cm.
    ISBN 0–415–11704–6. – ISBN 0–415–11705–4 (pbk.)
    1. Small business–management.   2. Corporate
planning.   3. Strategic planning.   I. Arthur, Michael B.
(Michael Bernard), 1945–   . II. Jones, Alan M. (Alan
Meirion), 1946–   . III. Title.
HD62.7.H47   1994
658.02'2–dc20   94–24394
                                                                      CIP

ISBN 0–415–11704–6
ISBN 0–415–11705–4 (pbk)

For our parents

Contents

Figures

Tables

Acknowledgements

This work has been six years in the making and stems from the collaborative efforts of a number of people and institutions.

First, we are indebted to the Centre for Corporate Strategy and Change at Warwick University which hosted this work originally, and to the Department of Employment which provided the initial funding. We are likewise indebted to City University and Suffolk University for their continuing support.

Second, we owe a great deal of thanks to many individuals who contributed in various ways. These include Andrew Pettigrew, David Storey and Stephen Batstone at Warwick University, for their constant source of ideas and help along the way; Paul Sparrow, at Manchester Business School, for his part in the original conception of the work; Ken Nixon and Jean Webb at the Department of Employment, for their sympathetic help in guiding the work on behalf of the sponsor; and the many who contributed ideas and material at various times, including James Curran, Mike Scott, Mark Dodgson, Peter Senker, Michael Daly, and Robert DeFillippi.

Third, although we cannot name them for reasons of confidentiality, we owe a special debt to the chief executives of the twenty enterprises that provided our case study material, and to the many people in those enterprises who generously gave us their time and candour. We hope this book justifies their cooperation.

Chapter 1

Strategy through people: an introduction

> I was brought up on the theory of the 'economies of scale' – that with industries and firms, just as with nations, there is an inevitable trend, dictated by modern technology, for units to become even bigger.
>
> (E.F. Schumacher, 1973: 64)

WHY THIS BOOK?

Several threads of argument can be woven together to introduce this book. First and foremost, it is concerned with strategy, or more specifically the strategy process, through which firms go about the fundamental business of competing and surviving over time. Second, the book makes explicit the link between the strategy process and the activities of people who influence and implement a firm's unfolding strategy. Third, and most distinctly, the book focuses unequivocally on a unit recognized to be of increasing importance – responsible, for example, for over 80 per cent of total employment in Japan, and for the majority of employment in the UK, USA, and most European countries – namely the small–medium firm or small–medium enterprise.

In assuming this focus we reject two commonplace inferences from the established literature, that 'small–medium firms are less important than large firms' and 'small–medium firms should learn from large firms', and reverse their sentiments. Smaller firms are both critically important in modern-day competitive economies, and often critically different from their larger counterparts. Within the constraints of more limited resources, they have much to teach larger firms, and certainly students of business and management, about the strategy process and operating effectively.

In declaring an interest in the strategy process, we associate this book with a growing body of work concerned with how strategy unfolds (for example, Quinn, 1977; Pettigrew, 1985), and with those economists and management theorists who see the interaction between a firm and the marketplace as complex and multi-faceted. So-called 'rational' models of strategic management, based on an omniscient and omnipotent chief executive as 'the architect of organizational purpose' (Christensen, *et al.*, 1987), can too easily deflect us from the multiple interactions, both within and beyond the firm, through which strategy comes about. To investigate the strategy process is to see a firm's strategy as something emergent rather than preordained, and affected by many factors rather than a few (Mintzberg, 1987). Our main title, *Strategy Through People*, reflects this position.

Our concern with people centres on human resources as a dynamic factor in strategy and organization. Human resources are part of and interdependent with the broader set of resources – including premises and equipment, finance, customer and supplier relations – that both inform and affect strategy as it unfolds (Grant, 1991). Human resources – like other resources – can be harnessed or neglected, built up or run down, over time. As an economic resource, people have a unique capacity not only to animate other economic factors (Zan and Zambon, 1993), but also to develop new capacities through learning and in the way they themselves combine (Penrose, 1959). They differ from other resources in the skills, knowledge and learning – at both individual and firm levels of analysis – which they accumulate. The consequences of today's strategy on the mix of skills, the development of knowledge, and the nature of new learning within the firm will inevitably affect the strategy of tomorrow. Adaptation and learning – signalled in the sub-title of the book – are therefore key processes in a dynamic perspective on small–medium enterprises.

These themes – strategy, people, and small–medium enterprises – are explored in the following pages through evidence derived from a study of twenty organizations, combined with the extensive use of secondary data.

WHY SMALL–MEDIUM ENTERPRISES?

In keeping with the European Community (now European Union) definition, a small–medium enterprise is viewed as a distinct business entity with not more than 500 employees. This is consistent also with US definitions of the 'small business'. As others have done (for example, Cambridge SBRC, 1992), we will in the course of this book use the terms enterprise and firm interchangeably, referring, for example, to 'small–medium enterprises' and 'smaller firms'.

Why focus on this kind of firm? Much management theory continues to emphasize large firms, even though their economic significance has receded. This gives a distorted picture of the industrial landscape, masking the fundamental importance of small–medium firms as a source of employment and as contributors to a dynamic economy. Small firms play a vital role in every local economy where they serve predominantly local needs. There are numerous such firms in service and retail sectors, whose ambitions for growth are limited to achieving a comfortable income for their proprietors, giving independence, and providing them with status in the local community. Such firms, often family-owned, persist through generations and are the bedrock of many provincial towns.

On the other hand, small–medium firms are equally important as a source of innovation and as the seed-bed from which new large firms can grow. As smaller units lacking market power, they offer lessons for managing in an increasingly volatile environment, and provide a focus for economic and management inquiry. In this connection, as the corporate restructuring of the 1980s demonstrated, they already serve as a model for large-firm decentralization.

A source of employment

To take the UK as an example, recent figures estimate small–medium firms employ around 71 per cent of the total workforce and generate the same proportion of financial turnover. Moreover, these figures, based on 1986 data, are up from 57 per cent and 50 per cent respectively just seven years earlier. Discounting very small and self-employment situations of five employees or less, small–medium firms still account for some 53 per cent of all employment (Bannock and Daly, 1990). In the process, the percentage of manufacturing employment in small firms with fewer than 200 employees has recovered from its low point in the years 1968–73 to levels not seen since the 1930s (Stanworth and Gray, 1991).

Similar US evidence shows such firms, excluding sole proprietorships and partnerships, employ about half the total workforce (Brock and Evans, 1989), and firms with fewer than 100 employees account for almost all net job creation (Birch, 1979, 1987). Many European countries show even higher proportions of small–medium firm employment (Storey and Johnson, 1987), while Japan has been reporting for some years that firms with under 300 employees account for over 80 per cent of the workforce – 88 per cent if agricultural workers are included (Chalmers, 1989). Clearly, small–medium firms, not large firms, have become the predominant employer in modern industrial society, and in the West are recovering their historical significance.

Embedded in these impressive statistics are a number of open questions. Do the statistics reflect disguised patterns of cross-ownership and accountability, as some observers would claim for Japanese *keiretsu* firms (Lawrence and Saxonhouse, 1991)? Are there consistent patterns of smaller firm dependency on larger firms that render defunct a notion of separate strategic direction (Imrie, 1986)? Do patterns of low pay and security in smaller versus larger firms imply that the latter provide the better models for social employment (Shearman and Burrell, 1988)? Do shifts in employment patterns merely reflect a shift in the location of jobs through large-firm outsourcing decisions (Shutt and Whittington, 1987)? All these questions are valid, but none deflect the underlying observation that small–medium firms have consistently reasserted themselves in recent years, in a variety of countries, within different employment systems (Loveman and Sengenberger, 1990).

Contributors to a dynamic economy

Several commentators draw a link between the high preponderance of small–medium firms in Japan and the level of adaptiveness and competitiveness of the Japanese economy as a whole (Clark, 1979; Gow, 1987). Japan's automotive industry in particular is deemed more efficient than Western counterparts because of its greater reliance on outside suppliers (Clarke, 1989). Small–medium firms can compete through 'flexible specialisation' and output flexibility. Depending on industry conditions, this can be a source of extra profit or greater survivability in periods of uncertain demand (Piore and Sabel, 1984; Fiegenbaum and Karnani, 1991). Developments in production technology and information processing have negated arguments for economies of scale which previously favoured larger firms (Carlsson, 1984, 1989). At the same time, productivity improvements have been fuelling a shift from manufacturing towards (frequently smaller) service operations (Bowen *et al.*, 1990).

Smaller firms still face a disadvantage in the labour market, where large firms – aided in part by monopolistic or oligopolistic circumstances – have traditionally offered higher pay and job security (Villemez and Bridges, 1988). Smaller firms in the UK are also prone to disproportionate costs through obligatory tax collection, legislative compliance, insurance obligations, and training and educational investments (Bannock and Peacock, 1990), while large firms in the USA enjoy tax subsidies that interfere with employee mobility (Mitchell, 1990). The economic contribution of small–medium firms prevails despite these disadvantages.

Sources of innovation

Small–medium firms are key sources of innovation, much of it the kind of informal, incremental changes smaller units are better equipped to introduce. However, explicit measures of patent registrations also confirm the major contribution to innovation that small firms make (Rothwell, 1986; Acs and Audretsch, 1987; Pavitt *et al.*, 1989), especially in new technologies where they have been playing an increasingly important role in European economies during the 1980s (Rothwell, 1989). In addition, the activities of smaller firms are a force against complacency elsewhere, and thus a spur to innovation in their large firm cousins. Even if on their own small firms are not the decisive innovating force, the behavioural advantages they bring to innovation are a vital complement to the material advantages which large firms possess (Rothwell, 1989).

Orthodox ideas about the growth of the firm have suggested successful innovation leads a firm on a predictable path toward greater size and stability (Quinn and Cameron, 1983). Tending towards the same conclusion, others have suggested that a small number of fast-growth firms are critical to national economies (Storey *et al.*, 1987). However, to presume innovation should lead to growth denies the distinctive advantage of staying small that may have generated innovation in the first place. Licensing and contracting-out are alternative ways of bringing a product or service to market, allowing a firm to stay small and take advantage of other firms' expertise (Furino, 1988). To focus only on fast-growth firms can deflect attention away from the importance of the small–medium firm sector as a whole.

A focus for economic and management inquiry

The concept of strategy provides a link between actions internal to and events external to the firm, and thereby an opportunity to bring economic and managerial perspectives together. However, this opportunity has gone largely unacknowledged as competing approaches on either side of the boundary of the firm have kept the two perspectives apart (Williamson, 1985). We agree with others who seek better integration of competing views (Rumelt *et al.*, 1992). Small firms, lacking market power, encourage greater attention to the use of internal resources in survivability and market adaptation, and to alternative ways of managing external relationships.

Studies of process and of people lead beyond the boundaries of all firms, but especially so in the case of smaller ones. Smaller firms rarely dominate over suppliers, customers or even governments in the way larger firms have been depicted as doing. Smaller firms must build inter-firm relationships, participate in industrial networks, draw on local labour markets, explore new business opportunities and derive new learning with little advantage beyond the raw intelligence and enthusiasm of their members. The emerging notion of the firm as a 'nexus of treaties' (as distinct from the more legalistic notion of a 'nexus of contracts') captures the essence of these activities, as well as implying something about the value of associated trust-building (Aoki, Gustavson and Williamson, 1990).

A model for large firms

The trend in employment levels of large firms has been clearly downward (Storey and Johnson, 1987; Advisory Council on Science and Technology, 1990). Pressure of market forces has brought direct effects, through layoffs, and also indirect effects through corporations such as Xerox choosing to 'Japanize' themselves through promotion of spin-offs (Giles and Starkey, 1988). Among these new firms there is evidence that small spin-offs outperform large ones (Woo *et al.*, 1990). Paradoxically, firms choosing to remain large, such as GE in the USA and Hanson Trust in the UK, have insisted on high levels of autonomy for separate business units. Such decentralization seeks to replicate the small firms' supposed advantages of flexibility and market responsiveness, high managerial motivation and employee identification (Hendry, 1990). The structural arrangements already exist, through widespread existence of separate establishments, for decentralization to go even further (Granovetter, 1984).

These trends have led to a revival of interest in dynamic views of the firm, displacing the belief in large-firm domination (Schumpeter, 1934; Penrose, 1959). Even in 'quasi-firms', where large firms enjoy the subservience of many small subcontractors, or 'non-owned subsidiaries' (Fitzroy, 1989), the potential for independent strategic action by the smaller firm is insufficiently recognized (Sato, 1989). An alternative idea of 'loose coupling' across autonomous, even if centrally owned, subunits is taking hold (Orton and Weick, 1990). The inherent flexibility of loosely coupled units, and consequently of employment arangements associated with them, can leave societies better prepared to deal with shifting demographic and technological variables (Arthur, 1992b).

SMALL–MEDIUM OR SMALL FIRMS?

While extolling the virtues and value of smaller firms, however, it would be foolish to overplay this theme. In terms of international trade, multinationals (or transnationals) are clearly the dominant players. As much as 80 per cent of the UK's manufactured exports, for instance, derive from multinationals (Dicken, 1992). At the same time, the vast majority of so-called 'small firms' – some 96 per cent of all firms in the UK – employ fewer than twenty people (McGann, 1993). This includes 'one-person businesses', while altogether around one in eight of the total UK workforce – nearly 3.4 million – is self-employed (Employment Department, 1992). Much self-employment is economically unstable and the self-employed are a vulnerable group. The same is true of 'micro' small firms. The death rate is greatest among the very smallest firms, and falls away rapidly with increase in sales (Ganguly, 1985). Likewise, some 60 per cent of all new firms registered for VAT 'fail' within three years (Stanworth and Gray, 1991: 11). However, only a relatively small proportion of these (some 15 per cent in the 1990–1 recession) are due to direct insolvency. A much higher proportion disappear by being sold – either to other individuals or into larger enterprises.

The conclusion we take from this is that 'small firms' on their own are not uniquely interesting or significant. While the processes of new firm formation and the support governments can give to them are economically important, survivability and growth are equally so. Nevertheless, academic and policy interest has been over-focused on small firms of under twenty-five employees. Small firm studies have consequently neglected the upper range within the Bolton Report's (1971) definition of 'small' (firms employing up to 200 employees), let alone the more extended focus in European Community, Japanese and American definitions. Our focus in this book, and in the research on which it is based, is therefore emphatically not on 'small firms' but on 'small–medium enterprises'.

The size of 'small' firms

Our research covered twenty small–medium enterprises (SMEs) in the range 25–500 employees, concentrating on firms in the mid-to-upper range of Bolton's definition (1971) and taking in a number having over 200 employees within the European definition of the SME.[1] Table 1.1 provides an overview of these in terms of size and other factors to which we will refer in due course.

Like the Cambridge Small Business Research Centre (1992) study, our sample was thus biased towards a select group of firms in the economy – less than 4 per cent of all firms, according to McGann (1993). Nevertheless, despite this broader reference, fourteen of our firms (or 70 per cent of the sample) were still in the lower range of 25–100 employees, which some researchers have identified as the most promising source for economic growth and job generation (Storey and Johnson, 1987). Complementing them, four of the six largest firms were also among the fastest growing (Fibres, Cable Co., Software Products, and Training International).

Size is, nevertheless, relative to sector – a point often submerged in aggregate statistics. Our Visitor Bureau, for example, with a very small number of full-time staff (around 30, plus 15 part-timers), regarded itself as a large organization in comparison with other convention bureaux. Similarly, two of the firms in the 201–500 range (Cable Co. and Fibres) were the largest of their kind in the UK, although by definition they were SMEs. In contrast, Bread Products was one of a handful of small independent bakeries in an industry dominated by large producers. Yet in terms of employee numbers it was the largest firm in our sample. Much therefore depends on the niche a firm defines for itself – in local, national, and international terms – and who its relevant comparitors/competitors are. Small firm studies frequently lack an appropriate strategic perspective of this kind.

With this in mind, one factor stood out. Almost all our firms saw themselves as either large or of average size in their sector. This reflected

Table 1.1 Case study sample

Travel, Tourism, Leisure
Visitor Bureau (P/I) [44] – West Midlands – 1980
Convention Bureau (P/I) [43–55] – West Scotland – 1984
Hotel Tourist (S) [45] – South East England – 1946
Hotel Heritage (I->S) [43] – West Midlands – 13th Century

Computer Software
Software Products (I) [130] – West Midlands – 1979

Training Consultancy
Training International (I) [130] – West Midlands – 1980
Skills Training (P->I) [60] – East Anglia/Northern England – 1990

Professional Services
Legal Services (I) [35] – West Midlands – 1981

Food and Drink Manufacture
Bread Products (S) [355] – West Midlands – 1962

Mechanical/Electrical Engineering
Aerospace Engineering (I) [61] – West Midlands – 1960
MOD Products (S) [100] – West Midlands – 1832
Pressings (I) [43] – West Midlands – 1826
Clean Air Co. (I) [39] – North Midlands – 1964

Electro-Optical
Glass Discs (S) [62] – North Wales – 1989
Fibres (S) [350] – North Wales – 1983
Optics (S) [93/180*] – North Wales – 1982

Construction
Construction Co. (S**) [270–330] – North East England – 1907
House Co. (S**) [57–81] – North East England – 1981
Cable Co. (I) [247] – North East England – 1968
Architectural Services (I) [81] – North East England – 1962

I = Independent; S = Subsidiary; P = Public Sector
[ ] Figures in brackets show number of employees
* The larger figure is for employees on all sites
** Subsidiaries of the same family construction firm
The final figure is the date of formation.

a significant fact about most of them, and certainly about the more successful. That is, a large number had secured themselves in a small, well-defined market niche, populated by a few firms of like size, or smaller, over which they dominated. In the process, most had done so on the back of one significant market lead or client which had enabled them to grow rapidly. Such phenomena of growth and market positioning are treated at length in Chapter 2.

Age and stage of development

The question of growth bears on a second point related to size – the age and stage of development of a firm. The firms we studied split roughly fifty–fifty between those formed before 1979 and those formed after.[2] Of the latter, many were market leaders in growth markets, and had achieved recognized excellence in their sector in a comparatively short space of time. Thus, although we did not explicitly construct the sample to target high-performing firms, we nevertheless obtained a large number which had enjoyed rapid success and growth (measured in both employee numbers and return on sales).[3]

On the other hand, in spite of the general pattern of success, both high-growth and retrenching firms had had to overcome periods of crisis, and manage difficult transitions. Some newer firms had only recently begun to face such difficulties, while older firms had often experienced repeated crises. (Managing watershed events associated with early growth and later traumas is a recognized major theme among small firms, which we will address in Chapter 3.)

One thing which nevertheless connected the older firms with the newer, fast-growth firms was that all were in some sense successful. All were survivors. The two oldest manufacturing firms, Pressings and MOD Products, for instance, dated back to the second and third decades of the nineteenth century. Since a high proportion of new firms disappear within a year or two of start-up, to reach ten years of existence and more still intact and with over twenty-five employees represents some kind of achievement from which something may be learnt. To survive a century and a half is even more remarkable.

In the preoccupation with new firm formation, it is too easily forgotten that the majority of small firms are not new.[4] Many are also by definition 'small firms' which once were larger entities. MOD Products, for instance, had shrunk from around 500 employees in the 1960s to 100 employees in 1990 as a result of technological improvements and vertical dis-integration through subcontracting non-core activities. The ability of such firms to reinvent themselves is therefore an important phenomenon which life-cycle, 'stages of development' models, preoccupied with the formation process, tend to overlook. Going for a broad-based sample with a wide variation in ages can therefore reveal important patterns of experience.

Larger, and older, small–medium firms may therefore throw light on the central questions of survivability, adaptation, and growth to the direct benefit of small new firms. The over-focus on small start-ups is a denial of the benefits that come from taking an historical view of developmental processes, and the lessons to be gained by studying small firms that have a longer and richer history.

Thus, we know far too little about what becomes of small firms which survive in some modified form. Until the recent survey by the Cambridge Small Business Research Centre (1992) there has been very little data available, for example, on small firms as acquisition targets and as acquirers in their own right. The tendency for the ownership of small firms to pass into other hands, which is largely undocumented, means a processual, developmental view is handicapped by excluding firms from study as soon as they have lost their independence. Our study also deliberately crosses this boundary.

Small firms and large firms

The UK economy, in fact, is unusually polarised between very large firms and very small firms (Bannock and Partners, 1990). In spite of the renascence of the SME sector, the middle range of companies – equivalent to the German *Mittelstand* – employ far fewer people especially in manufacturing. Compared with other European countries such as Germany, this is arguably a source of economic weakness (Hendry, 1994). It is not just that a country needs SMEs for their direct economic contribution, but that competition in the modern economy is increasingly between clusters or constellations of firms who provide services, innovations and product to one another (Best, 1990). It is not an issue of 'small' or 'large' firms, but the interdependency between them. SMEs provide a vital link between the large firm and the very small one.

In a sense, it is the small–medium firm which is the real endangered species, rather than the 'small' firm, and it is therefore important to give special attention to this category.

WHY PEOPLE?

If small–medium firms are important, why in turn should we study the people within them? A simple answer is that people are the actors through whom strategy unfolds, as a result of which firms succeed or fail. However, a more complete answer needs to recognize the diverse roles people play in representing the history and interests of a firm, in providing specific knowledge and expertise, and in contributing to both internal and external communication. There is also a need to capture the dynamic quality of these roles as events unfold, as knowledge and relationships change, and as the strategic positioning of the firm inevitably alters. People act, among other things, as owners, as entrepreneurs, as sources of skill and expertise, as collaborators, as participants in network and learning activities, and as agents of their own careers, all of which have a particular flavour in the small–medium firm setting.

Ownership and the small firm

The purist tradition of small firm research, in keeping with the pre-occupation with start-ups, assumes small firms are owner-managed. By definition almost, the person heading up the firm is then an entrepreneur. If we seek to understand strategic processes in small firms, this seems unduly restrictive.

People as entrepreneurs are credited with special qualities, such as strengths in judgement (Casson, 1982), a 'will to conquer' (Schumpeter, 1934) or a 'need for achievement' (McClelland, 1961), through which they succeed in founding new firms. Founding entrepreneurs may subsequently precipitate powerful cultural and family dynamics that affect the evolution of their firms for better or worse (Goffee and Scase, 1985; Handler, 1990). A resistance to losing control, for instance, is widely seen as holding back small firm growth, suggesting founding entrepreneurs, once successful, desert the very qualities for which they were once celebrated (Firnstahl, 1986). Economic renewal depends then on the rise to leadership of 'New Men' (Schumpeter, 1934).

Independent ownership certainly has important implications for the strategy of small firms, involving such issues as funding, ambitions for growth, expected returns, and time horizons. On the other hand, there are also widely recognized life cycle effects in the evolution of ownership patterns, in which increasing company age and size go hand in hand with dilution of ownership.[5] As a result, even many so-called independent small firms are not strictly 'owner-managed'. The line between independent and non-independent firms (i.e. subsidiaries) becomes less real, therefore, as firms age and grow.

The industrial restructuring of recent years reinforces the need to take a broader view beyond the influence or legacy of a single actor. Thus, behind the present forms of ownership in our sample, in both independent and subsidiary firms alike, there was considerable volatility. The recent history of the manufacturing firms in particular reflected the vicissitudes of the 1980s – a period of extensive industrial restructuring, when firms both large and small were susceptible to takeovers, mergers, reorganization by outside interests, disintegration and closure. Equally, a number of the independent service firms (significantly among the fastest-growing in the sample) had seen large companies taking shares in them and injecting capital during the relative boom of the late 1980s.[6]

By selecting in the first instance on the basis of size, our sample of firms were not exclusively owner-managed, although in deference to convention we ensured they constituted the larger part.[7] Again, the more varied nature of the sample exposed greater complexity and variety in strategic processes than a concentration on independent firms might have done, especially in revealing processes of adaptation (as we describe in Chapter 4).

Who is the entrepreneur?

The complexities of ownership and control invoke a critical theme in the discussion of strategy and people. This is the question of entrepreneurship. Is it appropriate to talk about chief executives who are not owners as 'entrepreneurs' when they cannot freely commit an organization's resources? Conversely, should one call a person who sets up a business and continues to own it 'an entrepreneur' even though the entrepreneurial impulse may have waned and he or she has settled for just a steady income? In Britain, for practical purposes these issues are normally avoided by talking about the 'business owner-manager'. As the discussion of ownership suggests, however, this raises other problems.

In our sample of firms, some of the most proactive, 'entrepreneurial' chief executives were in fact salaried managers.[8] Salaried managers in large firms also often command far more substantial resources to dispose of 'entrepreneurially' with far fewer practical contraints. (On this point, however, it may be that 'entrepreneurship' is better defined as, and results from, having to manage with minimal resources – that is, managing 'parsimoniously' (Starr and MacMillan, 1991).) Either way, the nature and extent of control, rather than ownership as such, is likely to be the more critical factor.

In practice, entrepreneurship may be exercised by anyone according to Schumpeter's (1934) definition of someone who 'carries out new combinations' – a view also implicit in Hebert and Link's (1989) reference to 'someone who specializes in taking responsibility for and making judgemental decisions that affect the location, the form, and the use of goods, resources, or institutions'. Other more generalised definitions, such as Kirzner's (1985) 'opportunity-taking' behaviour, lead to a similar conclusion.

Most studies of entrepreneurial traits and behaviour, however, have tended to restrict their focus to business owners starting their own business, implicitly associating entrepreneurship with direct ownership. It has been left to economists and to strategy theorists like Mintzberg (1990) to take a broader view and suggest that the hired manager is also a potential entrepreneur. Thus, many new firms have been spun-off by large firms rather than grown from one person's enterprise, and many established firms have been subjected to efforts of 'intrapreneurship' aimed at rekindling risk-taking and innovation (Burgleman and Sayles, 1985).

Focus on the single person, owner or hired manager, can obscure an even more fundamental issue, however. That is to say, the tendency to equate entrepreneurship with the individual detracts from the 'entrepreneurial process' itself (Hofer and Schendel, 1978). As a result, there has been the beginnings of a shift in focus and language in recent years to include notions of 'corporate entrepreneurship' (Guth and Ginsberg, 1990;

Sandberg, 1992) and 'collective (or team) entrepreneurship' (Reich, 1987; Eisenhardt, 1989; Timmons, 1990). Thus, Timmons (1990: 15–17) argues that what venture capitalists look for is a 'lead entrepreneur' and a team:

> A substantial amount of research, as well as practical experience, confirms that a team grows a business while a solo entrepreneur makes a living.

The value of a more team-centred view of entrepreneurship, which takes in relations between a 'lead entrepreneur' and collaborators, is clearly relevant where a large parent company puts in a professional team of managers to start up a new small company; or where large firms seek to rejuvenate themselves through 'intrapreneurship'; or where, in the case of small firms, survivors have had to reinvent themselves a number of times over (as in the case of MOD Products). 'Team entrepreneurship' may have special relevance in the smaller firm (even though it may be inhibited by ownership dynamics), since people there typically enjoy little of the 'slack' attributed to large firms (Cyert and March, 1963), and therefore may be more collectively motivated to succeed.

In particular, as we will argue in Chapters 4 and 7, broadening the management team – which often means creating an effective management team for the first time – is a necessary step for many small firms in realizing a change in strategy through raising the level and coherence of strategic thinking. Existing managers may need to be prodded and developed to think strategically, but nevertheless it shows that the 'lead (or founding) entrepreneur' has recognized his or her own inability alone to encompass all that a change of strategy entails. Other studies similarly have identified the importance of management teams in successful transitions (Macmillan *et al.*, 1987; Stevenson and Jarillo, 1990). From this point of view, adaptation and renewal is strategic change is entrepreneurship.

For such reasons as these, in company with economists like Schumpeter (1934) and von Mises (1949), it is important to define entrepreneurship, first, as a function or process, rather than tied to one specific person only; and second, again as Schumpeter (1949) did, to retain the idea of entrepreneurship as potentially a cooperative process. Such a processual or team-centred view of entrepreneurship will animate many of the subsequent chapters.

Throughout this book, we will therefore tend to refer to the person who most symbolises and identifies with the firm's entrepreneurial activities as the 'lead entrepreneur' (usually the CEO). Sometimes, more precisely when hierarchy or ownership is implied, we will refer to the 'founding entrepreneur'. Although such expressions may be cumbersome, it is important to discriminate explicitly between the person who happens to head up the firm and the activity of entrepreneurship which may be shared with or exercised by others.[9] At other times we will explicitly signal a shared leadership role by referring to 'team entrepreneurship' or some similar term.

Sources of skill and expertise

Turning to the generality of employees, people are of fundamental importance for the skills and expertise, or 'human capital', they bring to the firm. National systems of vocational and professional qualifications, and of training and education to meet them, provide frameworks within which individual firms operate. However, they are systems from which smaller firms have often been excluded, being viewed as 'peripheral' rather than 'core' employers, while larger, more powerful counterparts have determined occupational arrangements (Thomas, 1989). In the same way, the detailed specification and measurement of skills, through job analysis and performance appraisal, have been more characteristic of larger firms. In these areas, training and human resource management advice to smaller firms has been monotonous in its prescription of large-firm solutions (Arthur and Hendry, 1990).

However, recent government efforts, in both the UK and USA, to make policy-making and delivery of training occur at local levels, modelled after German Chambers of Craft Industries, suggest a new level of influence over skill specification for the smaller firm. While smaller firms have a strategic advantage in being able to respond more flexibly to near-term changes in demand (Fiegenbaum and Karnani, 1991), they may also respond more quickly and flexibly to new skill requirements. Through on-the-job training, on which for want of greater resources they have often had to rely, and teamwork, they are adept at developing new amalgams of skill to respond to new niche market opportunities (Hendry *et al.*, 1991c).

Collaborators

Beyond the direct skills they contribute, employees are prospective collaborators in the pursuit of a firm's goals. The point is emphasized by Western interest in Japanese management practice, and the contrast provided between impersonal scientific management traditions and more inclusive team-centred approaches (Schein, 1989). Popular programmes in quality assurance, competitive benchmarking, and changing organization cultures all reflect an underlying belief in the participative employee. So too do payment systems, which today more frequently include profit-sharing or employee-ownership components intended to reinforce collaborative efforts (Rosen and Young, 1991).

That small–medium firms provide a superior context for shared goals is fundamental to the 'small is beautiful' thesis (Schumacher, 1973) (although we reflect more critically upon this later on). Recent explorations in 'high-involvement' and 'high-commitment' management argue for a more 'communitarian' view of employment relationships in firms, and the advantages of small firms in encouraging this (Lawler, 1986, 1992). While landmark studies of Japanese management (for example, Ouchi, 1981) tended to emphasize large firm practices, the great majority of that country's employee participation in fact occurs in small–medium firms, without promises of lifetime employment these firms may be unable to keep (Koike, 1988). Likewise, the Mondragon worker cooperative community in northern Spain, which has flourished for many years while insisting on a maximum firm size of 500 employees (Whyte and Whyte, 1988), is an exemplar of employee ownership among SMEs.

Participants in network and learning activities

Beyond collaboration among members within a firm lies the issue of communication across firms. The growing appreciation that industrial markets function through a 'dynamic network' of changing, inter-firm relationships highlights a broader role for employees than traditional views of organization have allowed (Miles and Snow, 1986; Johanson and Mattsson, 1988; Reddy and Rao, 1990). Increasingly, people are expected to cultivate effective relationships with suppliers, customers and alliance partners that not only serve short-term goals but also make new knowledge available to their firm (Prahalad and Hamel, 1990). The parallel internal task of calibrating, interpreting and learning from this new knowledge underlies a firms's future competitiveness in a changing environment (Daft and Weick, 1984; Lounamaa and March, 1987; Hendry, 1994).

The emergent reality that most firms are small–medium firms lends a new significance to networking activities, and to 'horizontal coordination' across firms, as opposed to 'vertical coordination' within them (Hellgren and Stjernberg, 1987). Growth in the small-firm-dominated services sector is making face-to-face employee-customer relations now commonplace, in contrast with the remoteness of traditional arrangements in factory and office (Bowen and Schneider, 1988). However, even within large manufacturing firms, the acknowledged locus of organizational learning is becoming the individual, small establishment (Nelson and Winter, 1982). In such settings, even when employees are not connected to outside constituencies, their knowledge, and readiness to absorb new learning, depends increasingly on relationships they have developed inside the firm (Pucik, 1988) through networking.

Networking, moreover, is not confined to Person A in one organization linking across to Person B in another organization. People move between organizations and take their personal networks with them. A neglected but significant phenomenon, therefore, is the extent to which founding entrepreneurs and managers in small–medium firms move between organizations, from large to small–medium, and from small–medium to small–medium firm. As innovation studies have revealed, such movements are important ways of transferring learning and influencing strategy.

Agents of their own careers

Careers, in the basic sense of unfolding work experiences over time, occur for all working people (Arthur *et al.*, 1989). In their pursuit of employment, job changes, recognition and social support, people act out their career interests within and across the boundaries of individual firms. Career interests are therefore in continuing tension with a firm's strategic interests (Mody, 1989), representing both threats, through the potential loss of important knowledge, and opportunities, through the acquisition of new capabilities. The advantage has been traditionally assumed to lie with large firms, who could command loyalty in return for the job security and career opportunities their entrenched hierarchies provided. In contrast, smaller firms have been seen as offering fewer career rewards, with limited scope for an internal labour market (Siebert and Addison, 1991), putting them therefore at a strategic disadvantage.

However, if only through force of circumstance, most people are now pursuing their careers in smaller firms. Indeed, Tom Peters has publicly advised young people that they will enjoy greater stimulus and career opportunities by doing so (Peters, 1991). The new circumstances call upon people to drop their dependence on particular jobs and hierarchies (Weick and Berlinger, 1989), and to develop career goals across a series of firms anchored in the pursuit of employability and reputation (Kanter, 1989). A dramatic example of such new career forms in operation is the revival of the semiconductor industry among new firms in California's Silicon Valley (Saxenian, 1990). The growth in temporary and part-time positions at all levels of employment leaves the smaller firm no longer at a particular disadvantage in relation to large firms, while offering opportunities for smaller firms to capitalize on a freer labour market (Kirkpatrick, 1988).

Sectoral and local labour markets

Skills, learning through networks, and career moves tend to be focused in two ways – through the sector a firm operates in and the local labour market.

As Table 2.1 (p. 36) indicates, the sample of firms studied comprised a variety of sectors, split roughly 50: 50 between manufacturing (plus construction) and services.[10] The specific grouping of firms into ostensible sectors, however, is more a matter of convenience which turns out to have rather limited analytical significance.[11] This is often the case in comparative studies, but rarely acknowledged. The virtue of the sample in sectoral terms lies in the diversity of sectors and firms it covers (dispelling the idea that small firms are some kind of homogeneous group), rather than in particular opportunities to make comparisons according to Standard Industrial Classification (SIC) categories. This then allows for the identification of theoretical patterns which transcend 'sectors', grounded, for instance, in different types of production/service system. A good example of this is the classification and analysis of skill supply systems and strategies in Chapter 5.

Overlapping with sectoral linkages and career paths is the local labour market. In constructing the sample we aimed to capture a number of definable local labour markets (LLMs). Conventional wisdom and recent writing on 'industrial districts' suggests two particular circumstances pertaining to local labour markets are relevant for the ability of smaller firms to resource their skills.

One is the situation where a locality is dominated by a large employer. The larger employer supposedly provides a reservoir of trained people which the smaller firm can pick up from time to time. This may apply even where the large and small firm are in different lines of business, but make use of certain common specialist skills such as maintenance workers and engineers. In this way, the smaller firm can avoid responsibility for training to basic and advanced skill levels. The second situation is where there is a concentration of similar firms. This expands the general supply of common skills.

These two situations can clearly overlap in that a large firm may generate a cluster of smaller suppliers who share a common skill base. With the phenomenon of 'industrial districts' (Brusco, 1986; Lazarson, 1988; Antonelli, 1989) in mind, we were particularly attracted to the possibility of capturing examples of the latter situation where sector and locality overlap.

Such considerations were reinforced by research showing the significance of local networks and markets for small firms' activities (Sweeny, 1987; Aydalot, 1987), often involving unsuspected elements of cooperation (Pyke, 1988). At the same time, the training support system in the UK was restructured in the late 1980s from a sectoral to a local basis, with Training and Enterprise Councils (TECs) modelled on Private Industry Councils (PICs) in the USA and the regional Chambers of Craft Industries in Germany.

Within a range of labour market situations, we therefore sought to explore the nature and relative influence of such networks and interdependencies through concentrations of same-sector firms in the one locality. As a result, there are particular concentrations in three areas of the UK – North Wales, the Midlands, and the North-East covering both new and traditional sectors.

We have to say, however, that our ambition to sample the industrial district phenomenon was disappointing.[12] This may simply be a function of too diffuse a sample. On the other hand, the decline of traditional industrial districts and the failure to grow new ones, as we discuss in Chapter 8, may be a serious and widespread problem.

The counterpart to the industrial district, with its intensive concentration of skills, is the situation most of our firms actually found themselves in. As a result of the shakeout in the British economy during the 1980s and the decline of large plants, none of our sample firms were in local labour markets dominated by a large employer off whom they could feed. The problem for a number of firms was that they were isolated in their local labour market, neither able to recruit from similar firms, nor part of a cluster of firms that might act as an employment magnet and encourage the local education and training system to provide for their distinctive needs. Bread Products, for example, was particularly vulnerable in this way.

In this respect, a critical aspect of labour markets is the degree of 'closure' in skills – that is, the extent to which people are able to make job moves on a sectoral and/or local basis. The more specialized the skills, the more important the sector as a source of recruitment: the less specialized, the greater the importance of the local labour market. Such considerations play a vital part in skill formation and in firms' employment strategies. Since smaller firms may rely disproportionately on local labour markets, industrial districts are an efficient way of promoting skill development and overcoming the problem of inertia through people's reluctance to uproot themselves from their community.

Such issues have important implications for the maintenance and development of business strategies in smaller firms, and strong cultural overtones in the extent to which labour markets in countries like the USA and UK assume relatively greater employee mobility compared with Germany, Italy, and France.

Recognizing employees

These reflections on the roles that employees may take, which are important for the functioning of SMEs, point to a fundamental criticism of small firm studies. In the fascination with lone entrepreneurs, the workforce in smaller firms has been comparatively neglected. When employees have been taken into account, they have often been seen through the same lens which accords primacy to the founding entrepreneur. That is, as the employer would like to see them – docile, cooperative, willing to make material sacrifices through lower pay, for the satisfaction of working in a warm, friendly environment.

Thus, Ingham (1970) saw those working in smaller firms being governed by a 'non-economistic expressive orientation', while those with more instrumental-material orientations self-selected themselves into large firms. This kind of reasoning says more about the conceptual framework of industrial sociology at that time, however, than anything about real small firms. Nevertheless, it was perpetuated by The Bolton Report (1971), prevailed for some years, and is still often repeated on both sides of the Atlantic.[13]

The idealised view of the small firm and of employee motivations and relations has since been eroded by a variety of evidence. It is not employees who simply self-select: small firm employers are quite choosey about who they take on, while employees are often simply glad to take whatever job is on offer with whomever, and may readily move when other opportunities arise (Curran and Stanworth, 1979a). Loyalty and tenure should not be confused. The absence of strikes should not be surprising, moreover, given the difficulties for trade unions to organize in small firms (Curran and Stanworth, 1979b). This is compounded by the problem of labour instability which is in fact higher than in large firms. In any case, strikes are not the only measure of conflict and employee dissatisfaction. The employer in the small firm is in a position to exercise strong informal controls and discipline, which is why labour turnover may be the only option left for expressing conflict. Even employers do not take so sanguine a view of their employees as the earlier image suggested, and constantly complain about the difficulty of finding people with the right attitudes and skills (Scott et al., 1989).

While greater realism has therefore been introduced, two biases persist. First, the view of employment relations in small firms has been largely animated by an implicit comparison with large firms, in terms of formality versus informality (Rainnie, 1989). Early on this was seen to the small firm's advantage; latterly it has been seen as a 'problem' in which the employee is unfairly exposed to arbitrary control (Ford, 1982; Roberts, 1986; Rainnie, 1989). This is a distraction, however, from simply seeing the way small firms do things as different and maybe equally valid (Aitkenhead et al., 1992). The rise of human resource management (HRM) risks introducing a variant of this by confusing informal management with the deliberate practice of HRM (Marlow and Patton, 1993).

The second bias, which comes out of this interest in comparing large and small firms, is the predominant focus on employment relations and industrial relations. Employee relations, however, are essentially derivative to the primary need, which is to secure an adequate and appropriate skill supply. An aim of this book is to reframe the study of employment in the small firm in terms of people as a resource. The issue is how the small firm meets its strategic resource requirements within a labour market that it does not fully control.

The beginnings of such a perspective can be found in Rainnie (1989), where he connects employment relations to the economic circumstances of the small firm; in Scott *et al.* (1989), where they discriminate between the career and job orientations of scientific and technical versus other employees; and in Goss (1991), who introduces a fuller appreciation of the employer's dependency on the skills and commitment of employees under different conditions.

What is needed, then, is a perspective which takes account of the strategic imperatives driving the firm, in conjunction with a view of people in a labour market that is partly autonomous and partly structured by the activities of firms. This brings out the part played by people as 'input' to and 'output' from strategy, and the patterns of 'environmental dependence' and 'environmentally influencing' – a theme we develop at length in Chapters 5 and 6 and to which we now briefly turn.

STRATEGY AND PEOPLE

Two related distinctions can be drawn from the above set of roles which people fulfil, each of them relevant to the way the strategy of a firm unfolds.

The first distinction concerns people's roles within a firm as input to, or as an output from strategy. As an input to strategy, the person is part of the existing resource base from which strategy is drawn. Most obviously, this occurs through the specific skills and knowledge people bring to a firm and the way these are utilized. This is how we usually think about human resources. However, our discussion above points to a broader interpretation, where people's levels of commitment, network contacts and relationships, presence within internal learning systems, and participation in broad-based entrepreneurial efforts are part of a larger set of resources that can contribute to how strategy unfolds. The way people come together in a firm itself represents a new and unique combination in which competitive advantage is grounded and from which experience and learning develops (Penrose, 1959).

As an output from strategy, the person is treated as part of the changing resource base being prepared for the future. Again, most obviously, this occurs through specific investments in new skills and knowledge through training and development. Again, though, there is a broader truth, whereby the development of relationships with others – fellow workers, professional colleagues, suppliers, customers and so on – not only contributes to contemporary objectives and tasks, but provides the basis for future learning.

The second distinction concerns the relationship between the person and the firm, and the external environment. Both person and firm can be conceived as influencing and influenced by the environment – as free actors and as environmentally determined in their actions; as entrepreneurially acting on the environment and constrained within patterns of industry maturity.

The former presents itself in our image of entrepreneurship and in successful teams in sales, production, and services that make a difference to the company's welfare. Concepts of networking and inter-firm collaboration reflect a belief that people can affect a firm's control over its environment.

In contrast, the view of the firm as a product of its environment suggests a different pattern. Here, people may be seen as making choices about taking employment, expressing preferences and developing careers, over which the single firm – and most especially the smaller firm – has little control. The firm, buffeted by external forces, reacts by instinct and habit in order to survive. Strategy from this standpoint stems much more from outside forces than it does from determinations made within the firm.

Both sets of distinctions are important to our purpose. While the 'person as input' and 'person as output' viewpoints can be seen as dominating alternative views of strategic human resource management (Hendry, 1991), events in any firm are likely to reveal a mixture of the two. People recruited for one job may be switched for expediency to another. Insights gained or relationships inadvertently formed through one experience may prove valuable in another situation. Many current ideas about team building and quality assurance rely on incidental benefits accruing as a by-product of formal arrangements.

The distinction between people and firms as influencing and influenced by their environment is reflected in 'strategic choice' and 'environmental determinist' views of how strategy unfolds (Hrebiniak and Joyce, 1985). Again, events are likely to reveal a mixture of both, as demonstrated recently in the case of young semiconductor firms (Eisenhardt and Schoonhaven, 1990). Strategic efforts may not have the results intended, but may open up new, previously unforeseen opportunities. Environmental impacts, such as the unexpected loss of a key customer, may precipitate fresh efforts to develop knowledge in new product or customer areas. Chance experiences give rise to interpretations that lead to further consequences (Giddens, 1979).

THE USE OF CASE STUDIES

To learn more about the interplay between these distinctions, and thereby more about how small–medium firms succeed, calls for in-depth investigation of how strategy unfolds. However, such investigation has been rare in the small firm sector. Specialist journals have either emphasized a 'black box' view insensitive to the inner workings of the small firm (the tendency in the UK), or have pressed normative assumptions that smaller firms should imitate the comprehensive – and potentially stultifying –

management approaches of large firms (the tendency in the US) (Arthur and Hendry, 1990). There is a clear gap in our knowledge of how 'strategy through people' unfolds, for most people, and almost all firms, in present-day economies.

Instead, the dominant methodology of inquiry with small firms has been the survey method. Starting from a position where there was a need to accumulate some basic evidence by counting phenomena, and encouraged by the volatility of the sector to constantly update figures, the first question asked of any study tends to be 'how representative is it of the sector as a whole?' This tends to be detrimental to exploring the kind of questions addressed in this book. The obsession in the small firm literature with statistical sampling of a minute kind we see as a distraction from more fundamental questions concerning the phenomena of development and growth.

In contrast, case study research, with its focus on historical processes and real-life settings, can reveal the interaction between strategy and the people of an organization, which broader survey approaches fail to register. This book relies, then, on case studies with the aim of breaking new ground in this area. Although the research process is therefore important, rather than dwell on it here, the reader is referred to Appendix A (p. 227) for a detailed account of the background to the project and the methods used in developing the cases. Appendix B (p. 231) in turn provides a cameo of each case organization.

THE CHAPTERS THAT FOLLOW

The structure of the rest of the book is as follows. Two broad themes are discernable – the first emphasizing strategic positioning, adaptation and change; the second, the use of people in these processes. The first part of the book (Chapters 2–4) traces the broad strategic theme of how small firms position themselves, encounter crises, adapt and grow. The second part (Chapters 5–7) considers the role of people in these processes and in their labour market context.

This structure attempts to build awareness of how small–medium firms position themselves strategically before addressing the people implications. However, the distinction is not a sharp one, since the very nature of the strategy process makes the two themes inseparable. Thus, the 'strategy through people' theme flows through all of this book, as well as being highlighted in the final summary chapter (8).

Summarizing each chapter more fully, in Chapter 2 we provide an overview of how small–medium firms position themselves strategically, notably through exploitation of niche markets, customer relationships, and networking. In the process, we explore the role of the 'lead' entrepreneur, the development of skills, and the problem of gaining employee commitment. This leads on to two general forms of strategic change and renewal, through crisis and adaptation. Chapter 3 picks up the issue of crisis, its character and causes, and how it can contribute to learning and change. Chapter 4 then turns to the issue of ongoing adaptation, and identifies seven approaches to adaptation which were observable in the research. Each of these seven approaches has different implications for the use of resources, and especially human resources.

These chapters signal a variety of issues for people. An adopted strategy carries implications for a firm's investments in skills – the recruitment of employees and their development through training. This is the focus of Chapter 5. All firms, but notably smaller firms, are dependent on securing and developing resources, especially skills, for the fulfilment of business strategies – that is, they are 'resource-dependent'. Seven strategies of skill supply are described, in order to bring out the relationship of the small firm to its labour market and the means it uses to develop skills (including the contrast between formal training and the less visible, but often strategically critical, on-the-job training). This prepares the way for considering the tension between individual learning and learning for the firm. Chapter 6 focuses on individual learning and highlights the 'free agency' of a worker's career, anchored in occupational learning and opportunities for self-development in the firm. Chapter 7 shifts the focus back into the firm and reconnects to earlier strategic themes through the treatment of 'organizational learning', based in teams and work-based 'communities of practice' (Brown and Duguid, 1991). The concern here is with how learning is integrated into the firm, and with what consequences.

Chapter 8 offers our conclusions in which we connect our analysis of strategy and people in small firms to wider issues of economic change. The changing shape of modern economies, evidenced by notions of the 'flexible firm' and 'industrial districts', and the projection of these into the next century, has critical implications for how small firms make and implement strategy and how people develop the skills firms need to draw on.

WHO SHOULD READ THIS BOOK?

This book, we hope, will appeal to a number of audiences. At one level it has to be credible in terms of small firms themselves. It should be of interest, then, to all those who make a special study of small–medium firms, scholars, students, and policy makers alike, while challenging the limited focus this work has often had. We aim to expand the appreciation of issues about strategy and people, while reflecting the diversity of small firms which has also often been neglected.

Equally, the book is addressed to those in the strategy field. Many of the key debates there may be illuminated by evidence from smaller firms where strategic processes are more visible. This includes the respective contributions of entrepreneurial individuals, management teams, and the 'human resource' as a shaper of strategic options. Most of the chapters are framed around a key theme in strategy and small firm research, with detailed coverage of relevant literature. The book should appeal, therefore, to students looking for a comprehensive account of key issues and to scholars engaged in current debates.

A third group are those who take a specialist interest in human resource management (HRM). Too often the subject matter of HRM is the systems that human resource managers manage, not people at work. There is also little appreciation of people within a labour market and of the training and skills context on which firms are dependent. From this point of view, it is vital to build bridges between strategy and HRM to highlight human resource processes, including the development of skills. At the same time, HRM is over-focused on large firms where HR systems prevail. An appreciation of how smaller firms do things, on their own terms, is overdue.

Finally, by locating the strategy and people issues for small firms in the wider economic environment and current processes of economic re-structuring and change, we hope to make a contribution to the evolving debate about the 'new economic order'. This has implications for how policy makers, the research and training infrastructure, and larger firms value and support the diversity and dynamism of small–medium firms, and their overall place in the economic and employment milieu.

NOTES

1 The twenty firms in our sample fell into four broad categories:

Number of employees	Number of SMEs
25–50	7
51–100	7
101–200	2
201–500	4

The sampling frame therefore differed from Cambridge SBRC (1992) who defined four categories – micro firms (less than 10 employees), small (10–99), medium (100–199), and larger (200–499) – and thus included 'micro' firms.

Among the smallest (with 25–50 employees) were all the travel and tourist businesses – Visitor Bureau, Convention Bureau, Hotel Tourist, Hotel Heritage – plus Legal Services, and Pressings and Clean Air Co. in the engineering sector. The preponderance of service firms among the smallest is typical. The next group (51–100 employees) comprised Skills Training; Aerospace Engineering and MOD Products in engineering; Glass Discs and Optics in the electro-optical sector; and House Co. and Architectural Services in construction. Those in the range 101–200 were arguably under-represented, comprising just Software Products and Training International, although MOD Products is on the margin and if we include employees on a second site Optics would also be here. The largest group (201–500) consisted of two manufacturing firms (Bread Products and Fibres) and two construction firms (Construction Co. and Cable Co.).

2 Almost half the sample – nine firms comprising Visitor Bureau, Convention Bureau, Software Products, Training International, Legal Services, Glass Discs, Fibres, Optics, and House Co. – were founded since 1979, while one organization (Skills Training), originally formed in 1919, was privatized in 1990 and reborn under a change of ownership. This new firm formation reflects the emergence of new sectors (travel and tourism, opto-electronics, and computer software) and new opportunities in established sectors (Training International). Another five (Bread Products, Aerospace Engineering, Clean Air Co., Cable Co. and Architectural Services) date from the 1960s, having originated in the same way from changing markets and technologies. For example, Aerospace Engineering was formed to supply parts of fuel systems for jet engines for the expanding civil aircraft industry.

3 Table 1.2 shows the profile of the twenty firms in terms of their growth and decline. However, employment growth/decline is misleading (as the example of MOD Products illustrates). So is short-run profitability. Sales growth is more reliable. On this basis, while the relative performance of most SMEs in Table 1.2 stays the same, Pressings and Clean Air Co. also become fast-growth companies, each having doubled its sales over a 3–5 year period.

Table 1.2 Employment growth and decline in the sample of SMEs, 1984–89

Number of employees	Stable/Declining (up to 50%)	Medium growth (more than 50%)	Fast growth
25–50	Hotel Tourist Hotel Heritage Pressings	Clean Air Co.	Visitor Bureau Convention Bureau Legal Services
51–100	Skills Training MOD Products	Aerospace Engineering House Co. Architectural Services	Glass Discs Optics
101–200			Software Products Training International
201–500	Bread Products Construction Co.		Fibres Cable Co.

The sample also had a high proportion of seven SMEs (or 35 per cent) engaged in export – Optics, Fibres, Glass Discs, Software Products, Training International, Clean Air Co., and Pressings. Each had begun to export only since 1985 and all were expanding their export activity rapidly.

4 Within the limitations of sample size, our sample broadly reflects the age distribution of small firms in the UK – the 55 per cent of our firms formed since 1979 approximating to the Cambridge SBRC (1992) sample, where just under 50 per cent of firms had been formed since 1980 (their large sample, however,

ensuring a more even spread across the age range). These figures also correspond closely to figures for the USA, where over 57 per cent of 5,421,228 reported
firms were more than eleven years old (Report of the President, 1990: 158).

5 The Cambridge SBRC (1992: 9–13) survey traces ownership and life cycle
   patterns in its sample of 2,028 independent companies. One thing to emerge
   is the large proportion of chief executives who hold less than one per cent of
   the stock (probably indicating they are employees themselves). This becomes
   more common, as firms age and grow, within medium and large firms (defined
   as those with 100–199 and 200–499 employees respectively). Moreover, in a
   substantial proportion of the larger firms (18.5 per cent) the boards themselves
   held less than one per cent of stock. As the authors themselves comment, 'if
   board control of the stock is to be taken as a *sine qua non* of membership of the
   SME sector, a large proportion of firms which meet SME employment
   definitions would fail to qualify'. (Cambridge SBRC, 1992: 12).

6 A number of case examples illustrate these processes:

   • Optics was a merger of three businesses with very different histories. The
     oldest part was 120 years old, while the newest was founded in 1982 by three
     employees from the Pilkington company setting up on their own. By 1984,
     the company they had formed had over-extended itself and was in financial
     trouble. This led to its being taken over by a holding company which had
     already acquired two related firms in an effort to put together a modern
     electro-optics business.
   • MOD Products, after 150 years of independence, also lost its independence
     in 1982, to a privately owned holding company with world-wide interests.
   • In contrast, Aerospace Engineering had been part of a family business with
     mechanical engineering and electrical interests. In the early 1980s, it had
     been taken over by an investment consortium and split up. The engineering
     business was then bought out by the production director in 1985, at which
     point it reverted to private family ownership.

   Among the service companies attracting outside investment was Software
   Products, with two major insurance companies who were customers putting
   in money to aid product development, in exchange for seats on the Board. More
   emphatically, the founder of Cable Co. had just sold half his stock to an
   investment company, which planned to put together a group of specialist
   construction firms and float the whole as a public company.

   A third group – comprising Training International (80 per cent owned by
   two brothers, but with products licensed from its Danish parent), Glass Discs
   (a wholly owned subsidiary) and Fibres (an Anglo–American joint venture) –
   were set up with considerable front-end capital investment:

   • Fibres, for instance, was the most highly capitalized firm in the sample
     (although it kept exact figures secret to conceal the entry costs from potential
     competitors). As a joint venture, it drew on the technology developed by its
     American parent and the market knowledge of its British parent. In seven
     years, it had become the largest European producer of optical fibres, and the
     third largest in the world. It also displayed the greatest degree of formality
     in its human resource policies and practices, including the most thorough
     approach to training.

7 In all, the sample comprised three partnerships (Legal Services, Architectural
   Services, Skills Training); eight private firms where an individual or family
   owned 50 per cent or more of the shares (Construction Co., House Co.,
   Pressings, Clean Air Co., Aerospace Engineering, Training International,

Software Products, Cable Co.); four wholly owned subsidiaries (Optics, MOD Products, Glass Discs, Bread Products); two single establishments of a larger organization (Hotel Tourist, Hotel Heritage); one joint venture (Fibres); and two public sector companies limited by guarantee (Visitor Bureau, Convention Bureau).

In sum, thirteen of these were privately owned, including two (MOD Products and Bread Products) that were subsidiaries of family firms. However, two (Hotel Tourist, Hotel Heritage) were not strictly firms, but establishments (although the latter had only just lost its independence). This fact limited their capacity to develop and implement strategy.

8 A particular instance of entrepreneurial freedom and style among salaried managers was in the two public sector organizations, the Visitor Bureau and the Convention Bureau. In each case, the chief executive had rapidly expanded the organization's roles and activities, instilled a strong marketing mentality into staff, and gradually freed the organization of its civil service/local government culture, terms and conditions. Such people often overcome notional limitations on their freedom of action simply by ignoring them or managing them politically.

On the other hand, a high degree of formality had been introduced in some cases where formerly independent companies had been taken over by larger groups. For example, Optics and MOD Products had both been taken over and strict financial targets set. For MOD Products, this involved an elaborate planning and monitoring system, and tight restrictions on headcount. In other respects, nevertheless, both companies retained a high degree of independence and an arms-length relationship – not least, in a negative sense, in the absence of group-wide HRM policies and group support for training.

Only in the two hotels, which were the most integrated into parent group systems, were the managers largely constrained from both developing strategy and determining the level of required resources. In all companies elsewhere, those running the business on a day-to-day basis, irrespective of ownership, had considerable 'entrepreneurial' discretion.

9 A good example, which we will refer to from time to time, is Architectural Services where there were a number of partners but it was the most junior who had become the driving force.

10 The distinction between manufacturing and services in many ways is rather crude. All organizations in a sense must provide an element of service to compete effectively (Levitt, 1972; Shostack, 1977). What differs between types of firm is the mix of product and service elements in what they offer. Thus, Fibres not only provided fibre optic cable, but worked closely with end-users (one step beyond the companies which laid the cable), and prided itself on being able to provide almost instantaneous technical support if a cable broke. On the other hand, the 'service' that Software Products provided was a tangible product (a piece of computer software).

11 The three electro-optical firms, for instance, worked with glass in different forms, using different processing technologies, to create different products for markets in which they were not competing. They had neither customers nor suppliers in common, and common skills only to a limited extent in the case of Glass Discs and Optics.

12 The best candidate for a genuine industrial district was the electro-optics (or opto-electronics) industry in North Wales where a cluster of such firms had grown up. The large glass firm, Pilkington, had been influential in stimulating this concentration through businesses and technologies it had spun-off. One or two other companies had then formed as a result of employees breaking

away from Pilkington to set up on their own account – our case firm, Optics, for example. Regional grants administered through the Welsh Development Agency (WDA) had attracted others. More recently, the WDA had begun actively to target a number of high technology sectors to provide a firmer basis for local industrial development. Electro-optics was one such sector, and by 1989 there were over a dozen primary companies in the area.

However, as we note above, electro-optics covers a variety of technologies, markets, and skills. Even where there was close physical proximity, therefore, as between Fibres and Glass Discs on the same industrial estate, there was no interchange of staff. Only between Glass Discs and Optics, some 25 miles apart, was there any movement of employees. In such circumstances, it becomes very difficult to talk about a local labour market, and although an industrial district has other dimensions, these too are problematic.

13   As a much-cited paragraph in the Bolton Report puts it:

> In many respects the small firm provides a better environment for the employee than is possible in most large firms. Although physical working conditions may sometimes be inferior in small firms, most people prefer to work in a small group where communication presents few problems: the employee in a small firm can more easily see the relation between what he is doing and the objectives and performance of the firm as a whole. Where management is more direct and flexible, working rules can be varied to suit the individual. Each employee is also likely to have a more varied role with a chance to participate in several kinds of work. . . . No doubt mainly as a result . . . turnover of staff in small firms is very low and strikes and other kinds of industrial dispute are relatively infrequent. The fact that small firms offer lower earnings than larger firms suggests that the convenience of location and generally the non-material satisfactions of working in them more than outweigh any financial sacrifice involved.
>
> (Bolton Report, 1971: 21; quoted in Stanworth and Gray, 1991: 190)

Chapter 2

Strategic positioning in the small–medium firm

I think what [people] are really looking for is ideas that would make the world, and their own lives, intelligible to them. When a thing is intelligible, you have a sense of participation; when a thing is unintelligible a sense of estrangement.

(E.F. Schumacher, 1973: 84)

INTRODUCTION

This is the first of three chapters which look at how small firms establish themselves and the processes of change and renewal they go through at various times. All three chapters, which explore positioning, crisis, and adaptation, are linked by a common concern with how small firms manage and learn from their internal and external environments. While this is, at a pragmatic level, the archetypal task for the new small firm (Milne and Thompson, 1982), it is also of fundamental theoretical significance in understanding processes of entrepreneurship and organizational renewal. More and more, the respective weight given to the externalities of market power as against a firm's internally developed resources is becoming *the* central debate in strategic management (Rumelt *et al.*, 1991).

While the 1980s were largely dominated by Porter's (1980, 1985) analysis of market power based on barriers to competition as the source of abnormal returns, an alternative perspective emphasizes: (a) the efficient use of resource endowments (Hambrick and MacMillan, 1984; Williamson, 1991; Starr and MacMillan, 1991); and (b) the development of difficult-to-imitate resources (Rumelt, 1984; Lippman and Rumelt, 1984). Thus, according to Grant (1991: 117),

business strategy should be viewed less as a quest for monopoly rents (the returns to market power) and more as a quest for Ricardian rents (the returns to the resources which confer competitive advantage over and above the real costs of these resources).

Among the theoretical strands on which a 'resource-based theory of competitive advantage' draws, the evolutionary economics of Nelson and Winter (1982) is particularly relevant to learning and change. Difficult-to-imitate resources ('inimitability') come about from 'tacit knowledge' embedded in 'organizational routines'. A firm's ability to learn through repetition and the gradual perfecting of routines becomes central, therefore, to its success. However, it is difficult for firms to have a full and ready grasp of their own tacit knowledge and routines, precisely because knowledge and routines are 'tacit'. This is why many firms have difficulty in adapting quickly to changed conditions (Nelson, 1991). This also undermines the assumption that the strategic analysis of markets can furnish usable prescriptions for repositioning a firm.

The question, then, is: 'Where should strategic change start – in the analysis of markets or in the analysis of resource endowments and combinations?' As Grant (1991: 116) argues, 'a definition of business in terms of what it is capable of doing may offer a more durable basis for strategy than a definition based upon the needs which the business seeks to satisfy'. In the last few years, the pendulum has begun to shift in favour of resource theory, to the extent that Rumelt et al. (1991: 23) claim that

> Both theoretical and empirical research into the sources of advantage has begun to point to organisational capabilities, rather than product-market positions or tactics, as the enduring sources of advantage.

There have been one or two attempts to develop a synthesis between these two positions, either by drawing attention to points of theoretical convergence (Mahoney and Pandian, 1992) or by refocusing around particular concepts (Ghemawat, 1991). However, we think more will be gained at this stage by deepening appreciation of the resource-based perspective. This includes reinterpreting aspects of the market approach in resource terms, as in the understanding of organizational networks.

In Chapters 2, 3 and 4, therefore, while using our case material to exemplify practical and theoretical issues for the small–medium firm of a specific and parochial kind, we shall also draw out its more general significance for resource-based theory. Later, in Chapter 7 we will tackle this directly in relation to organizational learning.

At a mundane level, the tasks in establishing a firm are having a product or service, having the means to make and deliver it, and creating customers. While we will provide many practical illustrations of these processes through Chapters 2–4, our aim here is primarily to highlight three themes which stand out in the strategic positioning of the small firm. The first is to do with the fact that the great majority in our sample have succeeded in positioning themselves in niche markets. Related to this, and therefore treated as part of the same phenomenon, is the way this has occurred through dependence on often just one customer. The second theme concerns the building of network relations and the role of the founding or lead entrepreneur in this. The third is about creating employee identification and commitment.

Among the firms we looked at, a number were formed some time ago and have repositioned themselves at least once. The issues and phenomena around positioning are therefore not unique to any particular phase of a firm's development. They are, though, especially acute and salient at start-up and during early growth when they have to be successfully resolved, otherwise the firm will summarily fail.

NICHE MARKETS AND CUSTOMER DEPENDENCE

Starting with no reputation and limited financial and human resources, [new firms] must learn to compete, sometimes in industries dominated by large, established companies.

(Cooper *et al.*, 1986)

Cooper *et al.* (1986) note that the literature mostly advises small firms not to meet competitors head on, but to concentrate instead on specialized products, localized business operations, and products or services with a high degree of added value, through craftmanship and customer service – features inimical to large-scale operations. Such considerations point small firms towards the adoption of niche strategies where there are few competitors. This in turn implies serving a limited number of customers. The literature recognizes the prevalence of niche strategies, with dependence on a few customers (Shea, 1980; Finley, 1980; Davis *et al.*, 1984; Perry, 1987), but has not properly appreciated the significance of this for early growth, other than to caution against its drawbacks (Robinson, 1990).

The Bolton Report (1971) provided early evidence of the extent to which small firms in the UK are dependent on a few customers. The Cambridge SBRC (1992) survey confirms this picture, with a third of the 2,028 firms it sampled reliant on one customer for 25 per cent or more of its sales. The smaller the firm, also, the greater the dependence. Along with this, 43 per cent identified less than five serious competitors. Again, the smaller the firm, the fewer competitors. Other large surveys (Scott *et al.*, 1988) have observed the same phenomena. One interesting finding from the Cambridge survey, however, is that a third of all 2,028 firms saw themselves competing with larger firms. This tends to support Cooper *et al.*'s (1986) argument that small–medium firms can and do compete directly with large firms (although the Cambridge survey begs the question of what is a 'large' firm).

A similar pattern of niche markets and customer dependence was a striking feature in our sample of twenty firms. A large number (fifteen firms – or 75 per cent of the sample) had secured themselves in small (and occasionally not so small), well-defined market niches, where there were typically no more than half a dozen competitors, and often far fewer. These niches were defined by factors such as:

- a specialized product in which economies of scale were difficult to obtain;
- a regionalized market which put a premium on local knowledge;
- a fragmented market at an early stage of development.

Only two organizations could be said to be operating in direct competition with the major players in a genuinely oligopolistic market (Fibres and Bread Products), and both, in contrast, were committed to market penetration and cost leadership strategies that relied on automated plant and standardized products. It is noteworthy also that, as subsidiaries, both depended on technological and financial backing from parent companies, and, with 350 employees, were the largest of our 'small–medium' firms.

Although it is not impossible then for smaller firms to challenge large ones, the relative success of Fibres compared with Bread Products also shows the importance of timing for a small firm pursuing a market penetration strategy (Cooper et al., 1986). That is, Fibres virtually created the UK fibres market (and benefitted from its early fragmentation), while Bread Products was a 'follower', acting largely as an outlet for its parent company's milling business.

To reach their present position, around half the sample had grown on the back of one significant market lead or client. This excludes, moreover, a number, like the hotels and the convention/visitor bureaux, whose business precluded them narrowing their clientele in this way. Such relationships had enabled these firms to grow rapidly in their first few years or had given them long-term stability. Two examples illustrate the fillip to growth from customer specialization:

- In 1985, Training International gained a contract from British Airways to put its 36,000 staff world-wide through a culture change programme. At this stage it had just four presenters and operated from the chief executive's home. By 1990 it had 60 presenters, and in the immediate years after the British Airways contract (1985–86), revenue and staff were growing at 100 per cent a year.
- Aerospace Engineering was one of a number of engineering firms that sprang up in the early 1960s to produce parts for the new generation of engines for jet aircraft. It secured contracts with Rolls-Royce, and 80 per cent of its business in 1990 was still with Rolls-Royce. In the process, it had developed particular expertise as a jobbing engineering shop in machining difficult and exotic metals into unusual shapes.

Such relationships and focus can persist for many years or represent a refocusing within old-established firms.

- Having originally supplied light fittings to the ships of the Royal Navy in Scotland during the last century, MOD Products migrated into serving the railway industry, moved its premises south, and now specializes on a number of product areas with the Ministry of Defence (MOD) as its chief customer. Of its sales, 25 per cent are still in light fittings, and around 60 per cent in products of various kinds go to the MOD.

The value of a close relationship with one customer is that it enables a firm to hone its skills and products, develop its systems, and build its external networks in a highly focused, and therefore economical way (Wilson and Gorb, 1983; Gardner, 1983). Such a relationship propels a company up its particular learning curve more rapidly than if it were diverted in a number of directions by trying to serve and understand many customers. In other words, it benefits from early specialization, and from the reduction of uncertainty.

As a result, firms like Cables, Fibres, and Software Products had achieved a clear dominance in their chosen field, while at least half were recognized as firms of excellence in their sector, including five within their first ten years of existence.

How a firm creates and exploits customer dependence

Although customer dependence promotes specialization, 'specialization' is rather an inadequate description. It says nothing about the process of actually becoming more focused. For instance, in its early years, a new firm is often still trying to get a clear fix on its market and the precise nature and distinctive, marketable quality of what it is trying to make or sell. In a very real sense, products and market are developed simultaneously. This process is not assured and it can be slow. Thus, as a sales executive in the Visitor Bureau put it, 'You get to begin to understand what your business is all about only after five to seven years.'

Feedback from actual and potential customers is critical in speeding up this process. A classic tactic in new product development is therefore to persuade a potential customer to take samples of a product, to try it out, and to introduce it on a limited scale into their range. In this way, if successful, a significant and enduring commitment can be established on both sides.

- Glass Discs signed its first order to supply Philips with optical discs (for data storage) in 1984, three years before the business came out of the laboratory and became a limited company, and five years before it was spun-off altogether into the independent organization it now is. Ninety-five per cent of disc products are now supplied to Philips, to two factories in the UK and Holland, while export to Philips in the USA has begun, again, by supplying initial samples.

On the other hand, an initiative may come from a customer who recognizes a product as having significant benefits to its own operations.

- In the mid-1980s, having established itself as a specialist software house for the insurance industry, Software Products devised a package for writing insurance policies in customers' homes, which gave enormous improvements in accuracy and speed in issuing policies. To help its expansion, two of the UK's large insurance companies put over £5 million into Software Products to help it develop a package for their own use. Software Products is not strictly limited in its commercial relationships to these two companies, although they have taken seats on the board.

Power in the dependent relationship

The relative power of the small firm in relationships with larger ones is critical. The niche approach gets round this problem in relation to competitors, but is liable to replace it with a power-dependent relationship with a customer. This becomes apparent in pressure on prices and difficulty in getting prompt payment for goods – the latter probably being the more serious problem, certainly in the UK.

The smaller firm will therefore often try to achieve 'favoured supplier' status so that its own interests and those of its customer become indissoluble.

- Increasing sophistication in aerospace products and higher quality requirements led Rolls-Royce to reduce the number of its suppliers and to seek closer relationships with those able to meet its exacting standards. The combination of fewer suppliers able to meet these standards, with the increased volume of work that resulted from Rolls' success in winning long-term contracts to supply the American aviation market, strengthened the negotiating position of component suppliers. As a result, Aerospace Engineering had a stronger hand over pricing, and could therefore look forward to improving margins.

Such advantages, however, may be only temporary, and in this case knowing how Rolls-Royce had squeezed other suppliers out of business merely encouraged Aerospace Engineering to try to reduce their own dependence.

A more enduring source of power in relationships with customers is to have a unique product with qualities that, once adopted, locks the customer into it. This, of course, is conventional strategic wisdom not confined to small firms, although small firms are, of course, supposed to be especially innovative in products and services.

- Pressings has redesigned its basic product in such a way that, for the moment, it is unique throughout Europe and North America. This involves reducing the number of components in an industrial roller conveyor by putting bearings into a prefabricated housing and sealing it. This innovation reshapes the manufacturing chain. If adopted, therefore, as it has begun to be in both the UK and USA, it requires the roller bearing manufacturer to lay down production lines that lock them in to the component that Pressings uniquely supplies. The CEO of Pressings understands this very clearly, and for the same reason some customers are resisting the product.

Jobbers or marketeers?

This raises a critical issue for a small firm successfully positioning itself. At first sight, the development of a proprietary product represents a shift from the typical small firm 'jobber' to the 'marketeer' (Lydall, 1958). That is, instead of taking specification from customers and serving as a jobbing shop, the small firm markets its own product or service. The inference typically taken from this is that having products provides security: jobbing does not. By implying competitive strength comes from tangible goods a firm can put on the market, it buys into a market power perspective on competitive advantage. The importance of this issue for small firms can be gauged from the Cambridge (1992) survey where half the sample took on subcontract work, and for these firms, subcontracting provided 43 per cent of their turnover.

On deeper inspection, what Pressings has done in its new product is to bring together two sets of expertise, skills, and knowledge (pressworking technology and roller manufacture). It has to commercialize and sell the result, but what it is ultimately selling is the expression of a unique combination of expertise. Its other lines of work involve simpler, less specialized activities which customers can more readily recognize according to *their own* definition of requirements.

Other examples likewise show that the distinction between jobbing and marketing, based in an implied distinction between a product and skills, does not stand up. Architectural Services sells design skills; Clean Air Co. and Cable Co. sell installation skills; Construction Co. and House Co. sell building skills; Training International and Skills Training sell training skills. The successful ones among these have acquired a reputation for special sorts of work. Thus, MOD Products markets itself as providing 'high technology for harsh environments' through the design experience it has built up over the years, and its 'product runs' come from successful prototyping of 'jobbing' requests.

Implicit in these examples is also a blurring between concepts of product and service. Many of the small–medium firms in our sample thus stressed the importance of qualitative, service-related factors (such as personal attention to customer needs and the ability to respond quickly to customer requests) as a source of competitive advantage which goes beyond price factors in making a product.

The above examples serve, then, to highlight the extent to which competitive advantage is rooted in the development of resources, and how that comprises skills and information. One aspect of this, of course, is that not having a proprietary product can actually be a source of advantage in terms of flexibility. Skills are flexible, whereas a product or particular service is not and obsolesces more readily.

The returns to niche specialization

The result of niche specialization should be to generate resources for growth and high profitability, in some cases with opportunities for premium pricing (as at Clean Air Co.) because of factors associated with speed of response. Table 2.1 summarizes the recent profitability of our

Table 2.1 Sales/Profits (1988–89)

	Sales (£m)		Profits (£m)		Return on sales (%)	
	1988	1989	1988	1989	1988	1989
Visitor Bureau		4.0				20%
Convention Bureau		3.0		0.175		9%
Hotel Tourist		1.0		0.25		25%
Hotel Heritage		2.0		0.40		20%
Software Products		8.5		0.80		9%
Training International	11.7	n/a	2.9	n/a	25%	n/a
Skills Training		(not trading)				n/a
Legal Services	0.3	0.8	0.075	0.19	25%	24%
Bread Products		15.0	(loss)	0.75	–	5%
Aerospace Engineering	1.35	2.0	(.02)	0.035		2%
MOD Products	3.8	3.6	0.10	0.10	3%	3%
Pressings		1.5	profit	profit		n/a
Clean Air Co.	2.1	1.7	(loss)	profit		n/a
Glass Discs		n/a				n/a
Fibres	35–40	35–40	n/a	n/a		n/a
Optics		3.9	(loss)	0.10		3%
Construction Co.	14.1	19.5	0.064	(0.205)	—	—
House Co.	4.2	8.3	0.197	0.677	5%	8%
Cable Co.	3.1	5.2	0.294	0.270	9%	5%
Architectural Services	1.9	2.4	0.29	0.40	15%	17%

Note: n/a: some companies do not publish accounts, although they were usually prepared to indicate whether they were profitable or not sample of small–medium firms. However, this listing does not provide a definitive measure of their success or potential – it covers only a limited period, near the peak of the business cycle; nor does it allow for special factors which either depress profits (for example, reorganization and relocation costs at Optics), or which give a temporary boost to profits (such as the cost-cutting that is running down assets in the long term at Hotel Tourist).

For what it is worth, among those that provided figures the median pre-tax rate of return to sales in the latest year for which information was available was 11 per cent. This is rather higher than the 7.5 per cent for the large Cambridge sample over the three-year period 1987–90 which began to catch the effects of the recession.

BUILDING NETWORK RELATIONS

The value of networks in the early development of the small firm is widely recognized (for example, Birley, 1985), especially in the growth of high technology firms (Doctor *et al.*, 1989); while networks are beginning to be seen as a general strategic resource for firms of all kinds (Thorelli, 1986; Jarillo, 1988). Briefly, networks are the means by which firms gain knowledge of their customer markets and access to various material, financial and human resources for doing business.

The problem for the small firm, however, is often to be able to focus the vast amount of information available through various networks. As Woodcock (1990) has commented:

> The information available in the formal networks of business opportunity exchange systems is vast and so unwieldy that the smaller firm is simply incapable of getting to grips with it, quite apart from actually being able to find the links which are beneficial to it. . . . the smaller firm needs a network which links it with other networks.
>
> (Woodcock, 1990)

One policy response to this is to create bodies which act as a focus for the exchange of information, for instance in the area of technology transfer.

A more general solution lies in the early association with one customer. This overcomes problems of excessive, unfocused information (a) by narrowing the requirements for information, and (b) through the fact that a large customer has existing networks to which the smaller firm may gain surrogate access. Implicitly, these help the small firm to identify and concentrate on areas of significant advantage (Szarka, 1990) and allow it to build its external networks in an economical way with limited expenditure of time.

Among the examples in the previous section for instance, Training International gained a vast market through its association with the success of its British Airways customer care culture change programme. As other firms beat their way to British Airways' door to discover the secret of its culture change programme, so they then headed off in Training International's direction to get the benefits themselves. Had British Airways been less well-known, Training International would have attracted far less attention.

Some firms secure themselves further by going beyond their immediate customer relationships to the end-users of their products. The ability to do this depends on the structure of the industry – that is, it obviously helps if an industry is dominated by monopsonist buyers, since this simplifies the networks the SME has to engage with. This illustrates the general principle that small firms tend to be well down the supply chain and rarely deal directly with the retail consumer.

- Fibres supplies to cable companies who lay the fibre-optics they make, but it regards its relationship with the end-user as 'absolutely key'. (In the UK, this means British Telecom and Mercury.) Apart from working closely with them to identify their future requirements, it prides itself in offering immediate technical support and maintenance if a cable breaks, taking up the question of liability with the cable company afterwards.
- Faced with the resistance of British conveyor manufacturers to its new product, Pressings is seeking to overcome this by going over their heads to the end-user, British Coal, to influence their specification of sub-systems.

Diffuse networks

Focused networks on the back of limited customer relationships are not possible, however, for all kinds of organization. Some have to develop extensive network relations as a condition of operating. This is the case for those firms which trade on the qualities of their locality (travel and tourism), and for firms in the construction industry.

The chief executive of the Convention Bureau, for instance, defined its role as 'the maximum utilization of the tourism infrastructure', and its task as 'destination marketing' – that is, marketing the attractions of the city it served. To do this meant working actively on and with a great variety of suppliers, customers, competitors, and various intermediaries and gate-keepers. The tactics employed by the Convention Bureau show the range of activity in which a small organization may have to engage.

- Making suppliers of tourist services – hotels, entertainments, shops, and transport – aware of what it was doing, and changing attitudes to service and tourism (in a city that identifies with its heavy industry past), was a prime task. 'Destination lunches', for example, were held for local hotel managers so that they learnt to recognize the kind of visitor coming to the city and could include relevant information in their advertising. The Visitor Bureau went further and established an approved membership list, to promote standards. As hotel provision was regarded as a selling point, special efforts were made to work with the hotels to put together promotional packages. The Visitor Bureau also exploited its role in this network by opening a booking facility for which it received a commission from the hotels.

- Overseas tour operators were given tours of the area to see its cultural facilities, using the world famous Burrell Collection in Glasgow as a focus, while several major US airlines were persuaded to include the city on their routes, to bring in North American visitors. Similarly, staff of the Visitor Bureau attended trade missions, and exhibited at world fairs and specialist travel/tourism exhibitions all over the world to sell the merits of their home town.

- Academic and professional conventions were identified as target business markets where the city had a particular edge through its medical school and universities, and presentations were made to senior professors to get them to influence the holding of conventions there.

- Finally, the Convention Bureau developed links with its equivalent in Edinburgh to compete against centres outside Scotland and the UK for convention business. In like manner, both the Convention Bureau and the Visitor Bureau belonged to the UK British Association of Conference Towns, formed to address the overseas competition issue.

The two Bureaux thus play a role as brokers across a wide range of relationships, predominantly geared to information, but also involving exchange (or trading) relations. Managing this diffuseness of information meant an increasing emphasis on information technology (IT) systems (and IT skills in their staff).

In the construction industry, information brokerage (or 'wheeler-dealing') is also important, but with a larger part played by direct commercial relationships. Success depends on bringing together and managing a range of resources – above all people, but also in many cases land and finance. Consequently, all the construction firms, in their different ways – from Architectural Services to Cable Co. – have had to build and keep alive networks, in order to get jobs and to carry them through. Thus, networks are fundamental to the construction industry, but unlike the Bureaux are focused through a hierarchy of subcontract relationships.

- Construction Co. illustrates the general principles of contracting and the increasing importance of the broker role. Traditionally, a main contractor supplies a core of joiners, bricklayers, and general labourers, with 50 per cent of work typically subcontracted. The recent trend towards more self-employment among joiners and bricklayers has considerably increased this proportion, and therefore the ability to manage employment flexibility. Since profit depends crucially on performing contracted work on time and within budget, juggling the use of their own and subcontract labour, often between sites, is an important organizational capability.

- The role of the network is further illustrated by the way main contractors like Construction Co. develop strong relationships with two or three subcontractors in each trade. Typically, these will comprise 1–2 managers and up to 50 employees. A number of subcontractors of this size have built themselves off the back of work for Construction Co. While the commercial relationship is based on price, dependable relationships of this kind allow for more flexible site management and doing favours.

- Suppliers of bricks, timber, concrete, etc. are similarly an integral part of doing business. Efficient (and therefore profitable) site management relies on knowing suppliers who can perform and will look after you. The growing size of suppliers, however, is increasingly restricting primary relationships.

- The other critical factors in construction are the banks, as a source of working capital, because of the unevenness of cash flow in project-based work. It is important to maintain good relations with banks and to hold regular meetings with them to discuss both individual projects and the overall requirements of the firm.

- This pattern of network/contract relations in construction is becoming even more complex at the present time during recession, with bankruptcies disrupting networks, large national firms seeking smaller contracts, and smaller local firms moving up for larger contracts. Thus, Construction Co. has been collaborating with a large national contractor based in North East England to subcontract its own labour for work on foundations, brickwork, and joinery.

- While the sister company, House Co., operates on similar principles, in developing long-term relationships with well-run businesses for subcontracting and materials, it is a more speculative business. This has consequences for networking in two ways. First, in acquiring land, and second in off-loading risk:

> House building is all about outlets, the number and size of them being key features. Shared risk provides better use of finance and allows for putting eggs in multiple baskets.
>
> (CEO, House Co.)

- Consequently, House Co. has very strong links with a number of larger competitors in making joint land purchases and in pooling resources in schemes that are too big for it alone.

These examples show how local knowledge and contacts are the means by which regionally defined businesses gain a competitive advantage. Local knowledge and contacts create entry barriers and a defendable niche. Firms like House Co. and Construction Co. are then able to draw on their regional experience to enter into consortium arrangements, if they so wish, with prominent national contractors. As with joint ventures generally, however, this can have risks in safeguarding exclusive knowledge.

Networks as a capital resource

These examples of networking in operation illustrate two basic contrasting functions of networks. One is to bring together physical and other resources to perform a production task (the construction example), with such resources often being consolidated in contractual (or commercial exchange) relationships. The second is where networking is primarily concerned with gathering and disseminating information for marketing purposes. This may be fairly diffuse (the Bureaux), while in others part of a focused marketing effort (Pressings).

Networking is thus oriented to both sales and the resources to deliver a product or service. In both cases, the network itself becomes a key resource. It is the means through which opportunities are identified and secured (Dubini and Aldrich, 1991), and the means by which firms gain access to resources they do not control (Jarillo, 1989). Network theory recognizes this when it defines networks as 'market assets' through which firms gain access to other firms' 'internal assets' (knowledge of markets and production) (Johanson and Mattsson, 1988). Another way of putting this is to say that networking is a skill, and networks created are the realization of this skill.

Networking and networks can therefore be seen as a form of capital, even though their currency is essentially information. The tangible evidence of this is when the efficiently working network provides ready information and access to other resources, which saves time and money in extensive search (Dubini and Aldrich, 1991; Melin, 1987). Economists are beginning to recognize the economic value of networks in this respect (for example, Loasby, 1992), while the strategy literature implicitly acknowledges their capital value when it describes networks as 'strategic assets'. The innovation process, illustrated by the Pressings example in Chapter 7, shows how networks, in furnishing information, provide direct economic value. This is a strong argument then for locating networks within a resource-based view of the firm.

The entrepreneur in network creation

The founding entrepreneur is intimately involved in developing the new firm's position in its niche market, its relations with key customers, and its network relations with suppliers, other firms in collaboration, and intermediaries of various kinds. Jarillo (1989) regards such networking skills as the prime resource an entrepreneur has in making the early link between his/her perception of opportunity and the physical resources needed to make it happen. Beyond start-up, the entrepreneur continues to play a highly visible role in building and maintaining the network of relationships focused on customer relations and resource requirements. This is very clearly the case in the smaller firm where the head of the firm is often its chief and only salesperson.

It is also a well-observed fact that social relationships involving family and friends play a significant part in the lead entrepreneur's role networks, especially at start-up, in giving access to material and knowledge-based resources (Birley, 1985; Aldrich and Zimmer, 1986). Thus, family or friends remained highly visible in the management of eight out of twenty of our sample of firms, irrespective of actual ownership, while in two others (Optics, Hotel Heritage) such relationships had only recently dissolved as a result of internal wrangles and bankruptcy. These eight firms included Training International (run by two brothers); Construction Co./House Co. (run by two brothers, with a brother-in-law and a close friend of the former chairman in key positions in the Group); and Legal Services (three partners who belonged to the same charismatic church); while Optics, although now dominated by externally recruited managers, was formed by three managers leaving a large local firm and taking a core of employees with them.

Family and friendship networks, however, can be inward-looking. As Szarka (1990) notes, it is important that a founding entrepreneur moves quickly beyond his or her immediate social network to establish an 'institutional network' of formal links including banks, chambers of commerce, and consultants, to provide independent advice. Since they can filter information from a wide range of sources, they enable the small firm to identify and concentrate on areas of significant advantage – precisely the kind of benefit we have attributed to close links early on with one or two customers.

Cable Co. is a good example of a family network being supplemented and extended, both socially and formally, in ways which have contributed to its success.

• When cable-laying emerged as a significant activity in the construction industry, it used physically able gangs of unskilled labour who could outperform the traditional claimants to such work, electricians. Trade union objections were manageable, provided such gangs worked under the supervision of a qualified electrician. Cable Co.'s success has depended on bringing together two 'families': the founder and his four brothers, all time-served electricians, on the electrical side; and, on the cabling side, an ex-army group of former Royal Engineers, based in the north England town of Ripon where cable-laying originated in work for the military. Key management positions are now filled by three of the original brothers (one died, one left to set up a rival firm), with one son working lower down; and four ex-Royal Engineers from the 'Ripon connection', with four others of a younger generation from the same unit, in more junior positions. The army in Ripon continues to provide an active recruitment network, while the blending of the two 'families' has worked because of a common disciplinarian style.

- Having established cable-laying as semi-skilled work outside the electrical union's control, Cable Co. has also taken a leading role in establishing a rival cable-laying companies' association and latterly has been engaged in formalizing terms and conditions in the industry. This role at the centre of an industry network has given the company a new respectability.

Social networks beyond the family have an enduring functional value in one other way. In an industry like construction which is prone to instability, there is a pattern of 'firms going bust and starting again, while the personalities stay the same' (CEO, Construction Co.). Personal contacts thus provide some stability and continuity, and keep contracting relationships intact despite organizations changing.

While it is true, then, that founding entrepreneurs need to extend their networks beyond their circle of family and friends, their social network has an immediate and enduring value. For a new firm, the social network gets over the problem of entering into contracts and trading without an established reputation. Social networks overcome the initial problem of trust on which economic exchange relationships depend (Williamson, 1975; Henslin, 1981; Hodgson, 1988), since an existing social network provides a pre-existing basis of trust underpinned by an established set of norms. Consequently, Coleman (1988, 1990), and similarly Johannisson (1988), argue that the crucial resource an entrepreneur possesses, which is invested at start-up, is this 'social capital'.

As Batstone (1991) notes, this is in a sense 'free capital'. When the small firm extends its markets beyond the founding entrepreneur's own networks, however, it has to start paying to establish reputation and trust, through such means as advertising and employing sales staff. The ensuing reputation thus carries a cost and becomes diffused from personal reputation into 'corporate reputation'. Breaking out of dependence on a prime customer is a particular instance of this. This provides an economic rationale for the fact that the majority of small firms remain wedded to their geographic locality and complements a behavioural view to explain why small firm owners may be reluctant to grow beyond a certain point – namely, they lose control of a prime source of 'capital' and the returns from it. Such considerations help to locate networks within resource-based theory and add a further component to the theory.

Networks in theory and practice

However, we must not get too carried away by theorizing about networks or the capital the budding entrepreneur invests in a new business. The capital risks of entrepreneurship are real material ones and the tasks are basic behavioural ones, as the following quotation suggests:

> You have to be ruthless. You have to be tough – with yourself, with your employees, with your customers, and with your suppliers. Particularly when times are bad. You've got to be rock-steady when times are bad, because if you're not, the whole world will collapse about you. You have to be confident that you know what you are doing. Your employees, of course, need to have security of employment. And your customers need to be secure in the knowledge that your product will be there. Anyone who deals with us, has to have confidence.
>
> We've had legal disputes with customers; disputes with suppliers; industrial tribunals. But I have a philosophy which has always stood me in good stead – 'I don't care if it hurts me, Johnny, you're not going to get your way'. If you're prepared to be hurt in the process, then not many people in turn are prepared to be hurt in trying to overcome your resistance. It's a quality you must have, because if you falter at any point, the whole house will collapse.
>
> And you must be prepared to take risks. We've been through two very bad patches over the last twenty years. If I hadn't put my house on the line, we couldn't have financed the borrowings and the expansion. But if the wheels had fallen off in that period, my wife and children would have been on the street. I suppose I'm one of 'Maggie Thatcher's risk-takers'. I believe you'll never get anywhere if you sit behind your four walls and don't stick your toe in the water sometimes.
>
> (CEO, Pressings)

The other point about networks is that it is easy to overstate the involvement of small firm owners in networking. As Curran *et al*. 1991: 52–53 observe, drawing on a focused study of networking in 350 small firms:

> Owner-managers tend to have relatively small and non-extensive networks with even a lack of frequent resort to the most expected external contacts such as accountants and bank managers. Neither are owner-managers apparently greatly involved in networks based on family, kinship or social groupings.
>
> In some ways, the above findings are not very surprising. There is abundant previous research suggesting that small business owner-manager self-definitions stress independence, standing on your own two feet, and running the business in exemplification of these values. This produces a 'fortress enterprise' mentality in dealing with the wider

environment unlikely to go with high levels of participation in networks of all kinds. Moreover . . . demands on the owner-manager's time are very substantial, making any extensive networking activities unlikely. Finally, many of the more obvious external contacts an owner-manager might use cost money [and] they were very sensitive to these costs.

Despite the attractions of networking in theory, then, small business owners' contacts with their environment are much more limited and much less proactive than 'networks' and 'networking' in the literature imply.

Gibb (1984) likewise stresses the opportunity costs of networking activity, while Birley *et al.*, (1990) draw attention to the problem of small firm networks being intensive (dense) rather than extensive – or, as Hellgren and Stjernberg (1987) put it, being 'tightly coupled'. The dependent relationship with one customer is an extreme example of this. Such limitations point the way ahead from single entrepreneur towards team entrepreneurship.

CREATING EMPLOYEE IDENTIFICATION AND COMMITMENT

The third conspicuous activity which engages the entrepreneur is the need to build identification of employees with the business. In some ways this is a more substantial challenge than overcoming the initial technical problems of making a product or delivering a service, because the latter can conceivably be done by the entrepreneur alone. Managing a business acquires an extra dimension of complexity when employees are taken on. There is also a general consensus of opinion that the level of complexity increases significantly with the first employee, around 8–10 employees, and around 20–25 employees, while further significant growth points are said to be at 100 employees and 400 employees. Common to all of these is a problem of commitment and control which is customarily described in terms of culture and leadership style. In resource terms, the issue is one of maximizing the contribution of people and retaining ownership of their skills and knowledge.

As we indicated in Chapter 1, however, size is only one factor affecting qualitative changes in culture. Ownership and control is also a potent factor. Additional considerations are the nature of the business and its labour markets. The combined effect of the latter is greatly under-estimated in discussions of the small firm and Chapter 5 will attempt to transform the level of analysis and debate in this respect.

While size and ownership/control provide alternative explanations for differences in culture and style, both essentially play on the same theme – the extent to which commitment and control is managed in a personalized way, or impersonally through rules. One way of representing this is in the contrast between a 'transformational' and a 'transactional' style. A 'transformational' style of leadership seeks to inspire identification of employees with the product or service and with some 'elevated' mission; a 'transactional' style is much cooler and relies more exclusively on formal job specification and extrinsic benefits to do with pay and rewards (Bennis and Nanus, 1985; Shamir *et al.*, 1993). This, however, does not quite fit since personalized control in small, owner-managed firms is just as likely to be exercised in a dictatorial and oppressive way without regard to willing identification as often as it aims to inspire.

An alternative is Schein's (1983) contrast between 'founder/owners' and 'professional managers'. 'Founders' manage through a style which is personal and political, centralist and autocratic, emotional and impatient; 'professional managers' are rational and impersonal, participative and delegation-oriented, unemotional and impatient. While ownership may encourage all the behaviours listed, clearly all professional managers do not fit the opposite stereotype. Thus, there are professional managers engaged to run small firms who relish the prospect of relative independence and behave like founder/owner entrepreneurs – the CEOs of both Bureaux and Clean Air Co., for instance. Equally, some of the most dominating owner/managers (for example, the CEO of Pressings) served their managerial apprenticeship in large firms before becoming 'owners'. Thus, control is important as well as actual ownership, while leadership style is a function of both psychological and situational factors.

Eschewing more value-laden stereotypes, we will instead use the terms 'personalized' and 'formalized' cultures to contrast the way small firms create identification and commitment. As important as why small firms adopt a particular way of creating commitment, however, is how well this objective stands up to the pressures of business and labour markets to dissipate commitment and thereby to weaken firms' hold over employees' knowledge and skills. Chapters 5 through 8 develop this critical theme.

Personalized cultures in small–medium firms

The elements of a 'personalized' culture described here are not meant to be comprehensive. We simply identify a few of the key ones which stand out. Schein (1983) covers a wider range. The following four elements are, nevertheless, recognizable as key processes in a functionalist or institutional perspective on the firm – relating, namely, to goals, means, ideology, and identity.

Hands-on

One of the most conspicuous features of small firms is the leader's personal involvement in all important details. Such people are generally very 'hands-on' as managers. In some businesses, such as hotels, the patron's personal attention to detail is regarded by staff as a necessary quality, and personal recognition of their standards of performance by the boss is a key staff motivator. One of the problems at Hotel Heritage, for example, was the loss of this 'personal touch', following a change of ownership and its absorption into a large chain. Through a hands-on approach, the leader models and sets standards.

Goal-centred

A second feature is having a vision of where the organization is going and what it is about, and communicating this. In the Convention Bureau the enthusiasm for promoting Glasgow extended to the staff, who displayed considerable zeal in this task. While this drew on employees' local pride, the CEO's 'vision' was nevertheless communicated in a very task- and results-oriented fashion, through clearly-expressed marketing concepts. The emotional identification was thus grounded in hard-headed values:

> I'm pragmatic and results- and commerce-oriented. It guts me if I lose. As to style, I don't think I have a style, but you'd better ask my managers. What I do have is a very clear grasp of where this Bureau is going.
>
> (CEO, Convention Bureau)

Value-driven

A third element is the projection of a distinctive belief system. At Training International and Legal Services this was rooted in overt Christian beliefs:

> Training International is run as an extended family and is heavily influenced by my personal values more than anyone else's. This is quite overt. The fact that I am the major shareholder is secondary to me. Moulding the culture and manipulating it are the key things.
>
> (CEO, Training International)

The key values in Training International were a stress on business ethics, personal caring, trust, and openness, sustained by such features as a flat organization structure, first-name terms and name badges, an annual report which identified directors' salaries, and a fortnightly newsletter produced by the staff.

At Legal Services, the partners' values did not permeate the organization in quite the same way, although they all belonged to the same charismatic church. Their values were most visible in the fact that they marketed themselves as a Christian firm (which brought in important work in trust work for churches), and in the role of prayer apparently in their decision-making. Nevertheless, like Training International, they were also very profit-oriented, aiming to use their profits to further their church work. The Protestant work ethic was thus very much alive.

The downside of an 'inspirational' style of leadership, however, is that often it stifles true debate and necessary differences. There was a feeling at Training International, for instance, that the ethos had produced a situation where staff in general could not easily handle criticism. As a relative newcomer in the senior management team observed, 'our own flat structures make people loathe to criticize'. In each of these examples, one person's personality was central. Where that person happens to be also the owner, employees inevitably feel constrained from arguing with him or her.

Personal dominance

Only a few of our sample were so overt in projecting a set of ethical values. More often, power is reflected simply in the way one person dominates and provides the driving force. Although the CEO need not be the legal owner – as in the two public sector Bureaux which were nevertheless dominated by their CEOs – ownership does confer dominance. This is as likely to be autocratic as inspirational:

> My philosophy is when you're in charge of people, whether you're a teacher, an industrialist, an accountant, when you're put in charge of people, there seems to be an invisible line drawn in the sand somewhere, and somebody sometime puts their toe over that line and waits to see what you will do. And if you stamp on it really hard, then it won't happen again, by and large. But if you don't stamp on it, then all the other toes will proceed to go over the line, and you've got chaos.
>
> (CEO, Pressings)

In other owner-managed firms also, we observed behaviour from time to time which was downright bullying and aggressive. However, the close involvement of an owner-manager in a firm can also allow a curious latitude in relationships. Most of the more senior employees at Aerospace Engineering, for instance, had been together for a long time, since before the present owner was works manager and bought it out. One or two had therefore been of equal status to him at one time. As a result, they felt able to treat his moods with equanimity:

> The quality manager definitely bears the brunt of rollickings from Fred. They're old friends from their football days! He's been sacked a few times, but they still get on well, although the relationship is not now what it was.

The general easy-going atmosphere contributed a lot to the operating integrity of the company, so that, for example, employees took time at the handover between the night and day shifts to explain the status of work in progress. This is the kind of 'family spirit' which is supposed to characterize the smaller firm but is often hard to pin down.

Formalized cultures in small–medium firms

While personal dominance and a hands-on approach (that is, a 'personalized' culture) are especially characteristic of small, owner-managed firms, other types of firm also attempt to develop close identification with the business. The 'formalized' culture simply does it differently, by emphasizing consultation, teamwork, followership, and equitable treatment. Among the new firms, Fibres (a joint venture) and Glass Discs (a wholly owned subsidiary of another large company) had both put a lot of effort into developing a distinctive culture that avoided the adversarial relationships of their parent companies. Both were also run by professional managers. Other firms with a group of professional managers, like MOD Products and increasingly Construction Co., had similar embryonic traits.

Consultation

Fibres operated an elaborate and far-reaching consultative system, and sought to maintain a distinctive culture around this. This had three levels: a briefing three times a year by the CEO covering all aspects of the business; a monthly team-briefing, in which every supervisor received an authoritative, standard briefing which they then communicated, in cascade fashion, to all who reported to them, again on how the business is doing; and, third, 'the hub of the industrial relations wheel', an 'Advisory Board'. In addition to this three-tier structure, comprehensive information was posted on notice boards, so that 'No employee should be able to say, "I didn't know"' (Personnel Manager, Fibres).

The Advisory Board was an elective body of eleven members, elected on a two-year basis, and representing the major groupings ('constituencies') in the firm. They included representatives of management, a representative of the union which had sole 'representation', but not 'negotiating' rights, and various work sections. The Advisory Board was chaired by the CEO. It met monthly, received a review of the business, which it discussed, and advised on a wide range of personnel issues. This included making recommendations on pay awards, based on information it received from two sub-committees. These sub-committees were composed similarly of employee representatives. A number of training events had been held to improve the working of the Advisory Board, covering such things as negotiation, team-working, how to manage win-win situations, and how to handle reporting back to the members' constituencies.

Teamwork

The Advisory Board system at Fibres was a deliberate attempt to get away from the traditional culture of the UK parent on a greenfield site. Apart from putting work relationships on to a constitutional (and non-union) footing, the company also had a strong commitment to teamwork. The CEO had thought seriously about the nature of management in this regard:

> There has been a major change in how we manage a business. Ten years ago, I was managing a £100 million business of 2–3,000 people. I could manage it because I could make a reasonable stab at doing any of their jobs. But now it's impossible for anyone to get a total grasp. You can't manage anymore in the old top-down, hands-on sense. Management has become more of a 'secretarial' task, controlling the things people do.
>
> Meredith Belbin in *Management Teams* sums it up well. In the past, management was very much a matter of objective-setting and appraisal of individuals in formal ways. But now it's no longer about individuals, it's about teams and one person not being able to cope with it all. You can't be the 'big white chief' any more. You have to run it as a partnership and formulate joint plans.
>
> (CEO, Fibres)

In consequence, Fibres combined informality in personal relationships (at least among the top managers), and a high degree of formality (or 'constitutionalism') in employee relationships at large, expressed through the Advisory Board system. To the outsider, the latter seemed quite bureaucratic – perhaps an inevitable characteristic of legality and self-imposed rules. Company structure was also highly functional (reflecting the CEO's view that the modern organization is necessarily highly specialized). For this reason, teamwork across boundaries acquired a special importance and had to be worked at.

Followership

Glass Discs was also a greenfield site business that was conscious of trying to develop a style different from its founding parent. Management likewise stressed the development of teamwork, although they practiced it in less formal ways. One factor in this was that it was as yet of a size (62 employees compared with Fibres' 350) and age (in its first 18 months) where managers could personally get involved alongside the workforce – for example, in getting goods out the door when a rush order was on. In this way, they could powerfully communicate a culture of teamwork, lead by example, and promote 'followership'.

As the CEO at Fibres put it:

> The challenge is deciding what you want to do strategically, and then

influencing and persuading others by consensus to want to do it. The old bullying style is no longer appropriate. It's a matter of projecting a vision, a philosophy of the business, to create attitude change.

(CEO, Fibres)

While providing a forum for consultation, the Advisory Board at Fibres also helped with the general culture formation of the organization – 'away from the Ford approach, of workers making demands and management being responsible for managing the business' (CEO).

Equitable treatment

Finally, establishing equitable treatment through formal structures in areas like gradings, pay, and training, was seen as an important part of corporate culture in both Fibres and Glass Discs. A third company, Optics, was also coming to recognize that success depended on satisfying employees' aspirations over pay and job progression, instead of taking their cooperation for granted as they had done during the start-up phase. A fourth firm, Construction Co., combined industry standards on pay and job descriptions with profit sharing to underline its team-centred approach.

'Personalized' versus 'formalized' cultures

These examples stress order and equity in building employee commitment, centred on pay, gradings, training, and communications. 'Personalized' cultures, which tend to be, but are not exclusively, owner-managed, also give high priority to pay and other tangible rewards for developing commitment. Thus, there was a surprising breadth of provision in 'side payments' (although some of these entitlements were restricted to a few staff). Loyalty was widely perceived as a matter of looking after staff in tangible ways, benefits covering things such as pensions (60% of the sample), healthcare (30%), company cars (25%), a subsidized canteen (10%), a social club (10%), profit-sharing (25%), and financial support for external training (25%).

However, such benefits tend to be distributed in a more arbitrary fashion in 'personalized' cultures, dominated by one person, compared with 'formalized' ones. The result is that discontent in 'personalized' cultures is most likely to occur over lack of equity and order in pay, gradings, opportunities for training, and the like. In the next chapter, among other things, we will look at the circumstances which bring about greater transparency, openness, and order in these areas of human resource management.

The comparison between 'personalized' and 'formalized' cultures bears upon the issue of whether small firms are better or worse places to work – whether, indeed, 'small firms are beautiful' as some claim and others (for example, Rainnie, 1989) dispute. In this chapter we have not been directly concerned with this question, however, as much as with the different ways commitment is managed. An adequate analysis of small firms from this point of view needs to take account of size, ownership and control, technology and the product-market, and labour market factors. Neither type of firm described here can be simply equated with the form of ownership.

Thus, Fibres' culture was highly influenced by the exacting nature of product specifications, the sophistication of its technology, and the need to protect the finely-balanced system of production from disruption. While the Advisory Board system helped to ensure cooperation and stability, the control systems surrounding the plant contributed greatly to formality. Thus, every stage of the process, from specification by the supplier to delivery, was recorded and had to be signed off – including details of each production run, barometric pressure on that day, and progress through the plant for every single length of optical fibre made.

The complexity of influences on organizational culture is a warning against stereotyping the culture of small firms, or of other firms. In Chapter 5 we will develop a comprehensive model of these influences on smaller firms' management of employees.

SUMMARY AND CONCLUSION

In this chapter we have described three characteristic strategic issues small firms need to address as they establish themselves. The first is how successfully to position themselves in a market. Many do so by developing a niche and building on the back of one or two customers. The second issue concerns the building of network relations, especially to secure resources. The third is the need to create some level of employee commitment. In these ways, small firms begin to manage their internal and external environments.

In discussing these, we have had occasion to exemplify some of the principles embodied in resource-based theory. Working with a major customer helps focus activity and allows specialization. This promotes the efficient learning of skills and routines, and the development of a durable, 'difficult-to-imitate', specialization, which is relatively opaque to competitors (Grant, 1991). Networks provide access to resources of various kinds, and likewise tend to be opaque to competitors. In particular, Grant (ibid) suggests, the reputation established with customers may be more durable than the quality of a firm's technology, skills, and systems and thus function as a form of capital or source of competitive advantage.

Finally, teamwork (which is a feature of work systems in all but two of our firms) reduces the transparency of employee skills and the risks that they might transfer to a rival through employees leaving. The culture in which such skills are practised can further limit copying ('replicability') by rival firms (Grant, ibid).

The ways small firms manage these three strategic issues (positioning, networking, and commitment) thus exemplify some of the key criteria for a resource-based theory of competitive advantage – namely, the importance of durability, transparency, transferability, and replicability in protecting assets created during the formation process of the new small firm (Grant, ibid).

At the same time, a critical factor is who controls these resources, and hence who gains ('appropriates') the returns on them. There are three key players in this – the lead entrepreneur, employees, and customers. The extent to which a single entrepreneur retains exclusive access to the firm's customer networks, for instance, is a critical source of control and employee dependency. The shift towards 'corporate (or team) entrepreneurship' at a later stage of growth is therefore a major problem for the founding or lead entrepreneur to confront. Equally, where networks and skills and company systems are narrowly focused on few customers, all three kinds of resource are likely to be relatively transparent to the customer, and therefore transferable and replicable. Such power may be exercised then in downward pressure on prices.

In practical terms, the effect of a limited customer base and networks dependent on a single person is to fix resources in a way that limits and conditions subsequent strategic adaptation. Small firms risk getting 'locked in' to a set of routines and capabilities which hinder subsequent adaptation. The result is 'asset specificity' (Williamson, 1975), in which skills, organizational systems, and processes for the production and delivery of a product or service have restricted application. While this enables the small firm to grow rapidly in its first few years or gives some long-term stability, this strategy (often fortuitous) carries considerable risks. As a result, subsequent issues for renewal and adaptation, and the crises experienced, are highly conditioned by this recipe for initial success.

Chapters 3 and 4 will look at these consequences of customer-focus and dependence, and routes to adaptation, while Chapter 7 will pick up the critical theme of how adaptation is effected by building, transferring, and discarding tacit, organizationally embedded knowledge.

Chapter 3

Strategic change and renewal
Crisis in the small–medium firm

Life, including economic life, is still worth living because it is sufficiently
unpredictable to be interesting

(E.F. Schumacher, 1973: 240)

INTRODUCTION

Small–medium firms are prone to failure, especially in their formative
years. The literature suggests, for example, that between a third and a half
of all new firms fail within four to five years (Cromie, 1990), while an
American review estimates that 81 per cent fail within ten years (Dawitt,
1983). Short of outright failure, many also experience crises of varying
magnitude. The character of these is also said to change as firms grow and
mature. The unfortunate inference from this, however, is that smaller firms
face crises which larger firms grow out of. This is clearly nonsense. Large
firms have a nasty habit of disappearing, only more spectacularly. Equally,
firms which survive their early years, but stay small, may be no less prone
to crises. What is more, in such cases the underlying issues and causes
closely resemble those that afflict large firms. Here, then, is an area of
convergence in the strategic analysis of large and small firms. In practice,
however, each body of work tends to emphasize a different aspect of crisis.

In this chapter, we will explore the various facets of crisis through the
model of the firm derived from Miles and Snow (1978). Essentially, this
argues for the indivisibility of solving problems to do with the external
environment from solving internally focused resource issues. The advantage in studying smaller firms in this respect is that these twin processes
are more visible and concentrated than in the larger firm. Since they occur
on a smaller scale, the researcher can get closer and understand the 'micro'
aspects involved in managing them. This would also suggest that strategic
problems in large firms need to be solved at a finer level of detail than is
commonly allowed for.

We pause here to introduce the case of Pressings, an old firm beset by
multiple, successive and interlocked problems relating to both its external

environment (its customers) and internal resourcing (leadership, employees, and facilities).

Pressings: a case of multiple crises

Pressings was founded in 1826 to manufacture metal toys, and was owned by the same family until 1979, when the father of the present owner acquired the majority of the equity:

> The company followed the traditional pattern, where the great-grandad is full of business acumen and drive, and those qualities then become progressively more dilute. So at the end, the last two generations of the family really had no impact on the business whatever. The family merely lived off the back of the company.
>
> > (Geoff Brook, CEO, and all subsequent quotations up to p. 56)

In 1964, Geoff Brook's father was recruited to work for the family:

> My father took a loss-making company, teetering on the brink of collapse, turned it round, and made it profitable again – in the usual way by switching product range and moving from one area of the market to another.

From automotive and general presswork, Brook's father refocused it on to pressing heavy-duty components for industrial conveyors (particularly in coal-preparation plants), which is where the company remains today. In the period 1964–83, Pressings grew in real terms, but became progressively more vulnerable:

> In line with a lot of other companies who detect a relatively easy way out, too much of the turnover was tied up with too few customers. So if one customer had pulled the plug, there was a distinct possibility we would have folded.
>
> When my father died of cancer in 1983 and I came here in January '84, it was obvious his grip had started to go several years before that. The thing was in a state of decline. The fabric of the building was physically decaying. Plaster was coming off the walls. It was in decline, though not yet at death's door.

In January 1984, Geoff Brook inherited the majority shareholding, and left his job in a large mail-order firm to become sales manager and learn the business:

> In 1983, there was nothing here at all. I rolled up here on 4 January '84 in a howling gale. It was half seven in the morning, pitch black outside. I came in here after the fortnight's Christmas shutdown. The cups had been stood in the middle of the office for the fortnight. And the then

managing director [CEO] swilled a cup out and the fortnight's accumul-
ated verdigris was slung on the carpet.

The first task was to get hold of the organization in a behavioural and
personal sense. There was no guidance given to employees in terms of
what they did and didn't do. I'm not talking about formal job specification, but simply someone saying, 'that's your responsibility, and
that's yours'. There was no behavioural discipline, no job discipline in
terms of areas of responsibility. On the shopfloor, there was no respect
for authority.

Within a very short time, I was engaged in an industrial tribunal. I
sacked a bloke on the spot, because I will not have the tail wagging the
dog. We won the case, happily. But I wouldn't have cared if we hadn't.
I would have done it again. So we sorted that out. And I really haven't
had to sack people that much from the original workforce.

Before even getting to grips with the personal side of the organization,
however, there were customers to be encountered. In January 1984, 85 per
cent of turnover was covered by two customers:

And all of the main customers, those two included and the balance of
15 per cent, were on the point of giving us the sack. I didn't realize this
for a few weeks. So then the first job was to get on your bike and start
rescuing the situation.

The reason was primarily delivery, because in those days quality still
wasn't playing as major a part as it is today, even six years ago. We were
just so disorganized. We didn't know what we'd done, where we'd done
it, how we'd done it, where we'd sent it.

And it was very embarrassing at my first meeting with our biggest
customer, because at that point I was not a director. There was a
managing director [CEO] on site, and the last member of the old family
engaged in the business. They were very nice people, but in terms of
business acumen, they were non-starters.

So I went out physically to every single customer and stopped them
giving us the sack. Then I came back here and we tried to turn the place
round.

Keeping customers and getting new ones, then, was the immediate
priority. However, Brook (still then only the sales manager) proved too
successful at this. The company was ill-equipped in production facilities
and administration to cope with the unplanned increased turnover, and it
simply responded by 'throwing people and hours at the problem, rather
than expertise'. In consequence, the number of employees went from forty
to seventy during 1986–87.

The result was that from 1985–87 the company made big losses and
liquidity deteriorated:

Through '85–'87, I was dragging in too much work for the company to cope with. That created its own problems, and we were haemorrhaging pound notes. Like a lot of little companies, suddenly you find your skill base is zilch compared with what is required for the new level of business and the new quality level of business that you've just generated. We just couldn't handle it – coupled with our first venture into automation which came badly unstuck. And of course, when you automate, you rearrange everything, and if it doesn't work, you're up a creek without a paddle.

We were kept afloat basically by my sales pitch with bank managers and customers. But it was quite sticky for a couple of years, to the point where my house was on the line.

We will return to this case again when we discuss how firms manage their way out of crisis.

Crisis and renewal

Related to the nature of crisis is the pattern of crisis over time – specifically how it connects with periods of stability and growth. This has been explored through notions of evolution and revolution (Miller and Friesen, 1980, 1984), and convergence and upheaval (Tushman et al., 1986).

The convergence-upheaval argument begins with the observation that increasing maturity in an industry is accompanied by a sharper focus on whatever a particular firm does well and a reinforcement of its competitive strategy. In turn, the firm develops a tighter fit between strategy, structure, people, and systems. A major shift in the industry externally, from any one of a number of possible causes, or strains from within (such as quantum growth upsetting cherished values), disrupts this equilibrium. The result is either failure or 'frame-breaking' change (Tushman et al., 1986), involving substantial alterations to strategy, structure, people, systems, and processes, with long-term implications. Thus, periods of relative continuity are interspersed with sudden bouts of rapid change.

This observation of alternating phases in the life of a firm, or 'punctuated equlibrium' (Gersick, 1991), has a number of implications. It ties in, for example, with the argument that firms do not 'grow out of' crises. It also raises the question: 'How do firms stay in the competition over long periods of time?'.

Acknowledging such patterns raises questions about the ability of firms to transform themselves. Can upheaval (or 'crisis') be avoided through timely adjustments and adaptation? Conversely, does crisis have a positive aspect? Are the crises to which small–medium firms are prone 'upheaval' in this positive sense, since they bring renewal, or the result just of plain bad management – nuisances to be got out of the way as quickly as possible?

Following on from this are the consequences of crisis. Most managers (one presumes) do not seek crises, although the construction of crisis by powerful individuals or the use of crisis as an ally has been observed on occasions as a way of pushing through needed change (Pettigrew, 1985). More often, crisis strikes and people have to find a way through. What differentiates firms is which ones learn and which do not.

Against this background, the chapter explores three related themes:

1 The character and causes of crisis in the small–medium firm.
2 How crisis fits within the life cycle of the firm.
3 The consequences of crisis in terms of learning and future adaptability.

These themes are developed in three stages. First, we document the susceptibility of the firms in our sample to different kinds of crisis. Second, we consider the patterns in which these occur, in the light of contrasting models of the life cycle as a series of sequential stages or alternatively as periods of evolution punctuated by revolutionary upheaval. Third, and most critically, we analyse the impacts of crisis in terms of learning and how firms manage their way out.

THE NATURE OF CRISIS IN THE SMALL–MEDIUM FIRM

While a high proportion of the twenty firms we studied had enjoyed rapid growth, both high-growth and retrenching firms had periodically had to overcome periods of crisis and manage difficult transitions. In some of the newer firms these were just becoming visible for the first time, whereas older firms were often experiencing repeat crises. In a sense, of course, we were studying survivors and a true picture of crisis would need to include those many firms that disappear daily. That said, managing watershed events associated with early growth and later traumas is a major, common theme even when looking at the relatively successful.

Such crises were associated with a variety of events. For example:

- insolvency, or other severe financial difficulty;
- being taken over;
- loss of internal control from precipitate growth;
- loss of key employees;
- death of the founder/owner and succession problems;
- loss of key customers, especially where there is an over-dependence on a limited number of customers;
- product obsolescence.

Table 3.1 provides a brief characterization of the major crises experienced in recent years.

Interestingly, product obsolescence was the least common source of crisis in our sample. Firms faced with fading products or services were generally

Table 3.1 Characteristics of major crisis in the sample firms

Visitor Bureau	None
Convention Bureau	None
Hotel Tourist	High turnover in management and staff.
Hotel Heritage	Forced sale after family tax troubles, leading to takeover by major hotel group; high turnover in management and staff.
Software Products	None, although warning signs of owner losing control of rapidly growing business.
Training International	Major losses in USA followed failed attempt to export UK business formula.
Skills Training	Government privatization; loss-making training centres sold (with temporary subsidy) as alternative to closure.
Legal Services	None
Bread Products	Increasing quality requirements from major customer, creating intense cost pressures; part of new plant destroyed by fire.
Aerospace Engineering	Under-investment; acquired by financial holding company from family and sold back to production director; warning signs of over-dependence when largest customer temporarily reduces orders; over-geared after modernizing plant and office systems.
MOD Products	Under-investment; acquired by private family group; cuts in government defence spending hit major customer; loss of key staff when electronics side of business relocated; major redundancies as electronics business refocused cause other staff to leave.
Pressings	Death of owner; massive loss of customer confidence through late deliveries; physically run-down; subsequent over-trading and near insolvency.
Clean Air Co.	Suicide of owner; financial misconduct and major losses; CEO leaves with sales director and salesforce to start own company.
Glass Discs	None, in first 18 months from start-up.
Fibres	None
Optics	Insolvency and takeover by private group after rapid and uncontrolled initial growth.
Construction Co.	Collapse of local government housing programme (major customer); near insolvency and major losses; long-running family succession squabbles.
House Co.	Spun-off as separate business in response to parent company crisis.
Cable Co.	Near insolvency through lack of internal financial control.
Architectural Services	Loss of major contracts; senior founding partner forced to resign by younger partners.

very quick to respond. This is a tribute to the particular strength of smaller firms, in that they are most innovative around identifying market needs and in adapting to changing requirements (Cannon, 1985; Rothwell, 1989). It may be objected that if a small firm is a 'jobber' rather than a 'marketeer' (Lydall, 1958) it does not anyway have a product to obsolesce. As the discussion in Chapter 2 suggested, however, the distinction between product/service and skills, as the thing a firm trades in, is far from cut and dried, and skills may equally obsolesce. In this respect, our sample firms also appeared to be innovative and adaptive in keeping their skills up to date.

Otherwise, problems fall into two kinds – (a) loss of control, involving resources, whether of people, finance, or operating systems, and (b) limited markets. These are often intertwined (as in the case of Pressings) and often implicate the lead entrepreneur personally. In doing so, they provide a focus for management development and succession.

Miles and Snow (1978) identified a similar balance of internal and external concerns, in their model of adaptation – although, not being directly concerned with small firms, they tended to depersonalize the consideration of the 'entrepreneurial function' and underplay changes in leadership as part of the process of change. One may argue that, given the excessive preoccupation with visible 'heroic' leaders (Pettigrew and Whipp, 1991), in both the large firm and small firm literature, this is no bad thing.

As Miles and Snow saw it, the firm faces three interlocking problems which have to be constantly resolved – an entrepreneurial problem, to do with defining and extending a product-market domain (an external focus); an engineering problem, to do with establishing the means to produce a product or service, and control its operations (an internal focus); and an administrative problem, whereby risk is reduced through the stabilization of existing activity while mechanisms for innovation are created (a joint internal-external focus). Adaptation can start with any one of these, but adjustments in the other two areas must then follow. In defining crisis, we have expressed these problems somewhat differently, but the same principle applies, that in smaller firms crisis often appears in interlocking or sequential problems.

For pragmatic reasons, small firm studies have given more equal attention to external and internal issues than has the large-firm dominated, strategic management literature. This is because the accumulation and management of resources is relatively central during start-up, while product-market development and resource management are more obviously dependent on one another during early growth. Consequently, there is a more explicit recognition in the small firm literature of the need to manage both internal and external environments successfully (Milne and Thompson, 1982; Hjern et al., 1980; Birley and Westhead, 1990).

CRISES OF CONTROL

The first kind of problem is to do with loss of internal efficiency and control of key resources. Crises of control show themselves most vividly and dramatically in financial problems. More often, firms fail because they run out of cash, not because they run out of business.

• Serious cash-flow problems affected Cable Co. (1978), Pressings (1985–87), Clean Air Co. (1984–85), Construction Co. (1979–80; 1985–86), Optics (1984), and Hotel Heritage (1987), forcing the last two into a change of ownership.

Other firms made losses on the year's business from time to time due to market downturns, but these are easier to survive.

A factor particularly associated with loss of control is rapid growth and increase in size. Success is its own enemy here.

• Within two years of starting up in 1982, Optics had over-extended itself and was insolvent, having pulled in too many customers, failed to specialize, and become unable to meet deliveries and get paid. Likewise, Pressings, having recovered from the imminent loss of its two principal customers in 1984, was once again in crisis within two years through pulling in too much work. In other companies, like Software Products, there is even now an acute consciousness that growth is getting out of hand without the CEO knowing how to get to grips with it.
• In others, like Legal Services and Architectural Services, growth has generated overheads (particularly in office space and staff) which they will have difficulty covering in any downturn in business. A simple index of their becoming over-extended is the deterioration in the ratio of partners to other staff, which is important in professional practice. Furthermore, control systems which were good at one level of operation are gradually becoming overwhelmed.

The lead entrepreneur's responsibility for loss of control

While financial difficulties can result from circumstances over which the lead entrepreneur has limited control (such as high interest rates), loss of internal control, especially as the result of precipitate growth, is invariably the result of absorption in market-making tasks and/or personalized control systems. A crisis of control is thus often a hangover from the informality associated with dominant personalities. Such individuals may play a vital role in early company success, but often do not have the skills to create the company systems to protect that success and see the company grow.

Paradoxically, part of the control problem is a reluctance to let go of power and to relinquish involvement in the day-to-day activities of the company. This is typified by a lack of succession planning. Top succession crises and vulnerability to the departure of key employees (most damagingly from the firm's point of view, to start rival companies) are consequently related problems, resulting from a failure to prepare other people to take on responsibility.

- Five of the firms mentioned as having cash-flow problems faced related succession problems, although at Construction Co. this lingered on for several years until the death of the head of the family. Clean Air Co. faced the worst setback through key staff leaving, when its CEO, sales manager and four sales representatives left to form a rival business. Only Cable Co. managed its way through without changing its chief executive, and only then through the founder giving up some of his executive power to the finance director he took on.

The problem, though, is not just one of willingness to relinquish control. People develop dependence on the lead entrepreneur to take decisions and lack prior preparation for taking more responsibility.

- The CEO at Aerospace Engineering, for instance, tried to take a back seat in 1988 and pass more of the day-to-day control to other managers, but after a year found he had to resume full-time control.

Preparing others for a bigger role is consequently a major issue for human resource development in smaller firms.

A counterpart to personalized control is the tendency to settle pay on a personalized basis, and rather loose, supposedly participative structures. This was most visible in the newer service firms which had not yet suffered major reverses (Visitor Bureau, Convention Bureau, Software Products, Training International). Irregular habits of communication and participation reflect the tendency for management to be exercised as situations arise, rather than through having systems in place to project future needs, circumstances and situations. Both kinds of management activity – communication and decision-making – in other words are dependent on and open to the whims of the lead entrepreneur.

An implication from this is the degree to which informality in human resource activities might be a predictor of business failure. Considerable effort has gone into predicting small firm failure from accounting measures (cf. Keasey and Watson, 1990), not to mention elaborate mathematical models to aid venture capital decisions (for example, Amit, Glasten and Muller 1990). Such accounting measures, however, tend to be after the event when the problems have already come to a head. The firm that is ripe for failure from loss of control, by definition, is also unlikely to produce reliable accounts. Following Argenti (1976), Storey et al., (1987) and Keasey and Watson (1987a, 1987b) have therefore proposed the use of qualitative measures (such as lateness in declaring accounts and number of directors) as indicators of lack of control. More specific aspects of management practice, such as those identified above, could provide additional surrogate measures or insights into how decisions are taken and control exercised.

Recovery from crises of control

A common pattern in financial recovery for small firms facing loss of control is takeover and/or a change in management. Most studies of smaller firms confine themselves to independent firms, and therefore fail to document this. It is evident that small firms do not actually relish being taken over, citing loss of motivation, dislike of the large company ethos, loss of flexibility, loss of identity and job prospects, including opportunities for family members, and loss of face for founders (Cambridge SBRC, 1992). For most small firms, acquisition is a last resort to ensure survival. However, more positive attitudes occur in relation to succession when owner-managers want to retire, have no one to pass the business on to, and/or want to realize their capital (Hudson, 1987).

Takeover has advantages in that it brings in its train the formalization of pay, training, and employee participation.

- Acquisition by an outside group has been the impetus for introducing modern systems of accounting and control at MOD Products and Optics, through implementation of group-wide systems and the introduction of professional managers versed in their use.

On the other hand, absorption into a larger group can result in over-control and loss of identity.

- In the quality segment of the hotel market which Hotel Heritage operated in, the personal touch of the owner-manager and relatively generous resourcing were important to success. When it fell under the control of a national chain, the 'efficiency' experts took over and Hotel Heritage was forced to lose a number of staff and meet various profit and performance targets. This produced very conflicting messages about the strategic positioning of the hotel, and precipitated instability in staffing to add to previous financial instability.

The introduction (imposition?) of professional management is thus not an unmitigated good, even before any potential loss of entrepreneurial energy and freedom is taken into account.

There is a further implication here, in the extent and nature of control exercised. The examples in our study of crisis from loss of control tended to be predominantly in manufacturing and construction – sectors which experienced the greatest difficulties during the 1980s. The question then arises whether the lower degree of formality in the new, fast-growth service organizations is viable in the longer term. Does greater informality in service organizations reflect new-style HRM or just old-style organizational slack? Is the style of human resource management found in many of our service firms a function of industry life cycle, size, product-market and accompanying technology, or independent of all of these, and how will it withstand repeated recession?

CRISES OF CUSTOMER DEPENDENCE

The second kind of problem – limited markets – is the downside of the initial advantage obtained by focusing on a few customers, which was identified in Chapter 2. Niche specialization and the accompanying focus on a limited number of customers can generate high profitability. The downside is that the commitment of resources and attention (in essence, specialization) closes off, or postpones, other potential lines of development. It does so in two ways. One is by limiting networks; the other is in creating specialized skills. Both represent a 'fixing' of resources in some sense. This phenomenon has been recognized in the tendency for new small firms to get locked into strategies which change little after the first few years (Boeker, 1989; Romanelli, 1989).

Six of the twenty firms – all characterized by a narrow focus on a few customers – faced crises from actual or impending loss of key customers.

• In the case of MOD Products, Aerospace Engineering, and Bread Products, the danger was recognized before it became terminal – either being signalled sufficiently in advance by the key customer for them to begin to take corrective action, or by a lesser customer administering a manageable shock which alerted them to the greater danger. Even so, it is still too early to say whether they have been successful in responding, since broadening a product and customer base takes time.
• Three others (Construction Co., Pressings, and Skills Training) came much closer to seeing their entire customer base disappear before they reacted. Since completing the study, Skills Training has, indeed, gone out of business because it could not develop a new customer base in time.

In all these cases, the infusion of new management sparked a search for new directions.

While firms may claim that such problems were out of their hands at the time, such failure can be traced back to a faltering of vision and perspective through networks that had become too narrow, or 'tightly coupled' (Hellgren and Stjernberg, 1987; Venkataraman et al., 1990). Although management can be collectively guilty of a failure of vision, the firm dominated by a single entrepreneur is particularly prone through the perpetuation of (outdated) founding assumptions about what is the source of organizational success. As the CEO of the Construction Co./ House Co. Group put it (having lived under the shadow of his father and in conflict with him for some years over the direction of the business), 'family generations are twice too far apart to really suit a business'.

Where succession depends on the individual life cycle, a new perspective is not as readily forthcoming as it needs to be, and renewal can be delayed. Executive turnover is more frequent in the professionally managed firm, and less practicable in the owner-managed firm.

• The professional manager heading the Convention Bureau reckoned his boredom threshhold and the need to let someone else give the business a fresh impetus meant he should be looking for a new job by the time he had spent ten years there. At the time of interviewing, he had three years to go and has since left.

The other facet of the problem lies in the 'fixing' of resources in relation to employees' skills. One instance will suffice here, although there are others we will develop in the next chapter.

• Through its key contract with British Airways which triggered its growth, Training International perfected its skills in the face-to-face presentation of culture change programmes to mass audiences. Having pioneered this within the UK, it now faces a situation where companies are looking (a) to individualized training and personal development, rather than mass training, and (b) to ongoing consultancy, rather than one-off programmes, as the way to bring about cultural change. The presentational skills it has developed are, in consequence, in danger of becoming outmoded or inadequate, and, with its high overhead of training staff, its profitability (at 25 per cent return on sales) is seriously threatened.

PATTERNS OF CRISIS

Crisis is a common phenomenon among small–medium firms. We turn now to patterns of crisis, and how crisis fits within the life cycle of the firm.

Outright failure, as we noted, is most commonly associated with the start-up phase (Birley, 1985; Cromie, 1990), while the character of problems is said to change according to the firm's stage of development (Churchill and Lewis, 1983; Berryman, 1983). In the process, crises associated with the life cycle and increasing size raise issues about entrepreneurial competence, management development and succession (Churchill and Lewis, 1983; Clifford *et al.*, 1990). The life-cycle model has thus encouraged the view that smaller firms should move directly and as soon as decently possible from an entrepreneurial mode of organization to a professional management mode (Greiner, 1972; Flamhotz, 1986).

One thread of the literature has thus been concerned with the changing character of problems as firms grow. In an analysis of 364 small business cases, generating 849 examples of problems, Dodge and Robbins (1992), for example, found that external problems were more important early in the life cycle, but internal ones became more critical as the business grew.

Dodge and Robbins' conclusions, however, seem somewhat at variance with their data. Using a four-stage model of 'formation–early growth–late growth–stability', marketing problems appear to far outweigh management problems and financial problems throughout the life cycle. Internal problems relating to management become relatively more critical as the business grows, while both marketing and financial problems diminish. They argue that their results, nevertheless, are consistent with other studies and conceptualizations of the life cycle (cf. Anderson and Zeithaml, 1984; Chaganti, 1987; Churchill and Lewis, 1983; Gray and Ariss, 1985; Lavoie and Culbert, 1978; Moore and Tushman, 1982; Quinn and Cameron, 1983; and Stoner, 1987).

In contrast, Watkins (1982), from original sources, and Berryman (1983), in a review of the literature, find a much stronger bias towards finance and accounting problems generally – although Berryman notes this may reflect the fact that the examination of accounting records is the most frequently used method of analysis.

Other problems in such studies, of which Dodge and Robbins (op. cit.) is typical, are the assignment of firms to 'a priori' life-cycle stages, without a sense of actual time-scale; failure to distinguish size of firm; and failure to distinguish whether and how fast firms are growing or declining. The Cambridge SBRC (1992) survey of 2,028 independent small–medium firms avoids these faults, and their conclusions may be a better guide to the prevalence and pattern of problems.

Using firms' own perceptual data of constraints on growth rather than objective measures of crisis, the Cambridge study found that micro firms (with less than 10 employees) and small firms (10–99 employees) experienced appreciably greater limitations to do with finance, compared with those relating to markets and management, while the reverse was true for medium (100–199 employees) and large 'small' firms (with 100–499 employees). The same contrast distinguished newer firms established since 1979 from older firms. This may reflect the more rapid growth (ie. greater needs for finance) and the lack of a track record (to raise finance) in the case of newer firms, as against older firms' needs to move beyond existing markets and maturing products. Those firms growing fastest also experienced greatest difficulties in terms of finance and skills of all kinds, and, as one might expect, least in terms of competition and markets.

Clearly, in order to make a case for understanding crisis in terms of the life cycle, it is necessary to be explicit about such factors as firm size. Thus, although Fourcade (1985) and Cromie (1990) stress the distinctive problems encountered around the five-year point in a firm's life, Cromie's firms have an average of only five employees, and Fourcade gives no information on size (although the impression is that they are very small).

Among the most reliable things one can say about patterns of crisis in the smaller firm is that (a) fast-growth firms are most prone to resource constraints of all kinds – financial, managerial, and labour (Storey, 1985; Cambridge SBRC, 1992); (b) those which fail within their first 1–2 years probably never had a market at all and only survived while they ate up their starting capital; and (c) the cash-flow pattern which accompanies the launch and take-off phase of the product life cycle readily leads the under-capitalized, 'successful' firm into over-trading and illiquidity (Burns, 1989). At this point, the ability of the life-cycle model to provide accurate predictions and useful lessons peters out.

The extent of crisis

Table 3.1 (p. 59) and the discussion in the first section gave a qualitative analysis of crisis within the sample. Table 3.2 now summarizes the extent of crisis in terms of (a) customer dependency and market downturns, (b) control and resource problems, (c) accompanying changes in leadership and management, and (d) the extent to which these three sets of events are linked. Table 3.3 (p. 70) then expresses these in terms of the age of the firms.

Within the limitations of sample size, the overall prevalence of different kinds of crisis is reasonably in line with Dodge and Robbins (1992) so far as marketing versus finance problems are concerned, but way out of line in the greater frequency of management problems in our sample. Like Dodge and Robbins, we used inter-rater assessments (by the three researchers) of written case studies to ensure reliability. Unlike them, however, we relied on firms' own definitions of crisis and significant problems, rather than our own intepretations (rather as the Cambridge SBRC (1992) did in using firms' perceptual data for constraints on growth). We also have a sales, profits, and employment record over the most recent five years for above half the sample trading in the period. Although this corroborates problems in the market, it does not of course reflect resource and management problems. While such objective measures of crisis may seem nice to have, we have not therefore included this data, given also the difficulties of extracting it on a comprehensive basis from smaller, non-quoted firms.

The biggest source of crisis originated in the market (eleven cases).

- This included cyclical downturns (House Co., Architectural Services), as well as shifts in the market (Hotel Tourist, Hotel Heritage, Training International). However, while such external factors were the immediate trigger, the source of crisis was often the dependency on just a few customers (in six cases), representing a failure of strategy.

Table 3.2 Sources of crisis

	Market	Resources	Accompanying change of leader
Visitor Bureau	—	—	—
Convention Bureau	—	—	—
Hotel Tourist	m	r (p)	c
Hotel Heritage	m	r (f/p)	c/t
Software Products	—	—	(t)
Training International	m	—	(t)
Skills Training	m (d)	—	c
Legal Services	—	—	—
Bread Products	m (d)	r (a)	c
Aerospace Engineering	m (d)	r (f)	c/t
MOD Products	m (d)	r (p)	c/t
Pressings	m (d)	r (f)	c
Clean Air Co.	—	r (f/p)	c/t
Glass Discs	—	—	—
Fibres	—	—	—
Optics	—	r (f)	c/t
Construction Co.	m (d)	r (f)	c/t
House Co.	m	—	c/t
Cable Co.	—	r (f)	c/t
Architectural Services	m	—	c

c = crisis
(d) = involving a problem of customer dependency
(f) = involving a financing problem
(p) = involving a problem of key people leaving
(a) = involving an 'act of God'
c/t = crisis managed by addition to top team
(t) = addition to top team preventing resource crisis

Setting aside adjustments of resources following on from market down-turns, crises of resource management relating to a failure of control occurred in nine cases.

- These included situations where financial resources failed to keep up with expansion (six cases), plus Aerospace Engineering which, until it arranged a restructuring of its capital, found itself over-geared (too little equity, too much debt) after its investment programme. Also included are two cases where the organization failed to hold on to key employees (along with two others which had both people and financial crises). One other firm (Bread Products) suffered a serious fire which destroyed a section of new plant.

A number of these firms faced multiple and repeat resource crises (see Table 3.3, p. 70). If these are counted separately, resource crises outnumber market ones.

Putting these figures together, a total of fourteen firms (70 per cent) can be conservatively said to have suffered one or other sorts of crisis in the last twelve years. Those so far relatively immune were all formed since 1979. In seven cases, a resource/control crisis had combined with a market crisis.

- In some cases, the one may have been a direct result of the other, as at Hotel Heritage, where loss of key staff had led to a loss of competitiveness through falling standards. In a few others, there was a rapid sequence of different crises, as at Pressings.

Since specialization on a few customers is supposed to protect against resources becoming over-stretched, the two types of crisis ought to be mutually exclusive. To have both crises simultaneously or in quick succession is indicative, therefore, of extreme turbulence.

In twelve cases, or more than half, crisis was accompanied by a change in the chief executive. Although the frequency of chief executive turnover may appear to support the view that this is a necessary accompaniment of 'frame breaking' change, circumstances differ markedly.

- In four cases, it involved the death of the owner (Pressings, Clean Air, Hotel Heritage, Construction Co.); in five cases, it followed a takeover; while in one case (Hotel Tourist), frequent turnover of managers was actually a source of its problems. From this, we might conclude that change in the wider context of ownership is at least as important.

In one other case (Cable Co.), crisis was managed by adding to the top team without a change of leader, while in two others (Software Products, Training International) introducing other key people and making internal promotions helped firms to manage their way through incipient resource/control crises. In seven cases, moreover, change in top leadership was also accompanied by additions to and development of the management team. However, in all these seven instances, changes or additions to the management team followed the change in CEO and were initiated by the new CEO.

Whichever way we look at it, the overwhelming conclusion is that business crisis is accompanied by significant changes in top management. This is very much in line with observations of upheaval by others (for example, Tushman et al., 1986).

Life-cycle patterns in crises of markets and resources

Table 3.3 shows the age of firms in relation to the crises for which we have evidence. They have been regrouped according to how long after their formation the particular crisis occurred. Does our own comparatively small sample give any support to a life-cycle perspective?

A cursory inspection shows firms experiencing crises of all kinds across a wide range of ages. Equally, a number of the firms that had yet to experience any significant crisis, although all still relatively young, were by no means in their start-up phase. If there is any pattern it is that manufacturing and construction firms of mature age are more likely to

Table 3.3 Crisis and the age of firms

	Formed	Date of crisis	Elapsed time to crisis	Market	Resources
Glass Discs	1989	—	1	—	—
Convention Bureau	1984	—	6	—	—
Fibres	1983	—	7	—	—
Visitor Bureau	1980	—	10	—	—
Legal Services	1981	—	10	—	—
Software Products	1979	—	11	—	—
Optics	1982	1984	2	—	r (f)
House Co.	1981	?	?	m	—
Training International	1980	198?	?	m	—
Cable Co.	1968	1978	10	—	r (f)
Clean Air Co.	1964	1984–85/	20	—	r (f)
		1986		—	r (p)
Architectural Services	1962	?	?	m	—
Aerospace	1960	1988/	28	m (d)	—
Engineering		1989		—	r (f)
Bread Products	1962	198?	?	m (d)	r (a)
Hotel Tourist	1946	?	?	m	r (p)
Skills Training	1919/90	1990–91	71/1	m (d)	—
Construction Co.	1907	1979–80/	72	m (d)	r (f)
		1985–86		—	r (f)
MOD Products	1832	1981/	149	—	r (f)
		1987/		—	r (p)
		1988		m (d)	—
Pressings	1826	1984–85/	158	m (d)	—
		1987		—	r (f)
Hotel Heritage	c1350	1987/	547	—	r (f)
		1989		m	r (p)

Note: Periods of continuing crisis are shown thus: 1984–85
Separate crises are shown thus: 1985/
1986
The dates and elapsed time for Skills Training reflect both its original formation and recent privatization.

face a crisis of over-dependence on a limited customer base. There is therefore no particular evidence for a life cycle view regarding the occurrence of crisis in small–medium firms.

The real issue is whether firms are more likely to experience distinctive crises at particular points in their history and at no other time. It is therefore immaterial whether similar crises to those identified, but for which we do not have evidence, first occurred at an earlier date.

Firms also experience crises of various kinds across a wide range of sizes (with our firms ranging from 35 to 355 employees). We have not attempted to tabulate this, though, since we do not have precise enough data about the size of firms when they encountered a particular crisis.

On this evidence, we can say that crisis is recurrent, common, and not restricted to any particular age. Crises have affected firms between the ages of 2 and 158 years of age, with no perceivable difference in the type of crisis. This accords with Birley and Westhead's (1990) contention that there is little support for the life-cycle model (similarly, Holmes *et al.*, 1991). Kroeger (1974: 42) encapsulated this in observing that 'failure can occur at any stage of the life cycle' – even if the firm *is* most susceptible in its early formative and developmental stage.

There is, of course, considerable 'prima-facie' evidence for this perspective, not simply in the variety of firms that fail, but in the fact that the vast majority of small–medium firms remain that size (Perry, 1987) – founders' lack of ambition for growth notwithstanding. Thus, firms of all kinds have regularly to negotiate conditions of boom and slump at the industry, national, and supra-national level. This should suggest less a life-cycle view, than some kind of 'cyclical' model that captures the dynamics of market positioning and its accompanying resource building.

MULTIPLE CRISES AND RENEWAL

Table 3.3 lists more resource crises than does Table 3.2 because it distinguishes multiple crises in a number of firms. Seven firms, in particular – Clean Air Co., Aerospace Engineering, Construction Co., MOD Products, Pressings, Hotel Tourist, and Hotel Heritage – experienced multiple, consecutive crises, involving either interlinked resourcing issues or successive market-resource ones. Such chains of events and the actions taken to manage the way out of crisis are of critical interest, raising the question 'can any good come out of crisis?'.

The complexity and turbulence of the situation in certain companies exemplifies the notion of 'upheaval' in which 'frame-breaking' change (Tushman *et al.*, 1986) can occur, with wide-ranging alterations in strategy, structure, people, systems, and processes. When seen against previous (and succeeding) eras of relative stability, such complex crises illustrate the idea of organization development as a discontinuous process (Hedberg and Jonsson, 1977; Mintzberg, 1978), and provide a dramatic challenge to the simplistic notion of uni-directional phases of growth (Drazan and Kazanjian, 1990).

Concepts of upheaval and frame-breaking change, however, have been largely untested against the experience of smaller firms (with the minor exception of a study of four service firms by Pitt (1989)). Analysing these in relation to smaller firms can be particularly instructive because the origin of crisis, as we have observed, is often within the firm itself, whereas in larger firms 'upheaval' tends to be seen primarily in relation to changes in the external environment. There is scope, therefore, through the study of small–medium firms, to reorient the general theory of strategic management.

This does mean, though, that we have to be careful to distinguish between 'revolutionary periods' and 'revolutionary change' (Gersick, 1991). Crisis can occur without fundamental change taking place, and even more to the point, without learning. We need to be especially alert, therefore, to instances of ongoing adaptation, and how coping with crisis sows the seeds of renewal.

Renewal at Pressings

Pressings provides an exemplary case of renewal being managed out of crisis. As we saw earlier, Pressings had been almost overwhelmed by the combination of problems which the CEO, Geoff Brook, inherited in 1984. Solving one exposed or generated another. Between 1984–87, it gradually overcame these to engage in longer-term adaptive behaviour through an intricately managed process of building, repairing, and improvement in the firm's market position and physical and human resources. The first part of the story concentrated on the process of repair as the firm struggled to get over one crisis after another. We pick up the story in 1986 with the company still absorbed in building its sales base.

Sales, exports, and product innovation

In that year, the company got its first export order. At the time, it was supplying a UK company, which was then shipping consignments on to its American subsidiary and taking the profit on the mark-up. In 1986, the American subsidiary (Mechanical Parts) sent a representative over to see if Pressings could supply direct. To their surprise, they got the order. This imposed enormous demands on the disorganized, struggling firm. To cope with it, Brook laid down an order control procedure which the company has followed ever since. Coming when it did, the American business provided a financial lifeline and a base for subsequent product development.

Brook then set about deepening the relationship with Mechanical Parts through a series of visits to America during 1986–88. Having established a track record, Pressings were then invited to discuss plans for a new product, which coincided with work Brook and his technical manager were doing on a prefabricated roller bearing housing which they believed would revolutionize the market. After producing some samples and doing some redesign, the first order was placed at the end of 1988. The export relationship thus triggered orders for the first new product in at least a decade, allowing Pressings to build up a range of assemblies in different diameters and providing a platform for entry to the wider US market.

Using an agent to do the initial opening of doors, Brook made a week-long trip at the end of 1988 and four further trips in 1989–90. By then, the investment in new products and new customers had started to pay off, with a second overseas customer, and exports at 25 per cent of turnover planned to increase to 50 per cent within two years.

Company infrastructure

In the meantime, while diversifying in the UK, developing a new line of products, and building exports, basic improvements to the company infrastructure continued to be made – including a refurbished office and reception area, and new appointments in quality control and production management, a commercial director to oversee buying, selling, budgets, and costs, and front office staff.
As Brook commented:

Every single person in a key slot now is new since 1984. Then, we had two middle-aged ladies in the office, neither of whom could do short-hand typing. We had one switchboard with two lines on, which I learnt on when I was nineteen years old. And we had one mechanical typewriter with a fossilized roller, which was so hard that when you typed a letter the character disappeared through the paper. There was one filing cabinet with about three files in, and no correspondence. There were no office routines. We didn't know who our customers were, or where they were. The whole infrastructure had to be put in place while we were trying to generate business.

(CEO, Pressings)

Having reasserted discipline in the factory during the first period (described at the beginning of the chapter), the second stage in rebuilding the organization was therefore to bring in new people and create an operations and administrative structure to control the business. This only became fully effective in the period 1989–90, and in 1991 was due to take a further step forward with the computerization of office systems to improve planning disciplines.

Planning

Strategic planning during this time provided a rational framework for managing a way through crisis, although it remained largely in Brook's head and was never written down. It was based in the tailoring of aims to resources and limitations at each stage of development, with commitments to sales activity and capital spending allied to that:

> Basically you have to look at your product range with regard to your skill levels, your potential skill levels, your current market base, and your potential market base, and take a series of decisions on the basis of that. As a result, we decided to kick out some traditional stuff over twenty years old, concentrate on what we were obviously good at, and develop that in terms of our skill levels in manufacturing and design with the domestic customer portfolio in mind.
>
> (CEO, Pressings)

Forward planning was then based on a view of the time needed to develop sales in new markets:

> Each of our major accounts has taken at least twelve months to get. So we budget for at least twelve months before we get our first volume order. It took me two and a half years to develop America to where it is now, and that was from a flying start. Now we've just got this new order for assemblies which has taken three years. As you become more well-known, and as the practices and product become more well-known within the industry, you're going to find your introductory times come down. A lot come to us now, but I'm still there next day, and that's how we get our business.
>
> (CEO, Pressings)

Expanding sales, in turn, were accompanied by flexible investment plans:

> We have passed a series of board minutes or resolutions, 'authorizing' the company to purchase computerised equipment, 'authorizing' the company to invest in power presses of various descriptions. So it's planned. And then you wait the opportunity. You have to lay down the aims as a framework, and then you put the flesh on as circumstances allow.
>
> (CEO, Pressings)

Above all, projected investment in capacity was accompanied by a view of what skills might be needed and how expansion itself might stimulate new efficiencies and new skills:

> Now we've pencilled in Plan B, which is to open a warehouse in the States. I've made overtures to the Ohio State Development Corporation.

So my agent can run it. And he will then either have a choice of becoming an employee, or not remaining an agent.

So we're going to at least double our production, as I see it. And then your fixed overhead/cost per unit comes down with a thump. You acquire new manufacturing skills on the back of this vast increase in business, and you're forced to increase your efficiencies here. Then, through this metamorphosis over the next two to three years, we will be able to go into Europe, whereas if I tried it now, I'd come unstuck rapidly.

But already I speak German and have recruited a bilingual secretary who's German-speaking Dutch, has lived in Spain for six years and speaks Spanish fluently. And we both speak French. So we have the languages already here.

The life cycle revisited

The 'Pressings' case shows more than mere stumbling from crisis to crisis. It shows substantial organizational renewal occurring, significant learning, and a general enhancement of the organization's capability to cope with future opportunities and threats. In Miles and Snow's (1978) terms, there is a renewed entrepreneurial search for markets; a comprehensive overhaul of the production system for making and delivering products; the creation of administrative systems for planning and controlling this activity; and new product development. Although reported by the CEO in emphatic 'personalized' terms, there is evidence of broader firm-centred development. This renewal was managed by tackling problems one at a time – indeed, the solution of one problem tended to aggravate underlying weaknesses elsewhere and, in turn, to force attention to these. In the process, experience and confidence to tackle problems increased step by step.

The Pressings case illustrates how crisis can involve 'upheaval' that ends by transforming a small, very old firm. It is not presented as typical, and may not be so – given a less determined CEO and, perhaps, a different economic environment, many another small firm may have gone under.

While the above example appears to discredit the idea of life-cycle phases, it affirms it in one significant way which is generally overlooked. The question is, 'whose life cycle – the firm's or the firm's owner-manager?' The fortunes of independent small–medium firms may be more closely tied to personal life cycles than the strategy literature in general acknowledges. In the case of Pressings, and most of the other instances featuring multiple crises, a period of success and the near-demise of the firm is closely associated with an individual's life.

There is much anecdotal evidence and some systematic evidence

(Gersick, 1991) that periods of personal development and change ('personal careers') coincide with start-up and significant transitions in new firms. Phases of renewal and subsequent decline in firms of all ages may be similarly associated with individual life cycles. Even in relatively 'formalized' firms like Fibres, individuals make a difference. Personal life cycles therefore deserve closer scrutiny as a source of strategic action and organizational fortunes.

LEARNING AND CHANGING THROUGH CRISIS

In conclusion, it is possible to see crisis affecting organizational learning in three possible ways, bearing in mind the various facets of crisis presented through the chapter. These will tend to occur in sequence and in cyclical fashion, often ultimately precipitating a fresh crisis through renewed inertia.

1 Changing minds

The most common perspective on crisis is to see it breaking old strategic recipes, challenging belief systems, and overturning existing power structures (Miller and Friesen, 1980; Tushman *et al.*, 1986). Crisis first induces 'unlearning' by dislodging the interpretive schema by which organizations and individuals construe their competitive environments and disrupting the political systems which hold existing orthodox schema in place (Hedberg, 1981; Nystrom and Starbuck, 1984; Fiol and Lyles, 1985). Crisis forces attention to and re-assessment of information that was previously blocked or ignored. Crisis in this sense tends to originate in relation to the market, as a result of perceived deficiencies in market strategies.

The crises of customer dependence described in this chapter, often accompanied by succession traumas, are classic cases of this, triggering the search for new markets and products.

2 Elaborating organization

A second perspective is to see crisis not only as loosening attachment to the past, but helping to set in place a new configuration of roles, systems, and procedures. Crisis which stems from problems of internal control, resourcing, and succession is especially likely to lead to such a recon-figuring. Typically, such crises expose weaknesses in planning and control, and lead to more rigorous systems being put in place. Often, this entails new appointments to manage these systems. Pressings provides many instances of this kind of infrastructure development.

More generally, the external recruitment of a finance specialist is a typical role addition in the smaller firm (Storey, 1985), with production planning staff also. Many of our firms, like Cable Co., added such people. In this way, crisis can be functional for the small firm, especially one that is relatively young, by bringing about an elaboration of organizational structure and expertise, in place of the simple organization and single cohort it will have started out with (Pfeffer, 1983).

Put another way, crisis leads to a restructuring of those artifacts (such as roles) and operating procedures which theorists have seen as the carriers of organizational memory (March and Simon, 1958; Starbuck and Hedberg, 1977; Jelinek, 1979). Revised planning and control procedures establish new decision rules for situations that may be subsequently encountered.

However, while, in the short term, an organization may become more systematic and efficient in its search and decision-making through the establishment of planning routines (Walsh and Ungson, 1991), as Miles and Snow (1978: 28) note, in the longer term such procedures may become a strait-jacket and once again have to be broken or 'unlearnt': 'adaptive decisions tend to harden and become aspects of tomorrow's structure'.

This was, of course, the sense of Greiner's (1972) model of successive phases of evolution and revolution. Thus, tighter internal controls imposed at MOD Products after takeover were beginning to hamper its development into new markets through restrictions on recruiting sales staff.

3 Affecting psychology

A third possible impact that crisis may have, but which is least appreciated, is as a reference point in individual memories. It provides a lasting warning about the things that should be avoided. As such, it may reinforce the evidence and structures of formal planning, or override them.

Because crisis tends to reach throughout an organization and is present in many individual memories, it attains the status of an organization-level schemata or 'frame of reference' (Shrivastava and Schneider, 1984), which in time becomes myth and taboo. This helps to focus activity, while creating the risk that past crises over-condition subsequent behaviour. Equally, of course, success itself can have a similar impact by creating over-confidence.

Preoccupation with previous crises among those interviewed in our study indicated that crisis was a significant aspect of organizational experience and a major reference point in strategic action. In contrast, strategic advance for smaller firms is often presented simply in terms of more and better planning, both operational and strategic, to remedy what are seen as unstructured, irregular, incremental, reactive, and inadequate practices in small firms (Gibb and Davies, 1991). This orthodoxy is central, for instance, to government schemes to help small businesses in the UK. While laudable in terms of enhancing systems, it overlooks the psychology of crisis and the impact of such experience.

Future-oriented planning thus conflicts with the view that 'the future has no place to come from but the past' (Neustadt and May, 1986: 251). Awareness of the past (and, equally, lack of awareness of a past which constrains in unexamined ways) conditions present behaviour.

The benefits of crisis

These facets of crisis and renewal suggest it is often a cyclical process. At the point of renewal, however, organizational learning it seems can be affected in two sets of ways. First, crisis can contribute to both 'unlearning' (by breaking old recipes) and to new learning (by being constructive of new competences such as planning). Second, past crises and current planning can reinforce one another or alternatively generate conflicting messages.

The broad implication is that, for the organization that comes through it, crisis brings a number of benefits, not simply through being destructive of things that are outmoded, but by actually being constructive of new competences and systems. This is a broader perspective on crisis, as a factor in the development of small–medium firms, than is customary.

SUMMARY AND CONCLUSION

In this chapter, we have done three things. First, we have set out the essential character and various causes of crisis in the small–medium firm. These take two generic forms – a loss of internal control and problems that arise from over-dependence on one or two customers.

This is not to gainsay more general problems of lack of demand that can occur. Surveys of 'barriers to growth' invariably rate lack of demand highly and during the recent recession this has been elevated to number one position (SBRT, 1991). However, lack of demand may conceal more fundamental problems of strategy (as well as competence). The point to stress, which comes through very clearly in our case studies, is that customer dependence can generate crises whereas until then this may have been the route to stability. For that reason, it is all the more likely to be ignored until it produces a crisis. Surveys of the problems small business owners cite are unlikely to capture these underlying causes.

The second theme was to consider the evidence for patterns of crisis within the life cycle of the firm. We concluded that such evidence is tenuous at the least. Crisis in small–medium firms is recurrent, common, and not easy to associate with the age of a firm once a firm has survived start-up. If age cannot be distinguished, life-cycle stages are difficult to sustain.

The third topic was to consider crisis in relation to learning and the firm's future adaptability. This theme has tended to produce comfortable generalizations of a one-dimensional sort that are relatively untested against in-depth case evidence, and certainly in relation to the development of smaller firms. Generally, we lack a fine-grained appreciation of how exactly crisis episodes act on one another; how they add to and detract from the firm's capabilities in the medium and long term; and how they interact with entrepreneurial episodes which are more specifically oriented to adaptation in the market. Evidence of this kind needs to be set against such platitudes as firms emerging 'fitter and leaner' from recession, for example.

In this chapter, we have made a beginning in filling such gaps in our knowledge. In subsequent chapters we will take this further. Nevertheless, significant gaps remain, requiring focused research on critical incidents associated with crisis in firms.

Chapter 4

Adaptation and resource management

Into the making of the future enters that mysterious and inexpressible factor called human freedom – the freedom of creativity.

(E.F. Schumacher, 1973: 228)

INTRODUCTION

This chapter stands in contrast to the last in that it deals with adaptation – that is, the extension of the firm's product-market domain. Following Miles and Snow (1978) again, this includes the entrepreneurial, marketing-based activity of targeting an existing or new product/service at a new or expanded market/segment, *and* the development of resources and organization to service the expanded domain. To this extent, then, it continues the theme of treating entrepreneurship and resource-management as indissoluble parts of the overall strategy process.

As such, it challenges a perspective which has come to dominate recent work on the development of small–medium firms. This is the emphasis on entrepreneurship defined as 'the relentless pursuit of opportunity without regard to resources currently controlled' (Stevenson and Sahlman, 1989: 104; Stevenson, 1983; Stevenson and Gumpert, 1985; Jarillo, 1989; Stevenson and Jarillo, 1989; Timmons, 1990; Dubini and Aldrich, 1991). While this focuses on a significant behavioural trait in growth-oriented firms, we believe it produces a one-sided view of the growth process which is not borne out by the evidence of how small firm entrepreneurs behave or of how small firms grow.

The chapter also connects back to the theme of crisis by reflecting on how adaptation and crisis relate to one another over time. The convergence-divergence model (Tushman *et al.*, 1986), for instance, sees crisis as a radical shift in strategy, while adaptation is the process of incremental change between bouts of crisis. A second perspective is to see crisis as a trigger which ushers in 'adaptive' change. In this case adaptation simply describes change from an existing state. Crisis can initiate it or speed up processes and activity already at work (Pettigrew, 1985). But there is less sense of a radical change in direction.

Our own data is more akin to this second perspective in suggesting it is more appropriate to see adaptation and crisis as interdependent processes which feed off one another. In many firms, adaptive activity is going on all the time, in the form of product development and extension of market networks, but it just happens to be less visible. When a crisis in a firm's markets occurs, it is then tempting to attribute the initiatives taken to the crisis, when all that has happened is efforts are redoubled or work already going on in the background is brought forward. In other words, there is no single, linear causation between crisis and adaptive behaviour.

The extended example of Pressings in the previous chapter illustrated the intricate interweaving of these processes. In this chapter, we provide a more schematic view of the relationship by tracing the origins of the most radical kinds of adaptive behaviour in crisis or, at least, in incipient crises.

ENTREPRENEURSHIP AS OPPORTUNITY-SEEKING BEHAVIOUR

Stevenson and Sahlman (1989: 104) acknowledge that entrepreneurship should not be regarded as an all-or-nothing trait, but as 'a range of behaviour between extremes'. These extremes, defined as the 'promoter' type of manager and the 'trustee' type, represent, respectively, an orientation to opportunity and to resources currently controlled. Smith and Miner (1983) make a similar distinction between the 'craftsman' and 'opportunist'. Having developed the contrast, however, Stevenson and Sahlman appear to maintain a clear distinction between the two in which only the one exhibits genuine entrepreneurial behaviour. Administrative behaviour seems to be very much a poor relation to the opportunity-seeking entrepreneur. The resulting portrayal is not unlike that of Miles and Snow's (1978: 58) contrast between 'defender' and 'prospector' orientations:

> Unlike the Defender, the Prospector's choice of products and markets is not limited to those which fall within the range of the organization's present technological capability . . . entrepreneurial activities always have primacy, and appropriate technologies are not selected or developed until late in the process of product development.

While entrepreneurship without the orientation to opportunity is an empty concept, we believe it is necessary to go back to the definition of the problem in the terms in which Miles and Snow (1978) originally represented it. To repeat, this requires the firm constantly to resolve three interlocking problems that typically occur more or less simultaneously (1978: 21) – an entrepreneurial problem, to do with defining and extending a product-market domain; an engineering problem, to do with establishing the means to produce a product or service, and control its operations; and an administrative problem, which reduces risk by stabilizing existing activity while also providing mechanisms for innovation.

Crucially, in Miles and Snow, adaptation can start with any one of these, and the resulting strategies compare no less favourably in terms of aggressiveness or the exploitation of opportunities. The objective issue, it seems to us, is, rather, (a) whether opportunities are pursued within an existing domain or outside it, and (b) whether these are presented fortuitously (for example, by legislation or existing customers) or pro-actively sought.

Initial empirical support for taking a more balanced view comes from two UK studies of small firms. The first (Cannon, 1985) emphasizes how innovation frequently arises from solving problems customers put to them – that is, innovations are solutions to clearly defined, externally originated tasks which involve the firm in skilfully mobilizing its existing resources. This places resource management more squarely at the centre of entre-preneurial behaviour. At the same time, all firms in Cannon's study put considerable emphasis on improving existing production processes to secure productivity improvements. Storey (1991) found owner-managers in fast-growth new firms rapidly developed similar priorities.

It may be objected, of course, that such firms are not truly entre-preneurial. Indeed, Cannon (1985: 40) qualifies his own findings on the extent to which innovations are a response to customer-defined needs and problems, by suggesting that 'it may be that the major change type of development is overwhelmingly the preserve of the true entrepreneur'. The small firm is not by definition entrepreneurial, nor is the small firm owner or manager. On the other hand, pinning one's hopes on 'major change' as the only true expression of entrepreneurship seems unduly restrictive. Big breakthroughs are often the culmination of many small endeavours, and entrepreneurship, as Kirzner (1985) has argued, is displayed in many small ways.

The second study, sponsored by the UK Advisory Council for Applied Research and Development (ACARD), into barriers to growth in small firms, concluded that:

> The weight of evidence on market structure and the competitive positioning of small firms suggests that the really systematic and pervasive problems faced by small firms are internal to the firm, such as the technical base, the management systems and processes, appropri-ate organisation structures and the availability of skilled managers. In terms of positioning the firm against the market, small firms are specially handicapped by their limited resources and the restricted range of assets they have available.
>
> (McGee, 1989: 192)

Since this problem is so well attested, it seems perverse to stress the character of entrepreneurship as lying in the pursuit of opportunities beyond the small firm's capabilities.

A refocusing of the issue requires two things:

1 To redefine the field, either giving broader meaning to entrepreneurship or discarding it in favour of a more composite term like 'innovation'.
2 To view innovation and entrepreneurship in the established small–medium firm processually, by reference to the firm's existing strategic situation.

As a broader concept, 'innovation' brings more sharply into focus the concern with process improvements which small firms often exhibit. More importantly, it highlights the fact that the problem is often to transform a firm's existing knowledge base, which is derived from and embedded in its technology and in its accompanying work routines (Nelson and Winter, 1982; Spender, 1991). In contrast, the idea that 'the entrepreneur pursues opportunities in advance of existing resources', implies that resources are an 'add-on', and that the problem, once opportunities are located, is simply acquiring additional resources.

If we redefine the field in terms of 'innovation', it is necessary then to see it as a process in relation to specific circumstances. It is not just that innovation is a continuous process of adjustment in which constant small changes add up (Cannon, 1985). In establishing itself at start-up, the small firm typically creates a set of conditions which subsequently constrain. As Barber *et al.* (1989: 15–16) put it:

> The challenge facing the growing firm can be stated in terms of a move from relatively narrow market niches in which it exploits a narrow range of distinctive assets into a situation in which it serves a larger number of market segments with a much broader skills and knowledge base.

The chapter develops this argument by characterizing processes of growth and development among our firms, in the form of an empirically derived typology. We then identify the resource implications, human and material, that inhibit the pursuit of particular strategies and how solutions to resource acquisition are accomplished. In doing so, we note how a firm's original strategic positioning can act as a constraint. We then consider the nature of the firm's developmental activity, arguing that more radical moves are generated in response to internal resource issues ('capacity-push'), while the external environment drives only incremental development ('customer-pull'). In this way, the pursuit of opportunities is intimately linked to resource management. Our analysis is thus located within the resource-based view of strategic development originating with Penrose (1959) and recently restated by, among others, Rumelt *et al.* (1992) and Grant (1991).

SEVEN MODES OF DEVELOPMENT IN THE SMALLER FIRM

As Chapter 2 argued, a close relationship with a major customer and the lead entrepreneur's personal networks are important strategic resources in establishing a small firm (Casson, 1982; Johannisson, 1988; Batstone, 1991). On the other hand, such a limited customer base and networks dependent on a single entrepreneur have the effect of fixing resources in a way that limits and conditions subsequent strategic adaptation. The result is 'asset specificity' (Williamson, 1975), in which skills, organizational systems, and processes for the production and delivery of the firm's product or service have restricted application (Nelson and Winter, 1982). The characteristic strategic positioning of small firms thus heavily influences subsequent modes of adaptation and renewal, and the resources they need to develop.

The purpose of this section is to present a typology of modes of product-market adaptation or development derived from our cases, and to highlight the resource implications of these, pinpointing in particular the requirements for breaking out of over-dependence, tightly coupled networks, and asset specificity.

Our typology has a very specific character. First, it is a 'strategic' typology, combining marketing activity with consideration of resource requirements, especially human resource requirements (Hofer and Schendel, 1978). Second, it is a 'behavioural' typology, not a 'firm' typology. That is, firms may practise more than one behaviour at various times. This distinguishes it from Miles and Snow's (1978) 'defender–prospector–analyser–reactor' typology which implies firms' behaviour is invariant. In this regard, our evidence will challenge an unfortunate tendency in management writing generally – namely, elevating the description of tactics at a pragmatic level into over-determined typologies of firms. Third, it is an 'empirical' typology, about precise tactics for development – hence, we prefer to talk about 'modes' or 'ways of developing'.

The literature on small firms has relatively little, in fact, to say on tactics for developing markets, beyond adopting a model of broad strategy types (Covin, Slevin, and Covin, 1990; Davis, Hills, and LaForge, 1984), and has less still to say about the resource implications. Perry (1987), for example, states that a small firm must always follow a niche strategy, and then grow through market development and product development, in that order; while market penetration or diversification is not appropriate, except at a precise point in the early stage of the industry life cycle. As Cannon notes (1985), however, observing innovative activity over time undermines simple distinctions between types of product-market development, represented in the classic 'market penetration–market development–product development–diversification' matrix.

An exception to the broad strategy approach is that of Pitt (1989: 274), who characterized adaptive behaviour in general terms as 'the search for an extended domain'. More specifically, he identified four levels – (a) reacting to opportunities fortuitously presented; (b) deliberate targetting; (c) identifying latent capabilities; and (d) exploratory testing of existing boundaries. His study, however, covered only four firms. A second exception is Drucker (1985), who described seven sources of innovation which can be systematically searched for growth opportunities.

Our own typology consists of seven modes of adaptation and extends Pitt's, while retaining certain of his terms. It is organized in a similar fashion according to the degree to which the enterprise is departing from existing products or markets. The effect of presenting the typology in this form is to distinguish a range of behaviour which is about responding to customers ('customer-pull'), from adaptive behaviour which is driven by the need to fill capacity ('capacity-push'). This is a critical issue in the strategy management debate in arbitrating between the claims of a market-driven perspective and a resource-based theory.

The seven modes of adaptation or development are:

1 Capitalizing on environmental beneficence, as where new legislation comes into force that favours a product.
2 Incremental opportunism, adding services or products in direct response to customer requests, in an incremental and reactive way.
3 Developing a related package of services and products, in a more deliberate attempt to link diversification, possibly by setting up related companies.
4 Actively searching and targeting additional niches that have different demand characteristics, thereby spreading risk.
5 Building a flexible resource base so that the firm becomes capable of supplying a wide variety of customers and products.
6 Applying expertise in related product areas, through a developed design function and radical product innovation.
7 Testing markets and boundaries, by experimenting with new business, including international ventures, and mixing elements of strategy.

Table 4.1 summarizes the use of these strategies and tactics by the sample of twenty firms, over a five-year period from 1985–90. It excludes, however, specific examples of developmental strategy for Glass Discs, which was still in a start-up phase. Similarly, Skills Training was effectively in a start-up situation having been reformed through privatization and needing to build a paying client base from scratch. Hotel Tourist also has no entry since its owners, seeing no future for it in its present location, were operating an end-strategy of milking profits with minimal outlay on facilities. Hotel Heritage, owned by the same chain, was also in something of a hiatus after two changes of ownership in three years, and uncertainty

Table 4.1 Strategies for growth in small–medium firms

	Modes of Development						
	1	2	3	4	5	6	7
Visitor Bureau		•					
Convention Bureau		•					
Software Products	•		•				•
Training International					(•)		•
Legal Services				•			
Aerospace Engineering			•		•		
MOD Products					•	•	
Pressings						•	•
Clean Air Co.	•		•				•
Fibres	•					•	•
Optics					•	•	•
Construction Co.			•	•			•
House Co.			•	•			•
Cable Co.							•
Architectural						•	•
Glass Discs			no entry				
Skills Training			no entry				
Hotel Tourist			no entry				
Hotel Heritage			no entry				
Bread Products			no entry				

among the head office marketeers about how to position it. Conceptually, repositioning involves redefining a niche, while in practical terms it can involve any number of possible initiatives. Finally, Bread Products was intent on pursuing market penetration, with an emphasis on reducing costs, developing reliability through automated plant, and standardization of product. It continued to espouse the somewhat unrealistic strategy of becoming 'the lowest cost producer of bread in the UK', without any apparent attempt to adapt by other means.

The resulting examples of adaptation therefore comprise fifteen of the total sample.

The following section describes the approach to market development in these fifteen firms in terms of the seven modes of adaptation. First of all we characterize the particular behaviour in relation to the market (where and how the market opportunity arose), and then, in each case, we highlight the resource implications (what these are, and how and why particular firms responded the way they did).

1 Capitalizing on environmental beneficence

The easiest way for small firms to grow is by doing more of what they already do. This corresponds to the argument about growing on the back of just one or two customers to which we gave special prominence in Chapter 2. In another sense, it is what a 'market penetration' strategy is about. For the smaller firm, however, it is useful to be more specific about the conditions which help market penetration. The small firm is less likely to be able to influence the growth of its markets through marketing techniques, and unlikely to carry enough weight to influence market growth as such. Its growth is more likely to depend on fortuitous circumstances ('environmental beneficience') as the market expands around it, and opportunism in taking advantage of this. While Pitt (1987) used the term 'environmental beneficience' in a general sense, we were struck, however, by how often opportunities were specifically created by legislation.

Three firms, in particular, prospered in this way, as a result of new legislation coming into force to favour an existing product or service (Clean Air Co. and Software Products), or through deregulation of a customer industry (Fibres). For example:

- Health and safety regulations (COSHH – *The Control of Substances Hazardous to Health, 1988*), which became operative on 1 January 1990 in the UK, created new employer liabilities which provided a strong selling point for the company's fume-extraction equipment. Legislation transformed a 'luxury' into a 'necessity', and dramatically expanded Clean Air Co.'s market. The result in 1990 alone was a doubling of sales.
- In contrast, Fibres benefitted from a combination of deregulation in telecommunications and financial services, which boosted the market for optical fibre cable.

Those firms which are best placed to capitalize on such fortuitous opportunities will already be established in the relevant market, probably as a result of original product/service innovation. For them, 'reacting' to opportunities can be a most lucrative, and relatively risk-free course. The bigger challenge is likely to be in building an adequate resource base, requiring capital investment and the recruitment and training of additional employees. Since time is of the essence in being able to capitalize on the initial advantage of market presence, quick access to financial and human resources is critical. Privately owned small firms are often at a disadvantage because of limited capital. More especially, their owners are often unwilling to dilute their holding and weaken control by taking on board external equity finance (Aston Business School, 1991). Much therefore depends on personality, personal circumstances, and growth ambitions. Clean Air Co. and Software Products provide a contrast in this respect:

- The CEO of Clean Air Co. had to struggle against its owner's view of the company as a source of income, after the death of her husband, who founded it, left her with small children to bring up. It was therefore difficult for the CEO as a salaried employee to invest in facilities and expand the number of employees, while the owner continued to take out a substantial income and resisted outside investment. The company had also been struggling to rebuild its resource base after substantial (financial) losses in 1984–85 and the poaching of its sales force (human resource) in 1985–86 by the previous CEO.

- In contrast, Software Products had grown rapidly as a result of a major injection of capital of £5 million in 1988 from its two principal customers in the insurance business, who recognized its value to them and wanted to secure its growth and product development.

The fact that the owner-CEO of Software Products and the CEO of Clean Air Co. both previously worked in large international companies illustrates how those who have had management experience in larger companies are usually readier to give serious consideration to venture capital funding (Aston Business School, 1991). This may be because they are more confident in their management abilities; or because they personally do not bear the risk; or because they are more oriented to the rewards which size of organization brings through higher status and salary. The possibility that people are more risky where they do not bear direct financial risk is rather at odds with accepted images of the entrepreneur, although it fits with common observation (of entrepreneurs and ordinary people alike) that they are readier to spend other people's money than their own.

2 Incremental opportunism

'Incremental opportunism' is a way of extending activities within a broadly defined domain by means of relatively small sideways steps in the first instance. These are likely to arise from customer requests or as obvious ancillary lines generated by existing activities. It is thus customer- or sales-led, 'reactive', and opportunistic. 'Niche-based adventurism' would be another way of defining it. It illustrates the blurred line between product/ service development (new activities) and market development (expanding the definition of the market through a wider range of activities). Again, such activity depends on already being in the relevant market.

- Both Bureaux illustrate this behaviour through such activity as mounting training courses to support various aspects of tourism, taking over responsibility for managing tourist information centres, running tour guides, and establishing computerized booking facilities for events and hotels.

'Incremental opportunism' can generate clearly defined training needs, but requires a deliberately flexible style of organization to accommodate new activities. The risk is that the growth generated from adding services in an opportunistic and reactive fashion can take an organization down paths that are not an efficient and profitable use of resources. In the two Bureaux, undirected growth was held in check through the outline corporate plan their local authority sponsors required them to produce.

The part played by opportunism and reactivity can be overstated in other ways, too. In both Bureaux, growth was generated by paying attention to the whole environment of tourism. Both chief executives were constantly hustling and lobbying to improve the tourist infrastructure and attitudes to tourism within their cities, while building networks was integral to the activities of both organizations. Likewise, the CEO at the Convention Bureau constantly impressed on staff the need to market the city and to think in terms of 'destination marketing'. Opportunities that arose for expanding the role of the Bureaux were therefore the result of this 'front-end' investment.

'Strategic' investment of this kind in networks is important because it encourages 'happenstance' – the chance presentation of unsought opportunities. This theme recurs in connection with the internationalization of small firms (Hendry, 1994). It is also a key issue in determining how far the pursuit of opportunities should really be conceptualized as a resource-building activity.

3 Developing a related package of services and products

A more radical extension of 'niche-based adventurism' is where a company actively puts together a related package of services and products to gain more of the added value. A company can begin with a product and add services – for example, Software Products providing training and leasing of equipment; it can provide a service with bought-in products which it then decides to make for itself (as at Clean Air Co.); or it can add a further stage in a production process (as at Aerospace Engineering which bought a small electro-plating company to which previously it had sent out machined parts for finishing).

This mode of development can often mean setting up related companies. This avoids exposing the whole business to the risks in any one part, while allowing each to develop its own way of operating. A feature of this pattern of development, via related and subsidiary companies, is the employment of a wider raft of managers, with more varied backgrounds and experience. However, this complicates the structure of overall control, the demands on top management, and can create stress in the entrepreneurially dominated small firm (graphically illustrated in the case of Software Products).

A second problem of control with related services or products is that each is capable of losing money at the same time, while fixed costs also increase. Construction firms seem to have a particular tendency to prolifer-ate divisionalized activities like this, with various services, such as equipment hire and 'small works', being spun-off. An important resource issue is therefore the introduction of much tighter financial controls. Other kinds of business which generate inter-related companies in this way are real estate, and sales organizations which put agency agreements for servicing and supply into separate companies that are destined to outlast the sales operation.

A lot of such activity can thus be held apart from the main business operation. Where it involves genuine backward or forward integration, however – making products or components previously bought in, or adding a further stage in the production process – the addition of overheads becomes a serious consideration (which is one reason why neither is particularly recommended for smaller firms (Rumelt, 1979; Glueck, 1980; Pitt, 1989)). The financial constraints on the CEO at Clean Air Co. have already been mentioned in this respect, and affected also his desire to develop a simple manufacturing operation to secure more of the added value and to export:

> To make just a small move – to appoint an export sales manager, or a consultant for environmental matters, or a quality manager – none of which is a vast investment, could, if it went wrong, jeopardize the company. So we need to move slowly to build up funds to make new appointments. If I could encourage venture capital, we could grow to £10 million turnover in three years. If not (and I can't because the sole shareholder has an over-estimate of the value of the company and doesn't want to dilute her holding), we will probably see 20 per cent per annum growth, as against over 100 per cent per annum growth.
>
> (CEO, Clean Air Co.)

4 Actively searching and targetting additional niches

A related package of services and products, or simply products that are related to one another, compounds the risk associated with any downturn. Spreading risk by diversifying the product/service portfolio into areas that have different characteristics is, therefore, a fourth mode of develop-ment. We are still talking, though, about a domain characterized by broadly related products or services, rather than unrelated diversification.

Just as growth can often be built on the back of one good customer contact, so diversification can be managed through a series of such relationships in different markets. The original pattern of development, and the recognition of problems associated with it, can therefore provide learning for subsequent ventures. Legal Services, for example, had five lines of work – two involving the general public (conveyancing and matrimonial litigation), one channelled through the legal aid system (civil litigation), and two others (mortgage repossessions and trustee work for churches) which depended on the partners' personal contacts with a single client.

The development of different lines of work in this way sets up internal pressures for specialization, and the need for tighter administrative systems. In addition to encouraging specialization, diversification (even in related markets) can involve such different operating principles that it is best managed through separate companies.

- In construction, for example, there is a big difference between building to order (Construction Co.) and building speculatively (House Co.), with their different requirements for flexibility, cash-flow, and capital. For this reason, House Co. was eventually spun-off as a separate division from Construction Co. to allow its different culture to flourish.

Again, the demands of this kind of development are in a more complex management structure and the need for tighter financial control.

While the organizational implications of diversification under 'modes of adaptation' (3) and (4) are familiar in general models of organizational growth, the phenomenon of small firm owners generating a constellation of related companies has received less attention. In fact, small firm entrepreneurs often run a string of companies. One aspect of this, as recent research has shown, is that far from small firms being simply a target for large firms to acquire, small firms themselves are often active in making acquisitions (Cambridge SBRC, 1992), with one in five of the Cambridge sample having acquired another firm in the previous five years. Smaller firms are supposed to be simpler: acquisition activity and spinning off subsidiaries suggests this is not the case.

5 Building a flexible resource base

In Chapter 2, we observed that small firms often grow by establishing a close association with one or two customers and that this has certain advantages in focusing the development of resources through specialization. Such dependence, as long as the customer prospers, can give the smaller firm much-needed stability and security. Among other things, it allows attention and money to be given to systematic training. Reliance on one or a few customers may also influence specific human resource systems and practices.

Once such a resource base has been built, however, with one customer in mind, dependence can be reduced and further growth achieved by recognizing the potential to serve a wider customer base. The recent history of Aerospace Engineering illustrates this through two phases – first, through the building of a modern, flexible manufacturing resource, and, subsequently, in attempting to utilize this for a more varied market:

- As we previously observed, Aerospace Engineering had built its business on the back of a high degree of dependence on Rolls-Royce, and when the present owner/manager bought out the company in 1985, he set about securing its position as a component supplier to Rolls through major investments in CNC (computer numerically controlled) machines and training. The result was a modern, flexible manufacturing facility with capacity at almost double existing sales. However, having put money and effort in to secure Rolls' business, and needing to show a suitable return on the investment, the disadvantages of dependence started to become more visible. A lull in orders, when Rolls destocked following its privatization, acted as the initial trigger to think about seeking new customers, compounded by losses incurred in keeping together the highly skilled workforce. Continuing pressure on prices strengthened the resolve to broaden the customer base, and during 1990 the company began actively to seek other customers. This included the acquisition of an electro-plating facility to increase the service Aerospace Engineering could offer.

The investment in material and human resources thus opened up the prospect of better returns on existing business through improved efficiencies; the opportunity to look for higher added value sales from other customers from an enlarged and more flexible manufacturing facility; and the prospect of reducing its long-term dependence on Rolls-Royce.

However, as it soon found, there were other penalties from being customer-dependent, which held it back. These included limited market knowledge, lack of own products, quality standards specific to one customer, and a managerial structure over-focused on one person who also happened to be the prime link with the firm's main customer. Such factors are a major obstacle for a small firm in achieving 'break out' even when it has established a flexible manufacturing resource. 'Break out' requires additional substantial development in higher-level skills – in marketing, design, and product development – and the development of team management. We will return to this later since it is pivotal to small firm adaptation.

The resource issues involved in building a flexible resource base thus fall into two phases. First, is the physical resourcing, with the upgrading of relevant skills to make that work, to enhance what Miles and Snow (1978) call the engineering system. Second, there is the more specific addition of human resources to improve its innovative capability. The critical issue for the small firm, given its limited financial resources and the difficulty most such firms have in carrying 'organizational slack', is how to give time and resources to enhancing its capability in this way. Or in other words:

How can smaller firms satisfy their immediate requirements for economic and financial performance, while creating the conditions for longer-term development and learning?

The solution to this is in many respects *the* fundamental strategic problem for smaller firms and bears directly on our 'strategy through people' theme. In Chapter 7 we attempt a solution.

MOD Products, which was further down the track in building up a design expertise, and Training International, which had just begun to recognize the need to shift its skills and knowledge base, provide other examples of firms wrestling with this adaptation problem.

6 Applying expertise in related product areas

Once a firm has developed its own design expertise on top of specialist technological skills, it can then extend its range through new products. This can occur incrementally through product modification, or radically by the combination of new technologies, or even by switching to an entirely new technology.

- Thus, over a number of years, MOD Products had gradually migrated into new product areas, aided in the 1960s and 1970s by the Ministry of Defence's funding of prototypes. More recently, with the impending decline in defence work, the company had been using its design experience to try to shift its whole technological and product base towards electronics and factory/process control systems. This meant having to build up an alternative skills and knowledge base with the same kind of problems as Aerospace Engineering was facing, although it had the advantage of a mature design expertise in the other half of its business and stronger traditions of product development.

Two other firms (Optics and Architectural Services) already possessed flexible design expertise, being effectively solvers of problems presented by customers – Optics designing and assembling opto-mechanical systems, and applying thin film coatings to glass; Architectural Services specializing in leisure and tourism developments. A further two firms were active in more focused product development that came from seeing an opportunity and developing a product for it: Pressings with its invention of a prefabricated roller-bearing for use in heavy-duty conveyor systems, and Fibres with its technique for flexible installation of fibre optic cable in new buildings.[1]

7 Testing markets and boundaries

The final approach to development and renewal is where firms actively and consciously test the boundaries of what they currently do. Learning and discovery are central to this activity, and invite a deliberate process of strategic review. The important resource question is a human resource one, since it is initially about how such learning is acquired and played back into the firm.

In some respects, 'testing markets and boundaries' is like other examples already described – such as 'actively searching and targeting additional niches' – since it is about transferring lessons from one product-market to another. However, it is also the most creative, adventurous, and to that extent most genuinely entrepreneurial type of behaviour. In the same way, the motives which drive it are neither simply reactive to customers nor solely driven by the need to fill capacity. Above all, a firm's ability to experiment comes from building up expertise and resources elsewhere first, unlike in many other cases where the resource question is an afterthought. For this reason, we treat it *sui generis* as a distinctive mode of adaptation.

Our examples fall into two kinds – transferring lessons from one domestic product-market to another, and internationalization. New ventures and experimentation in these two arenas have the following in common:

- regularly testing the focus of existing activities, experimenting with new business, and looking for synergies between existing operations;
- a high degree of networking which gives the entrepreneur a foot in different markets;
- the transfer of skills and marketing tactics developed in one market to new ones which challenge industry norms;
- transferring learning from new markets (such as those abroad) back into a firm's traditional markets.

Transferring lessons between product-markets

All four firms involved in construction regularly tested the focus of their activities and experimented with finding new business or fresh synergies. As we noted in Chapter 2, networking is a condition of operating successfully in construction, and this is a skill put to good use in both growing and protecting the firm. Such experimentation at the boundaries of current business activity helps with understanding the subtleties of existing markets and learning about new ones.

- For example, after ten years of gradually evolving different business philosophies, Construction Co. and House Co. had recently begun to adopt elements of each other's strategy. Similarly, Cable Co. had begun to move back into conventional electrical work, having established itself using semi-skilled labour for cable-laying in which it undercut firms employing indentured tradesmen.

In each case, skills and marketing tactics developed in one setting were transferred to another to challenge industry norms.

Internationalization

Internationalization is a particular way of extending boundaries. Seven firms (35 per cent) in the sample had sales overseas (including Glass Discs).[2] The most successful, Fibres, had built up exports from nothing in 1986 to 45 per cent of sales by 1989, while Pressings had gone from nothing in 1985 to 25 per cent and had plans to increase this to 50 per cent of sales during 1991–92.

Internationalization comes about in different ways, however. For Fibres, it was a deliberate strategy to capitalize on its technological advantage and the development of markets in other European countries, and its move into exports was preceded by intensive market research. For Pressings, it had been initiated by the American parent of a UK customer wanting to buy direct rather than via its UK subsidiary. In the case of Software Products, exports were preceded by the development of relationships in the USA, through a minority shareholding in a Boston company (subsequently converted into a controlling interest) and a joint venture with a group of American insurance and finance companies.

An acquisition/joint venture approach reduces risk. Training International, however, launched its standard training package in the USA through a wholly owned subsidiary, much against the advice of some of the CEO's senior colleagues. The result was it very quickly lost £4 million. Testing boundaries can thus be an expensive process. The dominance of a single or lead entrepreneur (in this case, the CEO was the main shareholder) can mean that such testing is not as circumspect as sometimes it needs to be. It shows the advantage of building a position in a market via one or two customers, as at start-up, and directly parallels the fate of new products introduced without clear sponsorship by an existing customer (Cannon, 1985).

On the other hand, gaining a foothold in another country can have unforeseen benefits, by exposing a firm to trends in advance:

> What has been useful about the US experience is that it has opened our eyes about the training field and what is going to happen in Europe. The Americans have a different marketing concept. Their's is one of 'selling a process' not a stand-alone programme. Large corporations no longer want one-off programmes. We learned, albeit painfully, that large organizations want to buy an 'ongoing relationship over time'. Training is about becoming a colleague. The relationship is entirely different, and this is what is coming to Europe. We need to become a consultancy training organization.
>
> (CEO, Training International)

In the process, this has presented Training International with the same kind of problem as Aerospace Engineering, in that moving from packaged training delivered *en masse* means breaking out from an existing skills and knowledge base of trainers schooled in large lecture-theatre delivery.

In other cases, an overseas market can be the means to break back into the domestic market with a product which overseas customers have been quicker to accept. Thus, as Chapter 3 described, Pressings' prefabricated assemblies for conveyor systems were adopted by its American customer, which then used its influence on its UK subsidiary to do likewise. In turn, this has begun what Pressings hopes is a process of widespread adoption throughout the industry in both the UK and USA.

In all these examples of testing markets and boundaries, two processes stand out. The first is the transfer of competencies from one area to another; the second is the elaboration of networks. Internationalization, of course, has been described in terms of both processes. First, internationalization is essentially about leveraging domestic core competencies and transferring competitive advantages to new markets overseas (Dunning, 1988; Hendry, 1994). Second, the elaboration of networks is an essential part of the process in effecting this transfer (Johanson and Mattsson, 1988). In some instances (Pressings; Training International, Clean Air Co.), this involves the personal networks of a single entrepreneur; in others the development of a wider corporate network (Software Products). Above all, therefore, the firm which is active in testing its boundaries is one which works at extending its networks.

ADAPTATION: CAUSES AND CONSEQUENCES

In describing the adaptive behaviour of small–medium firms, we have tried to do justice to the intricacies of adaptation and growth. One consequence is to undermine the simplification which treats market development, product development, and diversification as if they are distinct activities (even though our typology broadly shows the greater frequency of initiatives focused on the market). A second result is to throw serious doubt on the idea that entrepreneurial activity involves pursuit of opportunities without regard to resources currently controlled. Developing resources is a vital part of most initiatives, either in implementing or conceiving them, and most chief executives were keenly aware of the resource implications of developments they were undertaking. This becomes clearer if we follow through the pattern of causes and consequences that surround new intiatives.

The causes of adaptation

The starting point in looking at the pursuit of opportunities is to ask what motivates it. From this point of view, as Figure 4.1 indicates, the seven

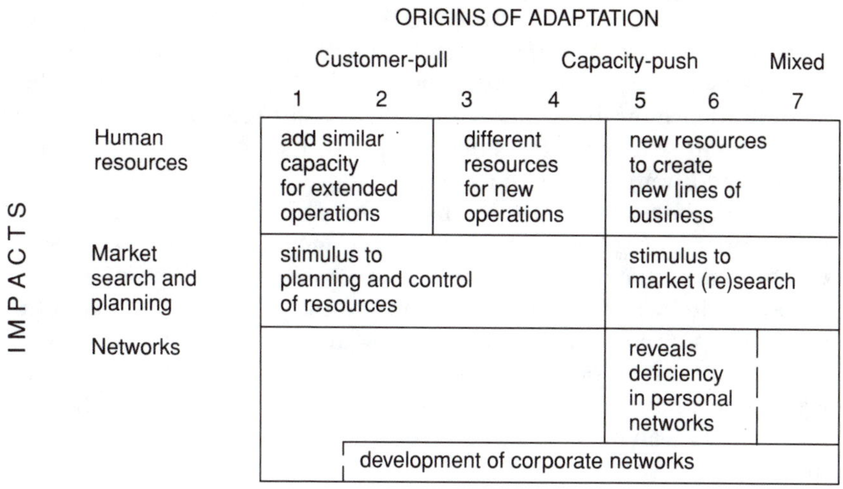

ORIGINS OF ADAPTATION

IMPACTS	Customer-pull 1 2 3 4	Capacity-push 5 6	Mixed 7
Human resources	add similar capacity for extended operations	different resources for new operations	new resources to create new lines of business
Market search and planning	stimulus to planning and control of resources		stimulus to market (re)search
Networks		reveals deficiency in personal networks	
	development of corporate networks		

Figure 4.1 Origins and impacts of adaptation in the small–medium firm

modes of adaptation fall into two generic types – customer-pull and capacity-push motivations. Types 1–3 provided fairly clear examples of initiatives undertaken in response to messages from customers or more broadly from the environment. Development through types 4–6, on the other hand, was invariably driven by the desire to utilize capacity more fully.

Type 7 ('testing markets and boundaries') is something of a residual category, with a mix of 'customer-pull' and 'capacity-push' motives behind it. Part of this ambiguity may be to do with the subjectivity with which an observer assigns behaviour to categories. The line between testing boundaries in an experimental fashion, adventurism, and active targetting of new niches, for instance, is uncertain in practice and subject to 'after the fact' rationalization (Mintzberg, 1978). On the other hand, the combination of such motives may be what gives type 7 behaviour its force.

The pressure to utilize capacity more fully is displayed in two ways – a straightforward need to cover overhead, and the desire to protect levels of activity by reducing customer dependence. The first of these – the simple need to cover overhead – is illustrated by the example of Legal Services, whose search for new areas of work was driven by a series of moves to larger premises. Other people-intensive professional practices, like Architectural Services and management consulting, reflect this pressure in the keeping of time-sheets and charging staff time to projects. Construction firms meanwhile are constantly juggling capacity (ie. people) within and between projects, and living with the anxiety of bringing new projects on stream to take up existing employee resources.

The second motivation – to reduce customer dependence – is vividly seen in a number of examples already looked at – in Aerospace Engineering seeking to reduce its sales dependence on Rolls-Royce; MOD Products its dependence on the Ministry of Defence; and Pressings since 1984 by the desire to reduce its dependence on two customers for 85 per cent of sales. In addition, Fibres had turned to exports and product development to avoid the risks of saturation in its home market for long-haul fibre optic cable; and Training International was looking at the possible eclipse of its whole market, as companies moved away from packaged training.

Alongside these immediate triggering factors, the development of the physical (as opposed to the human) resources of the firm also occurred as a condition of pursuing bigger opportunities (at Legal Services, Aerospace Engineering, Fibres, and Optics). Efficiency, reliability, and productivity – an internal focus – were prerequisites for expansion in all these cases.

In summary, then, the origins of 'entrepreneurial' behaviour in inwardly focused capacity issues is typically overlooked. The concern with customer dependence might seem to point outwards. However, the point about customer dependence in the above examples is that what focuses the issue is not dependence as such, but the realization of how much capacity is tied up with one customer or product. This is critical to managerial psychology. Up to the point of crisis, it is usually a matter of satisfaction to see capacity expanding as the relationship with a particular customer deepens (ie. becomes more dependent). As Jackson and Dutton (1988) and Shapero (1971) have observed in different contexts, negative factors and threats play a greater part eventually in precipitating opportunity-seeking action than do opportunities as such.

The consequences of adaptation

If we turn from the causes of adaptation to its consequences, we see that in many cases the consequence of these motivations to protect capacity is, paradoxically, a more radical pursuit of external opportunities than 'customer-pull' situations produce (see Figure 4.1, p. 97). Our argument is necessarily tentative, but the evidence tends to suggest that an actual or projected shortfall in capacity utilization stimulates:

(a) the building of a more varied human resource base or one that is substantially different;
(b) a search for new market opportunities, both informally and formally through planning; and
(c) the development of broader networks.

These processes, moreover, are intimately related.

Building the human resource base

Each of the seven modes of development raises questions about the platform of resources available to the firm. In the first two instances (1 and 2), it is simply a question of adding more capacity. Extra people have to be recruited or trained to take on greater volumes of business or ancillary tasks. In the next pair (3 and 4), new people are needed to put a new strategy into effect. All of these are primarily concerned with implementation of specific initiatives. Once we get to the fifth type of development, however – building a flexible resource base – there needs to be prior development of people to generate the learning that leads to new markets. New specialized skills have to be acquired as a condition of, or means to, break out.

In strategic terms, additional resources are a consequence of market development in types 1–4; but a means in types 5–7. In 5–6, this involves skills and knowledge, and ways of harnessing them within the business through team management; in type 7, it involves the utilization of external networks. We will return to these issues, and the collective firm-centred learning associated with them, in Chapter 7.

Market search and planning

The impact on planning is similarly variable and distinct. The effect of the first four types is to stimulate the adoption of systems that are concerned with control; whereas types 5–7 stimulate processes of market search and research.[3]

Planning is a 'multi-dimensional management system' (McKiernan and Morris, 1992), and it is important to distinguish the elements to which firms give particular attention and why. The distinction between systems concerned with control and those concerned with processes of market search is crucial in small firm development.[4]

This can be illustrated, first, by looking at the response to specific triggers. At Construction Co., Cable Co., Optics and MOD Products, for example, planning and control systems were instituted in the early 1980s after internal crises of control, and were geared to survival through the monitoring of project flows and attendant resourcing needs. In contrast, future performance at both Optics and MOD Products had become critically dependent in the 1990s on getting a handle on market prospects, the key to which was systematic market research. They were experiencing different fortunes in doing so, however. Thus, Optics had been able to develop a three-year sales forecast and for the first time to project its employee requirements and plan training and other investments accordingly, as a result of a marketing study commissioned outside. For MOD Products, however, the market was far more difficult to predict, and without convincing projections, the parent organization was unwilling to allow recruitment even of sales staff.

What a sales forecast does is to give confidence to justify recruitment and investment in critical areas of employee development which are essential to underpin growth. The case of MOD Products provides a pointed contrast between the growth needs of a business and the constraints of a heavily documented planning process.

The second way of illustrating the distinction between planning for control and market search is therefore where an organization is trying to change its strategic focus and begins concurrently to shift its style of planning and general approach to the market. Architectural Services illustrates this through two eras of development – from its contracts management system, developed in the 1960s, which sustained its success for twenty years and more as a regional practice, to the emphasis needed now on marketing skills and the development of political and commercial networks to operate in the national arena.

Developing networks

The third area – how networking behaviour changes – is harder to be categorical about. Search processes (and growth strategies) in smaller firms are said to rely heavily on the personal networks of the single entrepreneur (Johannisson, 1991), and necessarily therefore have an informal aspect which is difficult to pin down. It is harder, for instance, to say when the personal networks of the entrepreneur are active and successful, than it is to identify when they are proving inadequate and are being supplemented by other means, such as formal market research. Our evidence as to whether networking behaviour increases under the pressure of 'capacity-push' factors is therefore somewhat inconclusive. Certainly, the limitations of personal networks are most evident under the forms of adaptation 5 and 6. Developments under type 7, on the other hand, show the lead entrepreneur at his or her most active and influential. Even so, here and in many other cases, CEOs had brought outsiders into the top team deliberately to extend the enterprise's networks.

The general impression is that the breadth and reach of networks is the critical factor:

- as the source of customer-pull initiatives (types 1–3);
- as the means of targetting additional niches within an existing domain (type 4);
- as the inhibiting factor in 'break out' (type 5); and
- as the strategic resource exploited in type 7.

A tentative conclusion is that market development in the smaller firm owes as much to extended corporate networks as to the exclusive personal networks of the lead entrepreneur (Dubini and Aldrich, 1991).

Our own uncertainty on this score reflects the lack of detailed evidence generally about the precise ways networks change as a firm grows (Gibb and Davies, 1991), and what factors influence this. Size seems to be as much a factor as the type of market development. Thus, the individual entrepreneur's personal networks remain significant in firms of around 40 employees in our sample, but beyond that show limitations.

Developing people, planning and networks: a summary

Figure 4.1, p. 97 maps the accompanying developments of the organization's strategic resources – people, planning, and networks – on to the seven modes of development and their two generic forms, customer-pull and capacity-push. Although there is some ambiguity in the model, which requires fuller testing of the hypotheses implicit in it, the general thrust is clear. Pressure to utilize capacity more fully generates (or, at least, requires) a more radical response and a more thorough-going development of the organization's capability, than does environmental opportunity. Moreover, its impact is precisely to develop the means to process information about the market. What ultimately distinguishes firms' exploitation of market opportunities is the ability to handle such information (Batstone, 1991).

These challenges to develop the organization are reflected above all in our fifth type of adaptation ('building a flexible resource base'), represented by the Aerospace Engineering example. For this reason, it can be regarded as a pivotal strategy in small firm adaptation. We can discern four critical issues involved in 'break out' for Aerospace Engineering.

First, the 'tight coupling' with one customer first of all deprives a firm of a wider network and access to market knowledge (Hellgren and Stjernberg, 1987; Venkataraman *et al.*, 1990). The result is likely to be that marketing is undeveloped and the perception of opportunities and threats is limited. Thus, the CEO of Aerospace Engineering had only the haziest knowledge of other prospective customers, even within the immediate locality at the heart of Britain's engineering industry.

Second, Aerospace Engineering had developed as a jobbing shop working to Rolls-Royce's own designs, and lacked products of its own. This is not just a problem for the classic jobbing workshop, but for any firm whose product specifications are closely bound to a particular customer's requirements.

Third, dependent customer relations affect the relative emphasis given to quality and cost. This can work in one of two directions. On the one hand, seeking new customers up-market may mean extra investment in skills and systems to enhance quality (as Aerospace Engineering, MOD Products, and Optics had done in seeking the BS5750 standard to expand their potential customer base). On the other hand, the overheads a small firm like Aerospace Engineering has to carry to maintain high quality standards for a company like Rolls-Royce limits the scope for expanding the customer base to other firms that demand similar standards. In practice, though, high quality standards developed through a close alliance with one company are more likely to be a selling point than a burden.

A fourth constraint is that 'break out' is likely to require a more open style of leadership, compatible with building broader networks in the market, processing that information strategically, and acting on it. The conditions which produce the highly focused firm – limited network relations dependent on the entrepreneur personally – also encourage personal dominance.

Taken together, these factors provide a formidable obstacle to small firms acting 'strategically' and becoming medium-to-large firms or surviving in the longer term. Breaking out into a wider customer base means having to develop or add individual skills and capability in marketing, design, product development, and quality control, and this is a difficult, slow, and costly process. Added to this is the need to manage the more complex operation that results in an integrated way. This in turn implies a shift towards team-based management and the idea of entrepreneurship as a distributed function to which numbers of employees contribute (Stewart, 1989; Best, 1990; Timmons, 1990).

SUMMARY AND CONCLUSION

In this chapter, we aimed to do two things. The first was to analyse the way small–medium firms develop, adapt, and change in their markets and products, and the implications of this for their internal resource configurations. The second was to consider what triggers adaptive change and in so doing to draw the links between adaptive change and the forms of crisis, involving loss of internal control and customer over-dependence, which we laid out in Chapter 3.

In the process, we have argued for a broader interpretation of entrepreneurship, and for closer attention to the evidence of how small firms grow. The interlocking nature of entrepreneurial-engineering-administrative problems and challenges is apparent in the process of adaptation by which small firms develop their position in markets. Building an efficient and appropriate internal resource base – in advance, simultaneously, or in close succession to the exploitation of market opportunities – is critical in adaptation, since successfully doing the one depends on also doing the other. This is apparent whether we look (according to the chronology of adaptive change) at motivations, causes, the process of adaptation, or its consequences.

The need to give due attention to both the external market and internal resources might appear an unnecessary truism to be stating. The accumulation and management of resources has been a recognized theme in viewing the stabilization of the small firm through early crises during start-up and early growth. Issues of product-market development and resource management are closely allied during this period and, as we noted in Chapter 3, there is explicit recognition of the need to manage both internal and external environments successfully.

However, there is a tendency to separate the two, particularly in the literature on strategic change in large firms, where periods of upheaval are related first and foremost to changes in the external environment. Despite the balanced view articulated by Miles and Snow (1978) and by Hofer and Schendel (1978), there continues to be an excessive preoccupation with the external environment as a stimulus to strategic change. This has been the case in the treatment of large firms, and now appears increasingly so in relation to smaller firms. The result is to underplay the internal constraints on adapting to external environmental change, and in consequence to represent the process of strategic change imperfectly.

The characterization of entrepreneurial behaviour parallels this tendency in the strategy literature, to exaggerate the external focus on the environment. Kirzner (1985), for example, represents the market as a stimulus to learning, and interprets entrepreneurial activity as creative acts of discovery within the market. Others portray entrepreneurship as rooted in market-driven, opportunity-seeking behaviour (Stevenson and Sahlman, 1989; Timmons, 1990). The issue, however, is 'how do people, and particularly established firms, get drawn to opportunities, so that opportunities get identified?' The answer is that opportunity-seeking behaviour must depend in some way on 'selective attention'. Such selectivity is conditioned by people's involvement in particular activities, the range (or narrowness) of their experience, and the scope for inferring synergies and making lateral connections among the resources they have access to. The same is true of people in firms as of individual persons. Schumpeter (1934) recognized this when he characterized an entrepreneur as one who 'carries out new combinations' – in other words, that reconfiguring resources is an essential part of adaptation, change, and innovation.

It may well be the case that in the initial act of new venture creation the individual entrepreneur runs ahead of available resources. Equally, the externally facing activity of networking is peculiarly identifiable with entrepreneurial behaviour (Jarillo, 1989). However, from a transactions point of view, networks themselves might be better conceptualized as resources supporting the identification of opportunities. In this respect, one particular method of accessing external resources via networks – namely, franchising – may have unduly biased perception by representing networking as a substantive aspect of entrepreneurship.

Likewise, the continual development of a firm's capabilities may well

depend on pushing strategy beyond the immediate limit of those capabilities (Grant, 1991). However, the resource-based theory underlying
this proposition starts from precisely the opposite premise, being focused
on the building of resources and capabilities rather than on the external
pursuit of opportunity (Penrose, 1959).

Although concerned with smaller firms, our argument thus has broader
implications for the theory of strategic management. The more radical
departures from established product-markets and their attendant resource
configurations come from within the firm – from the need to utilize
capacity more fully. This realization has gradually begun to overtake the
conventional view that firms advance by responding to market opportunities (Porter, 1987, for example). An actual or threatened shortfall in
capacity utilization thus stimulates a search for new market opportunities,
the development of broader networks, and the building of a different or
more varied resource base.

Finally, since it may be argued that the more radical behaviour we
describe is stimulated by previous failures to be entrepreneurial, adaptation needs to be seen also in relation to crisis. As we noted in Chapter 3,
there is a growing body of work which documents the part played by crisis
as a trigger to major change and on how eras of evolutionary change are
punctuated by periods of crisis, both in large firms (Miller and Friesen,
1984; Pettigrew, 1985; Tushman *et al.*, 1986; Gersick, 1991) and in small
firms (Perry, 1985; Pitt; 1989). This needs to be supplemented, however,
by a more fine-grained approach which takes account of both crisis and
adaptation. In Chapter 3, we looked at the relationship between the two
through the Pressings case and in this chapter more schematically through
patterns of adaptation.

The classification of forms of market development outlined here provides, then, the basis for a closer analysis of entrepreneurial episodes and
of sequences of such episodes. However, beyond the present study, there
is much still to do to trace the precise chronology of what one might term
'entrepreneurial episodes'. This must include attention to such factors as
the sequence of successive acts of adaptation, development and change in
networks, the time-frame over which we view crisis and adaptation, and
the levels of interaction between the two.

NOTES

1   These examples, when taken together with the product/service innovation on
    which other firms like Software Products, Clean Air Co., Training International,
    and Glass Discs founded their businesses, reveal a fairly high level of product
    innovation (involving 45 per cent of the sample). It compares, for instance, with
    the Cambridge SBRC (1992) survey which found 60 per cent out of 2,028 new
    firms had introduced a product or service innovation in the preceding five years.
    Such figures support the image of small–medium firms as sources of innovation.

The role of small–medium firms in product innovation may, indeed, be increasing. The Cambridge figure is four times that estimated by the Bolton (1971) study of UK small businesses twenty years before. Supporting this is the surprising number of firms in the Cambridge sample which claimed to have either full-time (25 per cent) or part-time (75 per cent) in-house R&D staff. This contradicts the prevailing image of smaller firms lacking in technological resources (although there is a sharp increase in the R&D resource with increase in firm size).

Moreover, the rate of product innovation is fairly consistent across all sizes of firm up to 500 employees (ranging from 54 per cent of firms with fewer than 10 employees to 70 per cent of firms with the 100–199 employees). The main difference between smaller and larger 'small' firms is in innovation related to production processes and work practices where the very smallest firms lag and there is a fairly steady progression in innovativeness as firms get larger.

Most significant of all, however, is the very direct correlation between product innovativeness and rate of growth, compared with the relative lack of interest of the fastest growing firms in process innovations. There are various inferences that can be drawn from this. One is the fact (confirmed by other data in the Cambridge study) that fast-growing firms give greater attention to customer and market factors, compared with cost-efficiency-price considerations. In the period surveyed (1987–90) – that is before the onset of recession – they also performed better. The question is whether this is sustainable. Relative lack of concern with the efficient, internal control of resources may simply presage the kind of 'crises of control' described in Chapter 3 of this book.

The Cambridge survey incidentally finds little difference in product innovativeness between older and newer firms. On this point, it is interesting to note that MOD Products and Pressings, both product innovators, were the oldest manufacturing firms in our sample.

2 Our figure of 35 per cent of firms involved in export is close to the figure of 38 per cent reported for small–medium firms in the Cambridge SBRC (1992: 13) survey, and the average of turnover exported by SMEs of just under 38 per cent reported in a recent quarterly survey from the Small Business Research Trust (1990). Both these figures are biased, however, by the response rate and therefore sample structure. In contrast, in a review of 159 new start-ups in the North East in the late 1970s, Storey (1982) found only 1 per cent of firms exporting. In a second study, taking a random sample of small firms in all sectors of the UK, Storey and Johnson (1987) found only 6 per cent of firms had any overseas sales. Studying start-ups and taking random samples, however, induce their own biases, since the nature of product and services in certain sectors limits exporting, while older firms and larger SMEs are also more likely to export (Cambridge SBRC, 1992: 13).

3 The nature and extent of planning in this respect deserves closer attention. At first sight, there appeared to be a surprising commitment to planning, bearing in mind the tendency to think of smaller firms as unsophisticated and the evidence of most surveys (Stratos Group, 1990). As Table 4.2 shows, well over half the sample took a 2–3 year view of the future.

The level of detail invested in this varied, however, according to the inherent uncertainties that existed in their particular markets and the presence of specific operational factors. For example:

• Construction Co. took a two–three year view, based on a waiting period after tender of three–four months and construction periods of eighteen months. This was a fairly firm planning frame. In the short-term, however,

Table 4.2 Strategic planning timescale (years)

	0	1	2	3	4	5
Visitor Bureau	· · · · · · · · · · · ● · · · · ●					
Convention Bureau	· · · · · · · · · · · · · · · · · · ● · · · · · · · ●					
Hotel Tourist	· · · ●	5 year plans lapsed				
Hotel Heritage	· · · ●					
Software Products	· · · · · · · · · ●					
Training International	· · · · · · · · · · · · · · · · ● · · · · · · · ●					
Skills Training	●	impossible at present				
Legal Services	· · · · · · · · · · · · · · ● · · · · · · ●					
Bread Products	· · · · · ●					
Aerospace Engineering	· · · · · · · · · · · · · · · ●					
MOD Products	· · · · · · ● · · · · · · · · · · ●					
	1 on electronics; 4 on MOD work					
Pressings	· · · · · · · · · · · · · · · ● · · · · · · ●					
Clean Air Co.	· · · · · ● · · · ● · · · · ●					
Glass Discs	· · · · · ● · · · · · · · ●					
Fibres	· · · · · ● · · · · · · · · · · · · ●					
Optics	· · · · · · · · · · · · · · ●					
Construction Co.	· · · · · · · · · · ● · · · · ● · · · · · · · · ·>					
House Co.	· · · · · · · · · · ● · · · · · · · · · · · ●					
Cable Co.	· · · · · ●					
Architectural	· · · · · ●					

the key determinant was the annual wage settlement which had to be second-guessed in committing the firm to contract bids. Perhaps surprisingly for construction, they also prepared a ten year plan, updated annually.

- House Co., by contrast, as a speculative builder, worked to a six–nine month construction cycle; a two-year frame that allowed for site slowdowns in the event of adverse economic conditions while keeping in view the two-year limit on employment before redundancy payments became payable; and a five-year plan that covered land acquisition.
- A relatively large firm like Cable Co., with its privileged, dominant position in its industry, could confidently plan twelve months ahead with reasonable accuracy, while on individual contracts it could look as much as four years ahead.

Ties to a particular customer, especially where that customer itself works to long lead-times, also meant a predictable workflow:

- Thus, MOD Products could plan four years ahead on its defence work for the MOD. But for its electronics products in factory monitoring and process controls, it was unrealistic to plan more than a year ahead.

As these descriptions suggest, however, much so-called 'planning' is concerned with scheduling known activity and resource commitments and then deriving budgets, cash-flows, and so forth from these. The critical *strategic* factor, in contrast, is to be able to project a clear view of sales prospects. In practice, a reliable sales forecast is more significant than the planning process as such, which tends in most cases to be of only moderate formality. The Pressings example described in the previous chapter is a good example of this informality, and of the necessarily iterative, incremental process through which effective forward planning operates in many smaller firms. It contrasts with the widespread belief that a more formalized approach to planning is a necessary enhancement in a small firm's capability (Kudla, 1980; Stoner, 1983; Bracker and Pearson, 1986), even though many researchers have consistently failed to find a relationship between a formal approach to strategic planning and small firms' performance (Robinson and Pearce, 1983; O'Neill, Saunders and Hoffman, 1987; McKiernan and Morris, 1992).

4 Miles and Snow (1978: 23) perhaps unhelpfully conflate both control systems and systems for innovation within the 'administrative problem':

> Such a perspective requires the administrative system to be viewed as both a lagging and leading variable in the process of adaptation. As a lagging variable, the administrative system must rationalize through the development of appropriate structures and processes, the strategic decisions made at previous points in the adjustment process. As a leading variable, on the other hand, the administrative system will facilitate or restrict the organization's future capacity.

Chapter 5

Employment and people in the small–medium firm

Development does not start with goods; it starts with people and their education, organisation and discipline.

(E.F. Schumacher, 1973: 168)

INTRODUCTION

This chapter marks a radical shift in perspective. Hitherto, we have taken a strategic approach to small–medium firms in terms of their positioning, susceptibility to crises, and routes to adaptation. While positioning puts the development of an employee resource centre stage – or ought to – and crisis and radical adaptation stress the importance of developing a management team, a strategic perspective nevertheless tends to underplay the role of people in the firm. At one level this is inevitable as the emphasis is on firm-level phenomena and choices. At another, however, it is encouraged by the fact that in the small firm such choices tend to be invariably equated with the motives, ambitions, objectives, wisdom, capabilities, and preferences of the owner or individual entrepreneur. As Curran (1986: 33) has commented:

> Those who work in small enterprises might in many ways be called the 'invisible labour force'. The 'entrepreneur' and owner/manager are often equated with the enterprise itself with any contribution made by others, such as employees, made little of.

While there are good reasons for believing in the primacy of the single entrepreneur in establishing the new, small firm and in the making of subsequent strategic decisions, this should not be at the expense of ignoring the bulk of people in the firm. At a practical level, this neglect has been encouraged by the simple difficulty in research in getting access to employees to get their views and check out the often ego-centric perspective on issues and events of entrepreneurs themselves (Scott *et al.*, 1989).

In this chapter we aim to redress this neglect – not by presenting employee perspectives as such (although these do have relevance to the question of commitment), but by describing our firms in terms of their aggregate employment, conceptualized through patterns of skill supply. In this way, we will provide a fuller picture of the skill base small firms build through processes of positioning and adaptation and the managerial resources they are then able to call upon in times of crisis. Just as it is important not to generalize about employment relations in smaller firms (as we noted in Chapter 1), so, in focusing on their capabilities, we need to differentiate between firms on the basis of their skill structures and the means they use to secure them.

This does two things. On the one hand, it provides a broader perspective on small firm development by reminding how this is dependent on the mass of employees. On the other, and more radically, it locates the smaller firm in its labour market and shows how the realization of business strategies is contingent upon developments in the labour market. Common to both is therefore a 'resource dependence' perspective on the unfolding strategy process.

Skill structures are, first of all, the means through which firms do work and satisfy their immediate performance requirements. Second, they are the basis from which longer-term development is achieved, or not. More specifically, skill structures and skill supply strategies underlie:

1 the development and retention of knowledge and skills for present operational purposes;
2 the development of knowledge and skills for future adaptation and innovation; and
3 the development of management teams.

A description of a firm's present structure and supply thus reflects its current strategic positioning, but also exposes issues for future development.

At the same time, employees participate in a wider labour market. This may seem a banal thing to state, except that it conflicts with the well-known tendency of small firm owners to see employment relations in 'unitarist' terms (Scott et al., 1989; Gunnigle and Brady, 1985) and hence to assume overriding loyalty to the firm. In so far as employment markets become looser and job and career moves become more frequent over a person's lifetime, such tensions increase. However, smaller firms, by their very nature, may draw disproportionately on a local labour market and be more embedded in local communities, with the result that their stability is greater and their vulnerability to employee turnover is reduced. These tensions, reflected in Figure 5.1, bear directly on the theme which figures increasingly through Chapters 6–8 – namely, the conflict between innovation and individual skill development in and for the firm, and these processes in and for the sector and economy at large.

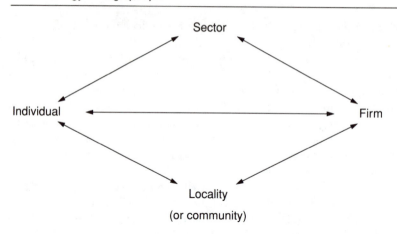

Figure 5.1 The inter-relationship of factors in skill development

This chapter, then, is intended to contribute towards a more differentiated view of smaller firms, while preparing the way for a broader
consideration of innovation and learning processes within the evolving
economic order in Chapters 6–8.

SKILL SUPPLY STRATEGIES AND STRUCTURES

To describe structures and strategies for skill supply two things are
necessary – first, a framework for describing external and internal influences, and, second, a way of grouping or conceptualizing examples into
common patterns. The framework and typology that follow are partly
derived from an empirical analysis of our sample, and partly an exposition
of existing models.

All firms can be described in terms of an existing structure of skills, and
all can be said to have a skill supply strategy, although the latter is often
only implicit and embedded in habitual recruitment practices. In broad
terms, a skill supply strategy comprises sources of initial recruitment,
further training and development, and various policies for managing,
retaining, promoting, and discarding people. Sonnenfeld (1989) con-
ceptualizes these processes in terms of a 'supply flow', through which
firms recruit in external labour markets, and an 'assignment flow', through
which they manage movements within an internal labour market. All but
the very smallest firms comprise a variety of skills and skill groups,
acquired and managed by different means. The result is that most firms
participate in a variety of intersecting external and internal labour markets
(ELMs and ILMs) which together make up the general labour market. As
Lovering (1990: 13) puts it:

The labour market as a whole can be envisaged as consisting of sets of internal and external labour markets, unevenly mapped geographically, offering a specific set of ELMs and ports of entry to ILMs in each local labour market.

Influences on skill supply

In terms of raw supply, the external labour market for a particular firm may well have local, national, and sectoral components. Our case examples show that the labour markets even small firms operate in are often quite complex, with sectors themselves operating on both local and national principles depending on how locally concentrated sectors are. The spread of 'local' labour markets moreover was often quite considerable, measured in terms of the distance employees travelled to work.

The labour market and the skill supply strategies with which firms intervene in it are subject to a wide range of influences, external and internal to the firm (Hendry, 1995; Peck, 1989; Curtain, 1987; Doeringer and Piore, 1971). Figure 5.2 summarizes these.

Externally, they include:

- The competitive environment, industrial structure, and stability of different product-markets, with the resulting requirements for operating successfully in the sector.
- The semi-autonomous nature of external labour markets, comprising various sources of labour from local and national sources, influences on levels of labour market participation, and the expectations and work motivations that employees import.
- The role of trade unions and professional associations in controlling the supply of labour.
- The infrastructure developed by the industry in which the firm operates, to service and regulate the external labour market – that is, sector-specific systems of training, and local and national pay rates.
- Government intervention in the labour market, through education and training policies, employment legislation and pay policies, with the influence of public opinion in helping to frame these.

These factors combine to produce the balance between supply and demand for labour which results in either unemployment or a tight labour market.

Internally, the individual firm generates its own dynamics which mediate these external factors. The internal factors include:

- The firm's business strategy.
- Its technology and systems of work organization.
- Its employment strategies, according to the management philosophy

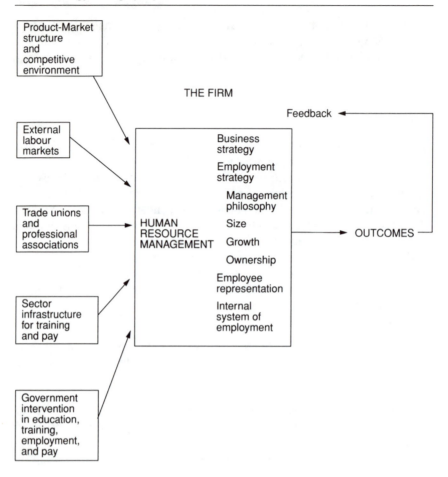

Figure 5.2 Influences upon a skill supply strategy
Source: Reproduced from Hendry, 1995

and capability, size, the growth stage of the organization, and owner-ship.
- The influence of trade unions, professional associations, or other collectives of employees over the internal supply of labour and its use on a day-to-day basis; and, in any established organization.
- The existing system of employment, which creates its own dynamics.

Within the firm, whether as a functional specialism or general manage-ment activity, human resource management (HRM) has the job of balan-cing external factors with the internal circumstances of the organization. This covers everything that makes up HRM and the management of employment, including recruitment, pay, training, work organization and job design.

Figure 5.2 is thus a more inclusive model than that of Rainnie (1989), for example, who sees employment relations in the small firm driven solely by its competitive position in the market, while it also takes into account employees' expectations and bargaining power (through the idea of semi-autonomous labour markets) as Goss (1991) does.

Even so, it is a generalized model which does not take special account of the features that characterize smaller firms. Scott *et al.*, (1989), for instance, have suggested that smaller firms have a greater tendency to rely on informal methods of recruitment, and thereby to recruit friends of existing employees, as well as to employ family members. This means that management legitimacy is often based in relationships other than the employment contract, with both positive and negative consequences. This puts the familiar stereotype of the smaller firm as 'one big happy family' in a more sociological light.

A second distinctive feature is the fact that small size restricts promotion opportunities, and hence limits the development of 'internal labour markets' (Siebert and Addison, 1991).

A third consideration is how small firms get set up and by what type of people. The 'craftsmen/artisans' who seek to practise their skills on their own account will probably recruit a group of similarly skilled employees, and this sets up a particular set of employment dynamics. Among these, according to Smith (1967), is the tendency of such owner-managers to practice a paternalistic style of management.

Patterns of skill supply

In addition to a framework for describing the influences on skill supply strategy, it is useful also to have a way of describing the resulting patterns. The literature offers various ways of conceptualizing skill structures and systems of employment. A recent example (Soeters and Schwan, 1990) brings together Williamson's (1981) ideas on internal labour market practices with Mintzberg's (1979, 1989) typology of organizational structures. More familiar are the distinctions between four types of employment system – the 'internal labour market' (ILM), the 'open external labour market' (ELM), the 'occupational labour market' (OLM), and the 'technical/industrial labour market' (TILM) – although some of the terminology around these has often been confused. As we characterize our firms we will indicate how they match up to these four types, illustrating in the process some of the salient features. A fuller description and a discussion of their historical origins can be found in Hendry (1995)

SEVEN TYPES OF SKILL SUPPLY STRUCTURE IN THE SMALL–MEDIUM FIRM

We now turn to a description of our sample of firms. In doing so, we will use our own 'naive' characterizations, rather than try to pigeonhole them into the typology of employment systems above. The principal reason for this is that ours is an attempt to characterize the firm, rather than any single labour market within it. A firm may operate a number of different systems. What is important is which predominates and the relationships between them.

In addition, our typology does three things. First, it highlights continuities between small and large firms, and thereby dispels some of the unhelpful mystique about small firms being uniquely different. Second, and in contrast, it can highlight some of the distinctive features of smaller firms. And third, it can then reveal particular gaps in existing typologies, since they do not noticeably discriminate between small, medium and large firms.

In describing the skill supply strategies of our firms, we are also reminded of the types of firm which founding entrepreneurs are said to set up. In the first of our categories ('specialized skilled'), for instance, there are strong echoes of the 'craftsman/artisan' (Smith, 1967; Hornaday, 1990); in the second ('technical process') one can see the influence more of the 'hierarch or salaried manager' (Collins et al., 1964; Hornaday, 1990); while the third ('flexible service') reveals the 'opportunist/promoter' (Collins et al., 1964; Hornaday, 1990). Bearing in mind, however, the criticism that these characterizations of small firm owner-managers are insufficiently empirically based (Stanworth and Gray, 1991), not to mention the fact that our firms are neither all owner-managed nor first-generation firms, it may be unwise to press these links.

Our analysis suggests there are seven reasonably distinctive skill supply patterns, although a wider sample might reveal more. They are:

1 Specialized skilled
2 Technical process
3 Flexible service
4 Unskilled mass
5 Professional market
6 Flexible casualization
7 Unstable market

We make no apology for describing these at some length since we see this kind of fine-grained case analysis filling a large gap in the human resources literature, let alone the literature on small firms. More to the point, without an appreciation of the intricacies of skill structure and sources of labour supply into the firm, it is hard to have a proper appreciation of the opportunities and inertia involved in business development. These patterns reveal issues in the resourcing of the firm in general and of management in particular, both of which may have significant implications for the development and implementation of strategy. Strategic implementation and development is 'resource dependent' – a dependency exhibited in the basic task of getting and retaining people and in securing sustained commitment.

1 Specialized skilled

The first type is the high skill workshop, dominated by skilled craftsmen within an 'OLM'. In its simplest form it works to customer designs and therefore has limited functional systems outside production. Its origins lie in the technical skills and knowledge of a craftsman who has set up on his or her own. Aerospace Engineering is the archetype in the sample. Indeed, in this case, both the original founder and the present owner who bought it out had the same kind of background.

Although highly focused on manufacturing engineering, the range of specialisms, even in such a focused firm, is quite varied. Moreover, in its efforts to break out into a wider market, this functional and technological variety in Aerospace Engineering was increasing.

The traditional feedstock for Aerospace Engineering was through engineering apprenticeships. Thus, despite recession, it had continued to train its own craft apprentices at one a year over the previous fourteen years (although latterly it had also taken a number of youth trainees and adult trainees at lower rates, as an economy measure). The result was a high proportion of time-served machinists who could work independently to exacting product specifications, while having acquired in-depth knowledge and skills specific to the product. The same was true of support staff in areas like inspection.

Within the aerospace components industry, people moved between a handful of firms well known to one another, and gravitated towards those like Aerospace Engineering which supposedly carried out the highest quality work. Thus, fourteen of the present employees had completed apprenticeships at other of these companies, while nine were apprenticed at Aerospace Engineering itself. For those who stayed with one firm, there was the prospect of progression into management roles, although personal knowledge of good workers meant a firm like Aerospace Engineering was always willing to take back and promote someone who had previously left. Since the industry had tended to settle in particular localities, pay also was highly sensitive to competitors' rates:

A lot of the skills originated from the shadow factories of the war and the 1960s' expansion. So they are city centre-based. Birmingham is a particular centre, and Coventry. People from the original firms set up their own companies, in the same locality. Three, for example, sprang from Aerospace Engineering, which are now bigger. And then around us you get specialist companies for materials and finishing processes.

We know which firms are reputable, which is why people tend to move between the same companies. People know you're qualified. The only question is how long you were there. When R . . . put up their rates, it affects us. The grapevine reacts very quickly.

(Quality Manager, Aerospace Engineering)

For such firms, the industry/sectoral network – at a very narrow, sub-sector level – is more significant for recruitment than is the locality as such, although local concentrations of firms, such as here in Birmingham/ Coventry, may obscure this. The existence of these within-industry networks means a lot of recruitment is by word-of-mouth. It also means it is not restricted to the immediate locality. Thus, the radius of recruitment for all grades for Aerospace Engineering was 25 miles ('this community and a bit more'), which took in 3–4 similar companies. Similar types of firm, in local sectoral clusters, can be found in many other industries (as Porter (1990) has detailed extensively).

The pattern of skill supply at Aerospace Engineering is shown in Figure 5.3.

Apart from the problems associated with breaking out into wider markets, described in Chapter 4, small firms like Aerospace Engineering encounter two kinds of recruitment problem. One is where an industry has experienced a downturn at some point in the past and this has left a cohort gap in the people entering and being trained. Aerospace Engineering, for example, had a preponderance of people in their late thirties/ forties, which reflected a downturn in the late 1960s. By 1990, it was having to compensate for the lack of qualified, recruitable people in the industry

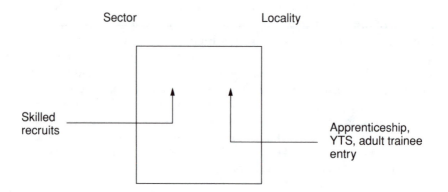

Figure 5.3 Skill supply at Aerospace Engineering

by increasing its own training, but to do so at acceptable cost it was having to diversify its sources of initial recruitment and take on cheaper labour. This risked a lowering of work standards, however, and threatened the very basis on which it competed – namely, quality through the accuracy and reliability of parts on which safe air travel depended.

The second problem is finding people with the right combination of skills in areas that are becoming increasingly sophisticated – in this case, testing and calibration. Here, successful recruitment for the smaller firm seems to be a matter of luck, and loss of people from such areas is a potential disaster. For instance, in Aerospace Engineering, because of the traceability and quality issue, there were only a handful of people who were personally authorized by customers to sign off for work completed. Without them, it could not conduct its business.

During the 1980s, engineering firms like Aerospace Engineering had to make major investments in new technology and systems. This involved systematic training of relatively large numbers of employees. As a small firm making a quantum leap in knowledge and skills, Aerospace Engineering carried out much of this off-site through equipment suppliers, supported by on-the-job self-paced programmes, or by using colleges of further education.

The range of formal training in such a firm is likely therefore to consist of:

- apprentice-type initial training, with on-the-job and off-the-job components;
- enhancement of skills and knowledge for individual specialists through (evening class) attendance at a college of further education;
- (re)training to implement new technology.

Significant development of skills, nevertheless, came more from working on specialized products on-the-job.

While shopfloor skills remained vitally important, the key resource issue at the present time, however, was to broaden the management team, to solve, at one and the same time, specific skill gaps and the lack of a strategic orientation.

A second example, MOD Products, had two labour markets with different profiles – one resembling Aerospace Engineering (in defence-related electro-mechanical work), the other (developing more recently in electronics) being closer in character to that of Optics and Fibres described in the next section.

In particular, MOD Products along with Aerospace Engineering illustrate a general phenomenon – that the complexity and variety of skills required by even small companies can be considerable. Many of our firms possessed a variety of skill groups and operated simultaneously within a number of labour markets. Highly differentiated internal labour markets in the smaller firm mean that recruitment and training can be very specific and focused, and that such firms may well operate within a series of tight labour markets. This can mean a high degree of interdependence in the development of skills at the firm, sectoral, and individual levels, and therefore a delicate balance which can be seriously disrupted by the business cycle or slumps in business caused by other factors. Operating highly specialized workshops, they are vulnerable in the retention and commitment of a group of skilled employees, and in getting and retaining uniquely specialized individuals.

2 Technical process

'Technical Process' firms are equally characterized by complex and varied skills, but such skills tend to be confined to a technical tier only. The rest of the workforce is less formally skilled, although they may acquire skills specific to the product or service. The effectiveness of such an operation, however, depends heavily on the attitude of the mass of employees, and much effort is put into gaining their willing cooperation and structuring attitudes towards quality. Recruitment to the two tiers of the labour force is divided between local recruitment for the mass, and sectoral recruitment for technical grades, with internal job ladders and promotion prospects for the latter within the limitations of organizational size.

This pattern, shown in Figure 5.4, is characteristic of all three electro-optical firms. Outside the sample, it is found in many process industries, and resembles, too, the electronics side of MOD Products.

The archetype of the 'technical process' firm in our sample was Fibres, its production system being a genuine process operation. As a smaller firm in transition, Optics illustrates the difficulties in moving towards this more automated kind of production system.

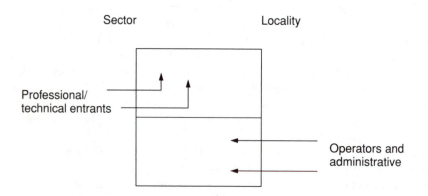

Figure 5.4 Skill supply in 'technical process' firms

Optics was put together from a number of businesses in the 1980s, and was based on three sites – design, final assembly, and testing in North London; manufacturing and assembly in North Wales (the largest site); and optical coatings in the South West. In North Wales, 'Optics' employed polishers of glass lenses (the key skill group); 'servicers' who did the pre-work, grinding and edging glass for the polishers; and quality, materials control, and production engineers/planners. The key groups in the smaller North London factory were optical designers and test engineers. These groups fell within quite different labour markets and had entered the firm by quite different routes:

1 All sixteen polishers had been poached from a larger local firm, where they had completed apprenticeships, when the business was formed by a break-away group of middle managers.
2 The eighteen 'servicers' had all been recruited direct from school at 16 years of age. They had expected to be trained as polishers, but had remained in mundane jobs. As a result, they were getting restless. Management, however, recognized how much they depended on their willing cooperation and felt an obligation to develop them better.
3 Quality, materials control, and production engineering/planning were becoming increasingly professionalized. Their skills were not unique to the glass industry and there was increasing movement into and out of the company.
4 Finally, optical designers (of which the company had four) stood quite apart from all other employees, having B.Sc./M.Sc./Ph.D.s in physics and being part of a select group nationally which the company estimated numbered only around twenty-five or so. There were also four less highly qualified test engineers.

Supporting these internal skill groups, there were concentrations of electro-optical firms in both North London and North Wales, resulting in a number of interlinked local-cum-sectoral labour markets and a need to maintain pay parities. In parallel with this, semi-skilled operators (the 'servicers') and administrative staff came from the local service and agricultural economy where there were few alternative manufacturing jobs and pay was low.

Skill supply was also subject to the influences of size and technological change, as Optics sought to create 'an engineering-driven optical manufacturing facility' (General Manager), with higher efficiencies. The centre-piece of this was the introduction of high-speed automated polishing lines which were about to change requirements radically by deskilling some of the polishers and formalizing the semi-skilled status of the 'servicers'.

Managers, meanwhile, came from two sources. First, there were those who had followed a career path in the industry – initially training as polishers, becoming supervisors, gaining experience in related production functions, and then becoming managers. The second group were professional managers from outside the industry who had special, transferable expertise in modern production management. The upgrading of quality, materials control, and engineering functions at this time made Optics attractive to younger managers with this kind of expertise. But the size of the company also made it difficult to hold on to them when further career moves beckoned. Moreover, with relatively few manufacturing firms around in a predominantly rural area, the supply of professional managers was limited, and three of the current management team had come from just one local firm during the previous year.

On the other hand, 'Optics' was large by the standards of its direct competitors in the UK electro-optical industry (with 93 employees at the main North Wales site and a total of 180 across all three sites), and it had a relatively high proportion of the nation's optical designers. However, the market for optical designers and test engineers extended to much bigger firms at the next level up, among its own customers, as well as to other electro-optical component firms in the London area. The unwillingness of these employees to move from the South East had consequently made the company cautious about relocating all facilities on to one site, although this made obvious commercial sense.

To sum up, the move towards a more 'engineered' system meant an erosion of craft jobs; dependence on labour drawn from local process and other unrelated industries for the shopfloor; and recruitment of engineering and production management from a wide range of industries – wherever, in fact, it could get experienced people. Once people had learnt to operate the new automated lines, training was then becoming focused on the maintenance of manufacturing standards, quality, and supervision. In these ways, Optics was shifting from the 'specialized skilled' Aerospace Engineering model to one more resembling the 'technical process' model of Fibres, as Figure 5.5 indicates.

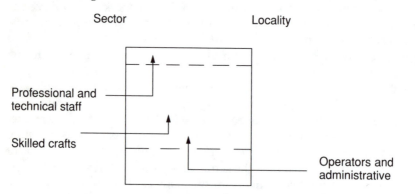

Figure 5.5 Skill supply at Optics

In these examples, along with Glass Discs, we see, then, the co-existence of two broadly distinct groups of employees, but with an effort to play down the divisions between them. There was a deliberate effort to get away from the divisive features of the technical/industrial labour market' (TILM), with its narrowly defined jobs, tight supervision, and adversarial relationships. Instead, management in all three firms, formed in the 1980s, had tried to create high levels of commitment (or 'high commitment systems' (Lawrence, 1985)), with a conscious attempt to capitalize on the opportunities afforded by relatively small size. They saw the resulting commitment as giving a major advantage in high productivity, high quality, and flexibility in response to customers.

3 Flexible service

'Flexible Service' firms are service businesses, which are people-intensive, and operate with a strong customer-orientation. They have a strong youth emphasis, high (and rising) educational standards at entry, and many more women in main-line jobs. Their dynamism is heavily dependent on the high levels of personal commitment they generate:

> I stay with the job because it becomes a way of life. You like it or you don't. I'm underpaid and it is expected you'll work long hours. They really look for people who can work almost to burn-out. But, as I said, you either stick with it and like it, or you get out.
>
> (Sales Executive, Convention Bureau)

Entry tends to be from a broad range of jobs, both locally and nationally. This is partly a matter of policy, with flexibility and personal attributes key factors in recruitment. Equally important is the new and evolving nature of the business. As skill definitions become more refined, a greater sectoral bias tends to creep in and to close down entry. The growing requirement for language and graduate qualifications in the Convention and Visitor Bureaux, as more courses specific to travel and tourism are established and external credentialism develops, is an example of this kind of shift.

An 'open entry' policy in the early growth of this kind of organization combines with the fact that the people these businesses attract tend to be mobile, in pursuit of enhanced pay and prospects and job interest. At Software Products, for example, many travelled 40 miles to work, with some travelling almost 100 miles. Having found an organization that satisfied their desire for intrinsic job interest, such employees tended to stay. In fact, all four organizations of this type – the Convention Bureau, Visitor Bureau, Training International, and Software Products – had achieved a reputation which resulted in many unsolicited requests for jobs.

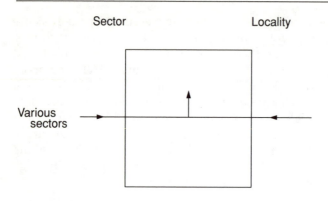

Figure 5.6 Skill supply in 'flexible service' firms

These were high commitment organizations, with relatively flat organization structures, giving a lot of discretion to employees, and demanding high commitment in return. In Mintzberg/Williamson' terms (as employed by Soeters and Schwan, 1990), they were 'ad hocracies' or 'relational team' organizations, with a very open labour market structure (as Figure 5.6 indicates). The environment in each case was dynamic and uncertain, and people developed firm-specific skills and knowledge as they grew with the business. There was a common interest, therefore, for employers and employees to stay with one another. Moreover, these businesses tended to attract similar kinds of people to the 'opportunist/promoters' who set them up (Collins *et al.*, 1964; Hornaday, 1990). The chief executives of these firms had a generally charismatic (or 'transformational') leadership style, with employee identification and commitment focused on themselves personally. Human resource management was less of a functional specialism and more of a general management responsibility to develop and motivate people (Soeters and Schwan, 1990). Thus, Training International had a deliberate policy not to have a personnel function. However, after a while, pressure may start to build for more order over things like pay and for training to be less dependent on CEO whim. Software Products (the oldest and largest of this group) had appointed a personnel and training director in response to this kind of problem.

Unlike the 'technical process' organizations, where commitment is managed through training that emphasizes teamwork and work standards, training in the 'flexible service' organizations is directed at individual improvement. There tends to be a strong belief in the incidental benefits to the organization of continuing personal development, and the initiative for this is expected to come from individuals themselves. In practice, the rapidly changing service portfolio of these businesses also meant that individuals had to acquire new skills and knowledge fairly frequently. The training culture thus tends to be geared to:

- off-site professional and knowledge-based education;
- 'ad hoc' training events;
- 'learning by doing', as new tasks have to be picked up.

It will be apparent from this that the conventional fourfold typology of employment systems referred to earlier in no way captures the particular qualities of 'flexible service' organizations, especially their team-orientation. The conjunction of young (plus unconventional) employees and a young organization is also not incidental or insignificant. Existing models, however, do not reflect this phenomenon, nor the challenge of maintaining energy and momentum in an evolving sector.

In fact, the small firm sector appears to have a significantly younger workforce (Curran and Stanworth, 1979b) than the population of firms generally. The examples here and that follow would seem to support the argument that small firms prefer younger people because they are more flexible (Curran and Stanworth, 1979b) – but in the sense that they may be prepared to work longer, less regular hours, and be able to sustain higher levels of stress from travel and the pace of physical work. On the other hand, new firms may require new skills and aptitudes that are not widely available, and young people may self-select themselves into such firms for the challenge they offer. Equally, an organization trying to grow a business on the back of ill-defined skills is likely to prefer that these come cheap, and young people will be more attractive for this reason too.

4 Unskilled mass

What we call 'unskilled mass' is the exact representation of the 'open external labour market' (ELM) referred to earlier, with low levels of skill and considerable labour 'leakage' into other low skill, unrelated jobs. There were two examples of this kind of firm in our study – Bread Products and Pressings. The employment profile of Bread Products shows the preponderance of 'unskilled':

Directors	5
Managerial (foremen, office managers)	12
Clerical/administrative	40
Fitters and trained bakers (skilled)	25
General unskilled	233
Van drivers (sales)	35

Of this workforce 75 per cent were Asian, almost all male, and almost all classed as 'general unskilled'. The only exceptions were the foremen who were also all Asian. All the skilled, semi-skilled, and managerial grades (except the Asian foremen), on the other hand, were white, male, and over forty. This included all the van drivers, all of whom were over fifty, with ten–fifteen years service. The latter came originally from the shop floor, and combined driving with selling to small independent grocers. There were only two graduates in the firm, and only three others with any kind of technical qualification. This profile reflects the deskilling of the bakery business through automation which Buchanan and Boddy (1983) have described.

The Asian workforce were attracted by the possibility of high earnings, and the proportion of Asians consequently far exceeded that in most other local firms. Because of unsocial hours premia and high overtime, the basic pay of £123 per week could be boosted to nearly £400 a week. At the same time (but not surprisingly since they would lose bonus), the workforce showed little inclination to receive training. Labour turnover among this group ran at around 30 per cent a year. At the same time, the company had difficulty in recruiting white workers in the bakery, and difficulty in keeping them. Unemployment locally was low and the long hours, shifts, noisy conditions, and boring work, following automation of production, was unattractive to white people who found alternative employment easier to come by.

At the top, the knowledge, experience, and skills of the directors, who were part of a very small national labour market, was paramount. Between them and the workforce there was a marked status divide, exacerbated by racial stereotypes on the part of the directors.

A similar structure existed at Pressings, with the business depending on just three of four people – the CEO who provided the marketing flair and drive; his partner, a former toolsetter, who provided the technical know-how for manufacturing and new product development; and a secretary and commercial manager who provided sales back-up. Pressings' work is noisy and potentially dangerous, while the quality of labour relations is shown in the CEO's comment: 'I often came in and found 'Brook is a bastard' scrawled across the walls.'

The resulting labour market for this kind of firm is shown in Figure 5.7.

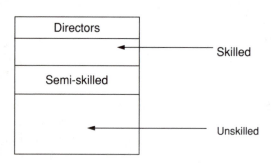

Figure 5.7 Skill supply in an 'unskilled mass' firm

5 Professional market

In all the examples so far, the industry has had relatively little impact in structuring the labour market within which firms operate, either through the setting of national pay rates or by determining the educational standards of practitioners. In some cases pay levels have been influenced by local norms and competitors, but in none of the cases so far have industry or 'federated' rates played a part. Nor have qualifications and entry standards depended on validation by external bodies, except for small specialist groups like engineers, notwithstanding the fact that some firms prefer to recruit craftspeople who have undergone apprenticeships.

The 'professional market' firms in architecture and law, by contrast, retain stronger vestiges of an 'occupational labour market' than many manual crafts. The profession in each case structures the labour market through formal qualifications and entry standards which are externally validated. The Royal Society of British Architects (RIBA) and the British Institute of Architectural Technicians (BIAT) also exercise some influence over pay levels through the profession's fee structure (unlike, however, the Law Society which does not operate a scale of fees).

External regulation and accreditation to practice, in consequence, mean individuals are oriented to the occupation as much as to the firm. They enter the organization already highly qualified; the hierarchy for promotion is then limited to one or two levels; and advancement comes from the opportunity to set up in practice for oneself.

Architectural Services typified many of these features, being characterized by an exceptional range of specialists (from contracts management to computer programming), without any career lines associated with them within the firm; and two major groups, architects (14) and technicians (13), with little differentiation in status within each group and no attempt at career progression between the two.

Architects were recruited from a national labour market, although in practice many came from two architectural schools with whom the company maintained a special relationship. On entry, they had already completed three years of formal study, and came for a year's practical experience, before going back to college for a further two years to study to Masters level. After that, they then spent their first year of full-time employment in professional practice completing their training. The quality of this recruitment to Architectural Services was perceived as critical to the image, reputation, and competence of the firm, and much effort was put into retaining them.

Technicians, on the other hand, were recruited locally. They spent four years working towards sub-degree qualifications through day-release and evening classes, followed by two further years of formal work experience and a final oral exam. Their training, therefore, ran parallel with their employment from the beginning. Architectural Services then expected to lose most of these people after they had completed their training, and regarded that as healthy for the individual and the firm.

Training was thus focused on the front-end of people's careers, with a major emphasis on on-the-job development. This culture of training young people extended also to general office level, with six trainees having entered on government youth training schemes over the previous three years. While training was substantially oriented to young entrant and initial professional training, the shift in strategy towards open competition for major national projects, with the attendant requirements to build consortia and influence clients, required a more active approach to professional development. This had led to the partner most associated with this strategy taking it upon himself to develop marketing and networking skills among the younger architects and acting as mentor to them.

Figure 5.8 describes Architectural Services' skill structure and labour market:

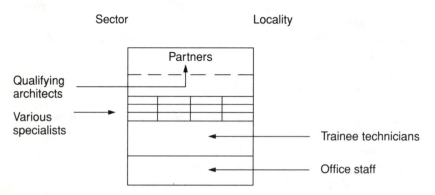

Figure 5.8 Skill supply at Architectural Services

There may well be differences of emphasis among 'professional market' firms, of course. With weaker demarcations between 'professionals' and others, Legal Services, for example, gave more encouragement to secretarial and clerical staff to undertake 'legal executive' training, and with the law also liable to constant change there was also more use of off-site seminars to update knowledge.

6 Flexible casualization

The three construction businesses we describe under this heading have a number of important features for the argument of this chapter and call for more elaborate treatment. First, they show how complex can be the factors that influence the employment strategies of small–medium firms. Second, they show how the viability of the firm as a commercial endeavour may, in consequence, be dependent on the workings of the labour market and the way the firm is networked into this. And third, they show how the conventional categorization of employment systems into internal labour markets, occupational labour markets, and what we have termed 'the open external labour market' (ELM) is often blurred in practice as a result of this interaction.

Company labour strategies in construction are a response to a complex set of factors. Among these are a commercial strategy having to respond to fluctuating competitive conditions; an external labour market that is partly independent of company strategies; government policies affecting employment status and training; and the industry regulative structures which firms, by themselves or with government support, have put together.

The starting point is the sensitivity of the construction industry to the general state of the economy, with the tendency to exaggerate recessionary and boom conditions. As a result, the construction industry has a long tradition of labour subcontracting and casualization. These provide flexibility to firms in a volatile market. In Britain, the ending of extreme casualization (the 'lump') in the 1960s was followed by subcontracting as a systematic practice for coping with the volatility of the industry in the 1980s. For Construction Co. and House Co., the flexible control of labour through subcontracting was thus one of the keys to profitability, while for Cable Co. it was *the* key. The prevalence of subcontracting is reflected in the industry structure in the UK whereby construction, compared with manufacturing and services broadly defined, is characterized to a far higher degree by very small firms with fewer than ten employees (Bannock and Partners, 1990).

The traditional image of construction simply as a casualized industry is misleading, though. Although Cable Co, for instance, had a rule never to carry idle labour, it also had a second one not to lay off people who had completed its 90-day probation period, during which they acquired the skills of cable-laying. Admittedly, only around one-fifth actually make it to this point. As a result, there was a clear core of around a fifth of employees with over three years employment with the firm, while 15–20 per cent of the workforce in 1989 were 're-starts'. One can view the latter as either casualization or the company keeping its links with former employees.

With Construction Co. and House Co., the situation was even more complex. Both operated with a core of staff (including site management and foremen) and a core of direct employees (principally bricklayers and joiners, with some labourers). In Construction Co., this core of 200 employees represented around 30 per cent and 50 per cent respectively of total employees in 1989 before the onset of recession, with around a fifth therefore leaving in any one year. There were then a large number of self-employed tradesmen and labourers (714s) whose numbers fluctuated considerably, and a wide variety of subcontracted trades working on sites at different times. At House Co., a more speculative business, the ratio of 'directs' (or 'cards in' employees) to self-employed and subcontractors in the same period was around 1: 4. This kind of skill supply structure is outlined in Figure 5.9.

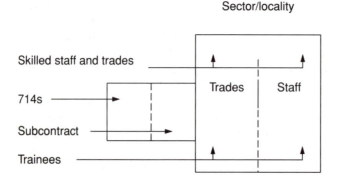

Figure 5.9 Skill supply in a 'flexible casualization' firm

These employment distinctions were reflected in three separate bonus schemes for staff, directs, and the self-employed. The prevalence of these, moreover, even for staff, and the high proportion of earnings they accounted for indicates the importance attached to matching labour costs to commercial factors. One estimate, for instance, was that 95 per cent of the site wage bill in these firms was through piecework payments. This is a related dimension of 'casualization' or 'flexible employment contracts'.

However, flexible labour is only one aspect of strategy in construction. As one manager in House Co. put it: 'Building a house is a mixture of timework and teamwork, but 80–90 per cent the latter.'

The importance of teamwork in construction is too easily forgotten. Teamwork is an integral part of on-site operations, and is easier to achieve with one's own 'direct' employees than with itinerant site workers. At the time of the project, teamwork (among staff and between staff and site personnel) was increasingly being seen as the key to improved performance and greater efficiency generally, and therefore a contribution to the overriding concern with costs. Apart from being harder to integrate temporary employees into teamworking, there is also the fact that construction firms have to pay them premium rates.

A stable workforce therefore has strategic value. However, there were also developments in the labour market independent of companies themselves which need to be taken into account. Principal among these was the emergence of the self-employed (known as '714s' because of their tax coding) to whom the Inland Revenue had agreed to give certain privileges as the only sure way of collecting tax from them. For their part, self-employed workers could divide their time between more than one employer, and this fed their sense of independence, even though net earnings might not in the end work out much differently from what 'cards in' employees got. This further weakened the direct control of companies over the industry's labour force.

The other labour market factor is the interdependency between local or regional and national labour markets. As regional firms, Construction Co. and House Co. both recruited locally, but were dependent on the state of the national labour market for skill availability. The national market in construction is made possible on the one hand by clearly defined trades, and on the other by the tradition of itinerant construction workers going where the jobs are. During the boom years in construction of the late 1980s, there was a large outflow of workers from the North East to London and the South East. Then, when the downturn hit construction in the South East first, this flow went into reverse – or as the CEO of Construction Co. put it, 'the trades have been coming home'. In other words, economic booms and troughs, combined with traditional mobility in construction, tended to produce feast and famine in local labour markets away from London and the South East.

The industry as a whole regulated this situation to some extent through national agreements on minimum wages, while local markets fixed piecework rates that reflected local circumstances. What companies, together or alone, did not do was maintain the supply of skilled people. In the recession of 1979–81, it was reckoned that half a million people left the industry, with the over-45 year olds leaving for good and many younger skilled men seeking more secure employment elsewhere. During the early 1980s, companies in construction stopped training, and supply had therefore not recovered to meet demand. The result was that the industry had been struggling against a downward spiral of insufficient basic training and falling standards since then.

Within companies, there are firmly established career lines for both staff and trades. Through office experience and part-time studies (notably for membership of the Institute of Builders), staff can achieve management positions in estimating and surveying; while trades people can rise from chargehand, through site manager, to contracts manager, and senior management roles. The industry is thus fairly unique in that such routes still predominate. There is also an occupational market whereby people in management positions tend to follow one another around between firms. The seniority structure and low volume 'small works' departments provide a way of retaining some experienced employees when they become less effective physically.

What we have termed 'flexible casualization', then, to describe the labour markets of small–medium firms in the construction industry is a complex system whereby occupational labour markets (OLM) struggle against skill dilution and external labour market (ELM) pressures for casualization, while companies try to create a necessary degree of stability through internal labour market (ILM) structures within. One further element in this, however, is critical, and that involves the effective extension of an internal labour market outside the firm.

At site level, a main contractor in a regional market like Construction Co. operates a network of relationships with labour subcontractors. Since profit depends crucially on performing contracted work on time and within budget, juggling the use of their own and subcontract labour, often between sites, is an important organizational capability for medium-to-large firms. However, flexibility over wage costs has to be traded off against reliability and the indirect costs of monitoring for and incurring poor quality. Consequently, main contractors like Construction Co. develop strong relationships with two or three subcontractors in each trade. Dependable relationships of this kind allow for more flexible site management and for extracting favours when it may be necessary to get someone on site at short notice. A number of subcontractors had built themselves off the back of such work for Construction Co.

A contractor like Construction Co. has a vested interest therefore in spreading its business around its favoured subcontractors to keep them all in play. In the longer term this ensures price competition among suppliers, as well as maintaining the system of favours. The indirect result of this is to provide greater stability in employment at subcontract level than otherwise would be the case. One can argue, then, that the benefits of an internal labour market are being replicated externally, as well as some specific costs being incurred in supporting favoured subcontractors (just as an ILM carries additional costs to protect an organization's assets). On a more individualized basis, temporary recruitment or engagement of self-employed workers works through a well-defined and active 'grapevine', which can reach out nationally.

These cases illustrate the argument of Bryman and colleagues, where they draw on a large-scale study of the construction industry to suggest that:

> a continuing relationship over time with certain sub-contractors may in effect act as a proxy for internal processes of probation and socialisation. . . . The 'authority' of the main contractor as such may extend beyond the specific terms and conditions of work for individual contracts, to a legitimacy more akin to that associated with the existence of longer-term employment relationships.
>
> (Bryman et al., 1987: 267)

In a sense, these kind of relationships in the construction industry – with Construction Co. participating at one level as a main contractor, and at another as a labour subcontractor to larger, national firms – represent the kind of web within which smaller firms in general operate. The construction industry, however, has evolved relatively sophisticated strategies for managing a volatile commercial environment through the labour market.

7 Unstable market

The construction firms illustrate the complex interaction between firms' commercial strategies, an autonomous labour market, government policy, and industry regulative structures. The last type, which we term 'unstable market', shows what happens when an existing balance of such forces begins to decay, and how that undermines a firm's capacity to deliver on its strategy.

The two hotels, which exemplify this, have characteristics in common with a number of other types. Like the 'professional market' (or 'occupational labour market') firms, they have a number of specialisms without a career structure in-company. Consequently, those like chefs with recognized skills tend to move freely within the sector locally and across the country. In consequence, hotels tend to suffer high turnover in key positions. Since they also employ such specialists in low volume in small units, there are advantages to the hotel industry in having institutions for centralized training and external credentialing.

At the same time, there is a tradition of itinerant employment among groups such as waiters, so that like the 'flexible casualization' firms they are subject to the autonomous working of the labour market. To cope with this, hotels use general and specialist recruitment agencies – Hotel Heritage, for example, using an agency which specialized in supplying continental waiters. Poaching staff is also rampant.

Unlike the 'flexible casualization' firms, however, there is no particular value in having casual employment. Up-market hotels and restaurants rely on providing a quality of service under sometimes extreme pressure. This depends on people knowing what they have to do and on team-working, without constant supervision. Stability of employment is therefore desirable. Far from operating a policy of casualization, hotels work more like 'total institutions' (Goffman, 1968). Thus, 75 per cent of the staff at Hotel Heritage lived in because of the unsocial hours they worked. Such businesses seek to maintain a relatively large 'core' of employees with a high *esprit de corps*, and in this respect they may be compared with the 'flexible service' firms.

This total institution quality in Hotel Heritage and in the hotel business generally has been eroding, though. The unsocial hours, low pay, and low status compared with other forms of employment produce considerable 'leakage' into unrelated sectors. The area around Hotel Heritage, for instance, had low unemployment, and the big employer locally (a country estate) provided many opportunities for young people to take apprenticeships and acquire 'real' skills in farming and estate work. By comparison, being a waiter has a menial image in Britain. In the scope for leakage into other sectors, hotels and restaurants therefore resemble 'unskilled mass' firms.

As a result, Hotel Tourist had a 60 per cent annual turnover rate (although this had reduced from 100 per cent over a period of three years), and Hotel Heritage had 85 per cent labour turnover. With this kind of employee instability, which is typical of the hotel industry as a whole, the unwritten apprenticeship system of learning on the job for long periods before getting promotion to senior positions and management had largely gone by the board. Appointment to management roles was taking place much earlier, fostered by both external programmes in catering management and, in the case of Hotel Heritage and Hotel Tourist, by an in-company management development programme. External credentialing and training was therefore stepping into the breach in the same way as for chefs.

However, company pressure for profit in both these organizations had reduced staffing. This was producing a 'vicious cycle' of work pressure, lack of time for training, crisis management, and labour turnover. Like the 'unskilled mass' small firms, these hotels depended increasingly on a few people at the top. But young managers and assistant managers in such circumstances were unable to acquire the necessary practical skills themselves and were unable to provide detailed guidance to staff. The 'tacit knowledge' which comes from experience was not being built up and the respect on which teamwork and the often patriarchal authority structure in such organizations was being undermined.

At the same time, the work environment was becoming increasingly a young person's environment because of the pace of work (the average employee age at Hotel Heritage, for instance, was 30), but young people were becoming less attracted to it because of the poor prospects, and the number of young people coming on to the labour market was falling.

Such instability risked fatally undermining an ability to sustain market position. The only relief from this seemed to be declining standards being matched by declining expectations among customers for a 'premium' service – effectively, encouraging a move downmarket. Alongside this, the widespread adoption of technological solutions to speed up the preparation of food was an attempt to reduce dependence on skilled staff in the industry at large.

Figure 5.10 summarizes skill supply in 'unstable market' firms.

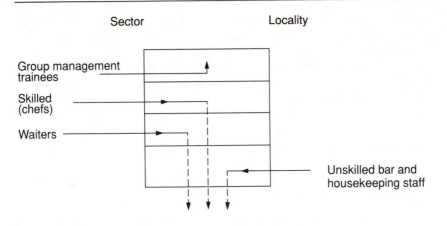

Sector   Locality

Group management
trainees

Skilled
(chefs)

Waiters

Unskilled bar and
housekeeping staff

Figure 5.10 Skill supply in an 'unstable market' firm

HYBRIDS: INCIPIENT PROCESSES OF SKILL FORMATION

The 'unstable market' example shows an employment system in a state of decay, or of endemic instability without having developed the mechanisms to regulate the external market. Elsewhere there are many firms, and outside our own sample there will be many such cases, where an employment system is in the process of forming or evolving into something new. This happens when a firm is between two types or operates two or more systems alongside one another because of a switch in market focus (as at MOD Products) and starts to employ different skills. Alternatively, a firm may be in the process of upgrading and/or downgrading skills (as at Optics) through technological change, and be moving from one type of skill structure and strategy to another. Another common situation is where different levels in a hierarchy operate on different principles. There are also true hybrid forms, as, for example, in construction where a system has evolved elements of more than one 'pure' labour market type.

One other situation, however, which may be particular (although not unique) to new small firms is where it takes skills from the labour market and applies them to a new activity, and in the process begins to create a new hybrid pattern. Skills and employment systems evolve, then, as the firm does. The 'flexible service' firms (Convention Bureau, Visitor Bureau, and Training International) provide an illustration of this. So also does Clean Air Co.

In Chapters 6–7, we will focus on the issues of skill formation and change which underlie employment strategy. Meanwhile, the example of Clean Air Co. is important because it captures the situation of many smaller firms that operate in the interstices of established labour markets, job categories, and skill definitions in the course of creating a new business niche. This in turn highlights the degree of interdependency between smaller firms' business strategy and the availability of skills. In other words it raises the question: How far does the success of the smaller firm in creating a new niche (as opposed to those small firms which simply duplicate what others are already doing) depend on the existence of reasonably approximate skills which can be adapted? We would argue that this is as important as the entrepreneurial identification of a niche. At the very least, it means that this question needs to be consciously addressed.

At Clean Air Co., installing fume and dust extraction equipment involved hybrid skills drawing on welding, electrical, and building skills. As the CEO said of these installation teams:

> I don't know how you would define their skills, there's no trades description – they have to be able to go into an empty site and fix the equipment. They're more akin to the building trade, even though they work with metal products.

In addition to the ability of these teams to work quickly and minimize disruption, the company depended for its success and reputation on sales engineers who could produce an engineering sketch of the intended installation and a bill of materials from which a quotation could be worked out. The skills here were an offshoot of the general heating and ventilation sector, which itself draws on the gas fitting and plumbing trades.

The poaching of almost the entire team of sales engineers in the mid-1980s, however, meant the company lost this accummulation of 'tacit' knowledge and skills. Nor could it recruit such people ready-made from the labour market because the specialism they represented did not exist outside, other than in two rivals set up by ex-Clean Air Co. employees. In this situation, the CEO and his sales manager were trying to speed up the process (a) by recruiting individuals with cognate skills, and (b) with formal and systematic training to underpin intuitive skills in engineering measurement and sales. This created difficulties with existing employees because of their low level of formal secondary education. The same problem arose with administrative staff where they were also trying to develop more formal skills associated with contract management.

This firm, therefore, may one day become more like the 'specialized skilled' firms, although its skills will be more firm-specific and not circulating within a true 'occupational labour market'. At present, though, it is but a pale reflection of these. Clean Air Co. is therefore representative of many such firms which have a low level of formal skills, but with the potential to upgrade and 'professionalize' these. To do so, means refining the source of skill and shifting from a purely local market to a sectorally defined one.

FLEXIBILITY: SMALL FIRMS IN THE LABOUR MARKET

One final issue concerning the skill supply strategies of smaller firms requires some comment in view of the tendency to see them as somewhat marginal within a labour market dominated by larger firms that are able to offer greater security and have more resources to provide formal training. This is the extent to which smaller firms rely on short-term contracts and part-time employment (or 'flexible' working).

Setting aside the question how accurate this picture of large firms is now, and also the extent to which larger firms themselves have come to rely on 'flexible' employment contracts, short-term contracts and part-time employment were quite prevalent among our firms, but for widely varying reasons. Mostly, this was 'strategic' rather than 'reactive' – that is, it was not because firms lacked clout in the labour market. For example:

- Because its success as a new firm was initially uncertain and to avoid getting a reputation as a hire-and-fire company, Glass Discs initially gave all new recruits three-month contracts (over and above the core who came from the parent company).
- Fibres had some 50 out of 350 employees, across a wide range of functions, on twelve-month contracts for a similar reason after its early growth briefly stalled. In this case, forced redundancy would dent the image and culture it had sought to establish through its Advisory Board structure.
- Of the Visitor Bureau's predominantly female staff 30 per cent were part-time, reflecting their perceived preferences and the short-term nature of events such as exhibitions they serviced. As at MOD Products, which used contract machinists from agencies to manage peaks in workload from a traditional pool of skilled men, the use of part-time and contract staff at the Visitor Bureau was seen as a valuable filter towards permanent recruitment which allowed a period of mutual assessment.
- In the construction firms, as at MOD Products, flexible labour was a way of managing fluctuating workloads.

All these instances of flexible working recruitment practice have a strategic quality. The desire to protect a reputation in the labour market and a core employment philosophy is significant because it is not one that is associated with the stereotype of smaller firms (albeit that Fibres and Glass Discs were offshoots of large firms).

A more 'reactive' and market-dependent example, on the other hand, was that of Software Products which relied on short contracts and part-timers extensively among its two key groups, programmers and sales/trainers, to cope with growth. Thus, nine out of fifteen programmers and up to twenty (out of thirty-four) sales/trainers were on short contracts. The software industry in general, however, has been characterized by a seller's market and Software Products' dependency was not especially associated with its size. On the contrary, its size actually helped it to retain such specialists who enjoyed the challenge of a growing firm and working relationships.

These observations on part-time and temporary work, however, should not be treated as saying anything representative about the small–medium firm sector. Service employment, which has grown disproportionately in recent years, is known to employ large numbers of part-time and casual workers (Hakim, 1987). What these examples show is the diversity in the sector, and reinforce the argument which has run through this chapter that small–medium firms have to be differentiated from one another, empirically and according to conceptually distinct types.

Flexibility (short contracts) for whatever reason, however, may have adverse effects on the learning of the firm, even though, in a buoyant economy, it may benefit individual learning and the stock of knowledge in the sector. The discussion of flexibility therefore provides the backdrop to Chapter 6.

SUMMARY AND CONCLUSION

This chapter has analysed the human resource base of a number of small–medium firms through the concept of skill supply. This concept was used to refer to the people and skills employed, where they came from, and how they were managed in terms of skill development and career progression. Other terms such as 'employment systems', 'skill structure', and 'labour markets' have been variously used by different writers to refer to the same set of phenomena and processes.

The analysis was supported by a framework for describing a wide range of external and internal influences, and a generic conceptualization of firm labour markets drawn from the literature. Our analysis, however, employed a sevenfold typology of our own, which characterized the firm, rather than any single labour market within it. While this reflected the system that predominated in each case, it also highlighted the relationship between different systems within the one firm.

The purpose of this was to generate a more in-depth view of people and skills in small–medium firms than is customarily the case. This does three things. First, it contributes to the necessary differentiation between smaller firms. For future use, it may, for instance, provide a sounder analytical basis for distinguishing firms than the 'a priori' classification into traditional manufacturing, traditional services, high-tech manufacturing and high-tech services (as used, for example, by Scott et al., 1989) which conflates a wide range of disparate businesses. Second, it shows in many cases the sheer complexity of the skill structures within relatively small firms. And, third, by locating such firms within their labour market, with all its multiple influences, it highlights how far the realization of business strategies is contingent upon developments in the labour market itself. In other words, small firms are dependent on employees as a resource for their performance and development, and not simply on an 'heroic' entrepreneur who takes 'strategic' decisions.

Employees participate in a wider labour market. Smaller firms are therefore engaged in a struggle to develop and retain the knowledge and skills of employees for present operational purposes, and to develop them for the firm's future adaptation and innovation. The way these markets work also determines the firm's resources for the development of management teams. This is, of course, true for all firms of all sizes.

The analysis of these processes in smaller firms, is nevertheless, distinctive from two points of view. First, because they are less able to sustain internal labour markets for reasons of size, smaller firms may be more vulnerable to the evolution of forces in the external labour market. They therefore provide an important testbed for viewing wider system changes. Second, they are organizations in microcosm and provide a focused environment for viewing processes of skill formation and change. If 'tacit' skills and knowledge are especially important in creating a defensible strategic niche (Nelson and Winter, 1982; Spender, 1991) and for the process of innovation, small firms ought to be a laboratory for observing the way these are formed and change.

Putting these two factors together, the innovativeness of small firms is dependent on the skill development of people, who participate at the same time in an external labour market. Small firms are caught then in the conflict between skill development in and for the firm, and these processes in and for its own sector and the economy at large. The following Chapters 6–8 take up this critical theme for strategy and innovation at the level of the organization, individual, and society.

Chapter 6

Individual learning through the small–medium firm

When people ask for education they normally mean something more than mere training, something more than mere knowledge of facts, and something more than mere diversion.

(E.F. Schumacher, 1973: 84)

INTRODUCTION

The aggregate skill supply activities explored in the last chapter are part of a larger picture. This is a picture of broader patterns of employment and mobility, impacting not only on firms but on host industrial sectors. As such, it is concerned with how 'the stock of knowledge and skill' in an industry 'accumulates as firms imitate each other and as personnel move among firms' (Porter, 1990: 120). In this larger picture, the accumulation of knowledge and skill – that is, learning – is relevant at three levels of analysis: the individual, the firm, and the industrial sector. What do our data suggest about individual learning? What do our data suggest about firm (or organizational) learning? What does the interplay between individual and oranizational learning imply for the sector in which this learning occurs? These are the principal questions we will pursue in the remaining chapters of this book.

The focus of this chapter is on individual learning. This calls for a broader frame of reference than the single firm. A person invests through work in an occupation, and thereby in an industrial sector that sustains occupational employment. The firm mediates between the person and the sector, and is a resource through which learning can be obtained. Learning can, of course, decay without employment (Lee, 1981). However, learning need not depend on a single employer. Firms can come and go, and win and lose on the labour market, while individual learning within an occupation may endure.

On the other hand, there are areas of learning that are specific to the host firm, and the strategic interests of the firm in developing a unique competence encourage the extension of firm-specific learning. The conflict between learning and skill development in and for the firm, and learning and skill development for individual occupational advancement, is a critical issue which the evolution of looser organizational forms pushes ever more centre-stage.

From the standpoint of individual learning, aggregate approaches to skill supply and training have several limitations. Firms, as some of the models from Chapter 5 imply, can discourage or restrict new learning. Or a firm's needs for new learning may not match the learning needs and interests of employees. Generic goals of training programmes can mask the distinct talents and experiences brought by individual participants. Work environments that provide learning for some may promote either boredom or worry for others at different stages of readiness (Arthur and Kram, 1989).

The above limitations of the firm for individual learning can be addressed through a focus on career development, that is on how a person's – any person's – work experiences unfold over time. A career development perspective offers a conceptual distinction between individual and organizational needs (Schein, 1978). This perspective overcomes the insensitivities of aggregate employment and training practices. For the organization, it presents a challenge to *stimulate* and *guide* an essentially individual developmental process in a way that is consistent with corporate needs (Beer *et al.*, 1984: 86).

However, in the wake of widespread industrial restructuring, the problems of subordinating individual careers to employing organizations are becoming clearer. For example, Dalton (1989) asserts organizations are dangerous if people expect: that those who work hard will be taken care of; that those making promises will be around to fulfil them; or that specialized knowledge or past achievement makes employment secure. Because both technology and organizational needs shift so rapidly, it is only people's ability to learn and adapt that prepares them for the future. Overlapping ideas about 'free agent careers' (Hirsch, 1987; Kanter, 1989) emphasize the importance of pursuing learning for one's own, rather than the employing organization's, purpose.

The writing on free agent careers has so far emphasized managerial and professional employee subgroups, but the case for broader application is not difficult to make. 'Blue collar careers' have historically been viewed as less significant to employing firms, and more susceptible to disruption for economic or technological reasons. Moreover, blue collar jobs, and increasingly service jobs, often exist in 'peripheral' rather than 'core' firms and in 'secondary' labour markets. In peripheral firms, the opportunities for training and upward mobility can be expected to be lower (Thomas, 1989). Employees in such situations can hardly be expected to embrace a firm's strategic interests as their own.

Pfeffer and Baron (1988) extend this argument to all firms, based on generalized trends in the externalization of work through the 'flexible firm' (Atkinson and Meager, 1986). Three particular trends – externalization of place, notably through work-at-home arrangements; externalization through diminishing employment duration, in the form of temporary or limited-term positions; and externalization of administrative control, through subcontracting or employee leasing – all signal more market-driven rather than bureaucratically controlled career structures.

In these circumstances it behoves all workers to seek learning and career opportunities for themselves. In turn, it requires both firms and governments, as custodians of employment policy, to better understand how individual learning can occur. In reality, however, governments (at least in the UK) do little to help employees in peripheral labour market situations to better themselves through training, preferring to see a ready source of cheap labour than to help employees extract themselves from such situations.

This chapter explores the theme of individual learning in a free labour market through four sub-themes:

- the nature of occupational learning, through examples from our small–medium firms, with some of the implications for people's careers;
- the specific strengths and weaknesses of smaller firms in providing for individual occupational learning;
- how people can make use of their employment circumstances to take up learning opportunities;
- managerial learning, in occupational terms and in terms of supervision and accountability for work performed as a generalized role requirement.

OCCUPATIONAL LEARNING

Old assumptions that occupational careers would evolve over a lifetime, frequently with the same employer, and concurrently with adult life stages (Miller and Form, 1951; Slocum, 1974), do not sit comfortably in the modern era. Super (1992), for example, has revised his earlier theory to propose that people recycle through sequential career stages after an occupational change. Dalton and Thompson (1986) have found that the four successive stages of engineers' and scientists' careers that they identify are not significantly age-related. Various other authors have explored 'dual ladder' career models which reward the pursuit of specialized knowledge instead of organizational seniority (for example, Mainiero, 1986).

A focus on occupational learning – that is, learning that in any way enhances people's skills and knowledge relevant to their present occupation – can avoid both age- and firm-specific connotations. Application of this focus to our case study data suggests four kinds of occupational learning. The first three – basic occupational learning, extended occupational learning, and learning from job context – correspond to distinctive entry, early, and middle career stages which are found in other models of the individual career (for example, Hall, 1976; Dalton and Thompson, 1986). The fourth kind of learning – learning skills that are new to the occupation – extends the dominant model of career stages, in that it involves new hybrid skills and the dissolution of old skill structures and attendant occupational career paths.

Basic occupational learning

This first kind of learning involves the pursuit of initial job competency or occupational qualification, and occurs through direct job experience, or a mix of job experience and formal education. This kind of learning is most associated with the *entry* stage of a career, and anticipates and overlaps with a person's first occupational role. Basic occupational learning usually takes between three to six months and three to six years to complete. Learning is directed toward recognized, and usually transferable, skill outcomes.

Informal on-the-job

At the lower end of the learning period came a diversity of manufacturing operatives (Fibres, MOD Products), fitters (Clean Air Co.), cable hands (Cable Co.), pressworkers (Pressings), domestic and catering staff in hotels (Hotel Heritage, Hotel Tourist), and – usually at higher levels of formal education – travel and convention guides (Convention Bureau, Visitor Bureau) and trainers (Training International). In all these occupations, basic competency was achieved through on-the-job learning within three to six months, although – with the exception of certain assembly workers and pressworkers – much could still be learned later.

Formal on-the-job

In engineering (MOD Products, Aerospace Engineering), toolmaking (Pressings), and construction trades (Construction Co.) arrangements for on-the-job learning were formalized into apprenticeships of around three years. A similar, systematic model applied for glass processing (Glass Discs) and polishing (Optics), supplemented by selected coursework. However, people in these occupations learned to perform useful work in a much shorter period.

Mixed informal on-the-job and formal off-the-job

Mixed formal and informal learning was undertaken among sample firms by surveyors (Construction Co.), architectural technicians (Architectural

Services), computer programmers (Software Products), legal assistants (Legal Services), and an array of secretarial and office workers – where informal on-the-job learning dominated – and by architects (Architectural Services), graduate engineers (Fibres, Glass Discs), and lawyers (Legal Services) – where formal off-the-job learning dominated, but complementary experience was required.

Formal off-the-job

Various other 'professional' roles (for example, in purchasing, contracts management and quality assurance) involved learning through certification courses, again typically in parallel with work experience. Certain key roles, such as calibration engineers (Fibres) and (especially) optical engineers (Optics), were learned through highly specialized degrees.

At the outset, it is clear that the opportunity for basic occupational learning is dependent on how skills themselves are defined. This is in part a function of the occupation itself, whereby firms (especially small firms) take their definitions of skills from outside the firm. Industry qualifications and attainment standards, along with common programmes of training, provide the standard for recruitment and basic training in many small firms. This is the case for traditionally defined craft skills in, for example, construction, catering, and engineering, but equally in the professions. The decline in traditional forms of apprenticeship training through which these skills have been developed in the past therefore poses a particular problem for small firms, and for the development of individual occupational skills.

In other areas, such as glass polishing (Optics, Glass Discs), the craft is not defined by a qualification structure nor by formal vocational training which individuals have been able to acquire through the public training system (although this has recently begun to change). This means the development of skills is entirely dependent upon firms, through on-the-job training combined with selective courses outside.

Difficulty in recruiting ready-made skills in this way may then encourage firms to automate and thereby deskill (as, indeed, had happened at Optics). In other cases, firms had deskilled following trends in the industry at large (in the restaurant side of the hotels, and in Bread Products). Cable Co., on the other hand, had built its business on the deskilling of work traditionally undertaken by apprenticed electricians.

In contrast, the availability of higher-level skills and knowledge coming out of the education system can generate new definitions of occupational skills, while some firms themselves may take the initiative in defining new standards. A combination of such factors was at work in the policy adopted by the Convention Bureau to recruit only people fluent in a second language.

These observations are a salutary reminder of how far the opportunities for occupational learning remain with firms themselves and in access to the education system. 'Free agent careers' may be curtailed before ever a person gets on the ladder of opportunity represented in initial occupational choice. To that extent, 'free agent careers' may be a middle-class concept.

Extended occupational learning

This second kind of learning involves developing further skills beyond recognized job competency or qualification levels, and occurs through extended job duties and selective formal education. This kind of learning is most associated with the *early* stage of a person's career, usually lasting for several years after occupational entry. However, extended occupational learning can last indefinitely, provided new challenges continue to be faced. To that extent, it overlaps with 'learning from job context'. Learning is directed towards recognition for prolonged experience, often linked to the reputation of employing firms.

Most of the occupations above, in skilled and semi-skilled trades, in the professions and clerical work, encouraged extended learning. As one informant commented:

Qualifications open doors and then it is experience which has to count most of all.

(lawyer, Legal Services)

The skilled engineering firms, Aerospace Engineering and MOD Products, for example, both emphasized extended occupational learning, drawing on the 'tradition of regional skills' based in the apprenticeship programmes of large firms and smaller firms like themselves, and on the circulation of qualified employees among similar SMEs. As the production director at MOD Products put it, the aim in extended occupational learning was to 'make staff as flexible as we can', to 'lead them to think for themselves, try new things and get them to have the right attitude'.

The conventional wisdom of human resource management suggests that extended learning should be promoted through the formal employment system, with new skills acknowledged by regrading and promotion. Optics, which was introducing a 'skills matrix' system, and Glass Discs, through its 'employee competency development' structure, were going down this route. The advent of 'national vocational qualifications' (NVQs) in the UK is encouraging many more firms to devise or to adopt such schemes.

However, the greater tendency in our small firms was for employment systems to be more geared for pay equity and control, with extended learning left to the idiosyncrasy of particular managers. The positive attitude of the computer manager at Fibres, while exemplary, shows how firm-sponsored extended occupational learning is often dependent on exceptional managers:

> People are attracted to a job by job interest, training, a boss that is interested in their work, and salary. I try to create here a semi-academic environment, where people have the time to discuss professional issues around computing, and where everyone has the right to be wrong, and I broadcast that.
>
> I have worked all over the world and been impressed above all by the German belief in training. When I came here I made it clear that training would be paramount. A guy gets demoralized if he is not able to do a good job for lack of training. I sought therefore to put into practice all the things I found wrong in my early career.
>
> (computing manager, Fibres)

The range and depth of developmental activities supported by this manager was probably greater than anywhere else in the sample. It included individual training plans for all twenty staff; a two-year pro-gramme of external courses for new entrants, and continual topping-up courses for all staff; a progressive career structure, with opportunity for non-professional entrants (that is, computer operators) to move into the professional stream; grooming of his two section heads in management tasks so that either (or both) could succeed him; and making provision for women staff to work from home after maternity (through work stations linked to the office) in order to retain their skills. The outcome was continuous learning for employees and a reciprocal loyalty to the firm, with just one resignation over an eight-year period (and that only because of a family move).

The formality of continuing development (or HRD) in general, however, was low. While the great majority of our firms attempted to implement some kind of policy for continuing development, it was mostly on an 'ad hoc' basis and depended very much on the CEO and managers of particular functions who had a commitment to training and development – often because of significantly good or bad developmental experiences in their own careers.

Just as occupations can define basic training structures, so can occupa-tional and sectoral factors also support or limit extended occupational learning through career progression. Thus, some types of small firm retained natural job ladders – for example, in construction on both the manual and staff side, with top management in Construction Co. made up of people who had come through both streams. In contrast, in larger firms in construction there are signs of increasing recruitment of graduates and MBAs which foreshorten learning and career opportunities for those trained in the building trades. In other cases, the competing interests of different occupational groups can result in truncated career ladders and learning opportunities for certain groups – as in the Architectural Services example:

• Architectural Services showed a trade-off in the opportunities for extended learning. The firm maintained an excellent regional reputation for its training of architectural technicians, but regularly lost people by the time they had served out their qualification period or soon after. Investigation of the problem revealed that while similar firms were willing to offer experienced technicians more challenging (and perhaps more lucrative) work, Architectural Services reserved such work for young architects in order to accelerate their development and position the firm for greater national prominence. A learning environment favourable to one group was by the same token detrimental to an adjacent group.

Learning from job context

The third kind of learning involves the development of skills that extend beyond the direct content of a job and formal occupational definitions of skill. Such skills usually stem from collaboration with others in the workplace, and represent the point at which 'tacit knowledge' and 'tacit skills' become significant in the operations of the firm and in the achievement of occupational mastery.

This kind of learning is most associated with the *middle* or advanced stage of a person's career, although it is not necessarily aimed at higher formal position. Learning from job context can persist indefinitely, but relies on a regular flow of new challenges or opportunities becoming visible to the job-holder. The learner moves from algorithmic competence and the learning of routines to heuristic mastery in coping with novel problems and unfamiliar situations. This stage of learning is recognized in Burke's (1989) model of skill development through the specification of three types of job performance variable:

1 The *contexts* in which the performer will have to operate, including likely locations and their salient features.
2 The *conditions* under which the performer will have to work – for example, degree of supervision, pressure of time, conflicting priorities, availability of resources.
3 The *situations* which the performer may encounter, covering such factors as client types and demands, tasks to be tackled, interpersonal events, and emergencies.

As the learner advances, he/she is able to cope with greater diversity and uncertainty in contexts, conditions, and situations. Similarly, Dreyfus and

Table 6.1 The Dreyfus and Dreyfus model of skill acquisition (adapted from Benner (1982))

Level 1	*Novice*
	• Rigid adherence to taught rules or plans.
	• Little situational perception.
	• No discretionary judgement.
Level 2	*Advanced beginner*
	• Guidelines for action based on attributes or aspects (aspects are global characteristics of situations recognizable only after some prior experience).
	• Situational perception still limited.
	• All attributes and aspects are treated separately and given equal importance.
Level 3	*Competence*
	• Coping with crowdedness.
	• Now sees actions at least partially in terms of longer-term goals.
	• Conscious deliberate planning.
	• Standardized and routinized procedures.
Level 4	*Proficient*
	• Sees situations holistically rather than in terms of aspects.
	• Sees what is most important in a situation.
	• Perceives deviations from the normal pattern.
	• Decision-making less laboured.
	• Uses maxims for guidance, whose meaning varies according to the situation.
Level 5	*Expert*
	• No longer relies on rules, guidelines or maxims.
	• Intuitive grasp of situations based on deep tacit understanding.
	• Analytic approaches used only in novel situations or when problems occur.
	• Vision of what is possible.

Source: Dreyfus and Dreyfus, 1984

Dreyfus' (1984) five-level model (Table 6.1) emphasizes job context at the upper level by reference to a person's 'intuitive grasp' and 'vision of what is possible' in responding to problem situations.

The characterization of skills which Glass Discs developed to underpin what it called 'employee competency development', incorporates the kind of thinking found at the upper level of the Dreyfus model. In the example shown for a team leader in manufacturing (Table 6.2), the learner was expected to accummulate increased representational and communications skills over time. At the pinnacle, but still out of the same job context, came 'qualified proficiency', incorporating team leadership, product knowledge, market knowledge, and customer care components.

Table 6.2 An example of employee competency development at Glass Discs

EMPLOYEE COMPETENCY DEVELOPMENT
JOB TITLE: Team Leader Manufacturing
GRADE: B

Proficiency	Competency	Measurement
Level 1	Reasoning/communication/ decision-making abilities.	Acceptable performance at Team Leader Assessment session (including, interviews aptitude tests, etc.).
	Manufacturing experience, i.e. fully competent in at least 1 out of the 4 processing areas.	Training undertaken and skills demonstrated in practice (min. 18 months experience).
	Supervisory experience.	e.g. 'Standing in' (min of 5–6 occasions).
	Basic supervisory/Man Management training.	SDI or equivalent (e.g. Industrial Society courses).
	Supervisory experience.	Min of 12 months as Team Leader (or Foreman).
Level 2	Manufacturing experience, i.e. fully competent in at least 2 out of the 4 processing areas.	Training undertaken and skills demonstrated in practice.
	Specialist skills/knowledge.	Training and practical experience in • communication/team briefing • interviewing • appraisal • discipline/grievance handling • 'trainer training'
Level 3	Manufacturing experience, i.e. fully competent in 2 out of the 4 processing areas and a suitable working knowledge of the core manufacturing skills in the other 2 processing areas.	Training undertaken and securement of appropriate knowledge in the 2 remaining processing areas with skills demonstrated in practice.
	Supervisory Experience.	Min of 2–3 years as Team Leader.
	Advanced Supervisory Training.	SD9 or equivalent (e.g. Industrial Society courses).
Qualified Proficiency	Supervisory/Man Management Development.	Completion of in-house training programme covering • product knowledge • the marketplace • customer care. Completion of NEBBS Supervisory qualifications or another recognized vocational qualification.

Other examples of learning from job context included the response of a junior at Legal Services, who appreciated an environment 'where people let you find out about things you've never known about before, and about your job and you as a person'; and the way skills were perceived and developed at Aerospace Engineering beyond basic occupational competence:

> We need to have people who can think actively and respond to a wide range of customer requirements. We can't standardize on the basis of products, but on the kind of questions to ask. They all lay out the programme, operate it, and inspect it.
>
> Attitude, what I call 'integrity', is important – to develop a sense of responsibility from beginning to end for machine jobs. I don't know that I can explain how we develop that. From day-to-day experience they see what matters, what's important, because they see things go to other stages. They see some jobs from beginning to end; others they pass on. Jobs go between the two shops. Individuals see all sections of the two shops. A trainee might get a job in one shop, then be brought to the other shop to finish it, although it's not allocated to them on the 'layout' that sets out the stages in the job. The pass-off system then supports the sense of responsibility.
>
> (manufacturing manager, Aerospace Engineering)

In these and other situations, the job context provides the potential for people to learn from supervisors or teammates, and to benefit from participation in shared project, quality, and customer service goals. Learning from job context is particularly associated, therefore, with the furtherance of reputation – with suppliers, customers, and co-workers.

Learning from job context, however, poses a problem and a challenge. The goal of scientific management has long been to specify exact job performance, either by simplifying prescribed tasks and/or by absorbing more and more of the secret art of a craft into programmable work, in manual or on machine. The competency approach, embodied in NVQs and in a customized form in the Glass Discs example, derives (in part) from this same motive to specify and control performance in the job. As the work of Orr (1990), however, has shown, it is extremely difficult to pin down and articulate the intricate logic of skilled performance. Likewise, our managers had a similar difficulty, as the Aerospace Engineering quotation above suggests.

More important, the achievement of higher levels of organizational performance depends on informal initiatives, at individual and group level, to interrogate the complexity and variety of work situations. In a similar vein, designers and managers of advanced manufacturing systems are finding it pays to allow greater scope for the 'human element' and to design for lower levels of automation (Bessant, 1993; Hendry, 1993).

There is thus a basic conflict between the organizational aspiration to be able to describe, specify, evaluate, and control competency in the job, and the extent to which true proficiency is buried in 'tacit skills', which are only partially 'describable' and destroyed by attempts to prescribe them. Learning from job context is an arena, therefore, for the continuing struggle for control over learning between organization and occupation. The question is, whether smaller firms exercise greater or lesser control in this respect and allow greater or lesser scope for individual learning.

Learning new occupational skills

This involves learning at the forefront of one's chosen occupation, ahead of the generally recognized skill base in the industry. This kind of learning extends beyond the assumptions of orderly career stage models. It draws upon a person's involvement in an entrepreneurial setting, and tends to flourish where previously untried approaches to job performance can be explored. Learning is directed toward innovation in the occupational role performed, and the subsequent value attached to the innovation in the marketplace. It does not necessarily mean 'better' skills, though, but 'different' skills.

An interest in new occupational skills underlies Flynn's (1988) 'skill-training life cycle' originally applied to the development of technological change (Table 6.3). The model suggests that individual firms promote the learning of new or modified occupational skills, which over time become 'routinized' and transferred to the sector as a whole. With new occupational skills, there is a 'tacit' component at the outset. The interest of the originating firm may then be to keep hold of it as a 'firm-specific' skill – even to prevent the emergence of a newly defined occupationally transferable skill.

- Glass Discs, for instance, realized that its requirements were not bounded by traditional glass industry training models. Instead, experience in any kind of clean air environment (with the disciplines and attitudes that requires) was a qualification for shop floor (laboratory) jobs. However, employees subsequently learned to work with computer-controlled equipment and technical drawings, and were encouraged to take external studies in glass-processing designed with the needs of Glass Discs in mind. In due course, this began to set new standards for the industry as a whole, and was making the workforce attractive to a wider range of employers.

As this and other examples indicate, the definition of new occupational roles, skills and knowledge is often preceeded by recruitment from unconventional sources. If the skill is unclear, so is the person. For this reason, greater emphasis is often given to personal attributes (such as

Table 6.3 The skill-training life cycle

	I Introduction	II Growth	III Maturity	IV Stability or decline
Tasks	Complex	Increasingly routinized		Segmented
Job skills	Firm-specific	Increasingly routinized		General
Skill training provider	Employer or equipment manufacturer	Market sensitive schools and colleges	Schools and colleges more generally	Schools and colleges some skills provided by employers
Impact on job structure	Job enlargement new positions	Emergence of new occupations formal		Rigid job hierarchy with education and occupational work experience requirements

Source: Flynn, 1988.

flexibility, willingness to work, and team orientation) as the foundation for continuous learning beyond what is immediately foreseen.

- A second example was the Visitor Bureau. As the first such organization to be set up in the UK, it rapidly evolved a range of activities. All staff were required to have a wide range of technical skills (including basic accounting, foreign language proficiency, and selling), and to engage in marketing and research tasks. Alone, none of these represented a 'new' skill or occupational expertise, but the combination of these, with knowledge of travel and tourism and familiarity with the database and administrative systems of the organization, was a relatively unique blend. As the Bureau's activities and systems gained outside recognition, it had begun to dictate the type of skills required in other organizations set up in imitation. The result was that Bureau staff had become doubly attractive in the travel and tourism labour market, and key staff had moved to set up comparable systems in other cities. What had begun as firm-specific learning, therefore, was becoming an occupational standard – especially through the influence of the Bureau's CEO on travel and tourism courses in the local education system.

As this example suggests, a 'new' occupation is often the result of applying old disciplines in new job contexts with a different knowledge base. The example of Architectural Services provides a similar instance where new disciplines in architecture (namely, marketing) were applied to an established technology (building design) in the course of refocusing the business.

- By degrees, Architectural Services had moved from a regional practice to competing for work nationally. Entry to the national market required specialization in design, which it did principally through leisure centre design, with transportation and urban redevelopment as additional strings. Such work had to be more innovative; required projection of a 'house style'; submission to open competition for design awards; and a higher proportion of commercial (non-public sector) work:

> It means avoiding the grubby image of community architects and claiming the moral high ground through excellence in design, coupled with a strong commercial viewpoint. It means getting alongside developers, not beneath developers.
>
> (partner, Architectural Services)

Above all, it meant learning to market – being more aggressive and hustling for work; instead of accepting a brief as given, researching proposals so that the firm had a clearer view of the commercial and market aspects to inform the design; spending money speculatively in advance to secure projects; networking with agents, developers, and engineers to build proposals and assemble their own consortia; projecting themselves through the media, via journal editors, and mounting exhibitions to gain reputation and image:

> Positioning for new work calls for networking and political skills that are not a natural part of the architect's education or socialization. Relationships are of fundamental importance to the complex nature of contracts needed to pull things together.
>
> (partner, Architectural Services)

Finally, it also meant a higher proportion of non-billable work, longer lead-times to projects, and managing a higher level of risk, all of which imposed additional management skills.

Since the profession did not develop networking, marketing, and political skills, Architectural Services had to do so itself, and one of the partners had taken on the mentoring of younger staff to introduce them to these skills. In this way, we can see close affinities between new occupational learning and the learning from job context in the previous section.

Common to all these examples are three phenomena: first, the role of the individual firm (and in this sample the smaller firm) in promoting new learning through its entrepreneurial activities; second, the emergence of new skills without support from the training establishment; and third, the role of the individual learner as the carrier of new occupational skills in the host industrial sector. Indeed, a high proportion of our twenty firms could point to the creation of new occupational skills and specialisms to complement and support entrepreneurial business activity – in relatively low-skilled environments (the development of 'skilled cable hands' by Cable Co., and 'shell' specialist toolmaking at Pressings), as well as in high-skill environments (computer programming for laptops at Software Products, and mass presentational skills for culture-change programmes at Training International). This is a role not generally associated with the smaller firm.

THE MAKING OF LEARNING OPPORTUNITIES IN SMALLER FIRMS

The above evidence from our sample of firms suggests a generalized model of occupational learning, covering the learning of basic, extended, job-context driven, and new occupational skills. The occupational learning model also allows us to see a firm's skill supply activities in broader relief, as intermediary between the individual learner and the host industrial sector. While we have identified some of these dynamics between the firm and sector, influences on change in occupational skill structures, and some of the conflicts between learning in and for the individual versus the firm, we have not explicitly considered what advantages and disadvantages the smaller firm may represent for individual occupational learning.

The advantages of smaller firms for individual learning

The advantages that smaller firms offer for individual learning centre around the related factors of size, growth, and market uncertainty, and the consequent requirement for flexibility.

Small size means some employees at least have to perform a wider range of tasks than normal occupational definitions might require. Growth means some employees have to perform across a wider range of situations and respond to a wider variety of people than they might encounter at similar levels of experience, age, and career in larger firms. Both factors enable, and require, employees to extend their competence over a wider performance domain, accelerate learning, and give increased responsibility. These influences of size and growth are, of course, moderated by technology and the complexity/routineness of operating tasks, which may restrict opportunities to a limited number of employees.

Market uncertainty (or novelty) impacts in a number of ways. First, as we noted above, a high proportion of our firms contributed new occupational skills and specialisms as part of their entrepreneurial business activity. Niche specialization (see Chapter 2) means more specialized skills. Second, the degree of flux in the markets of both new firms and older ones means that smaller firms often find it more practicable to keep their definitions of tasks and skills flexible. As a result, tasks are often put together in unusual combinations, and jobs and skills are loosely defined and subject to change. Even where forces such as technology can be expected to sharpen task and skill definitions, the special circumstances of smaller firms may mean skills are practised and developed in unconventional ways. Third, the process of becoming established means tasks being devised and added bit by bit, and as growth occurs this continues to be the pattern through the augmenting of existing jobs.

In these circumstances, real day-to-day issues form the basis of learning; the relationship with the sectoral infrastructure for training and specification of occupational skills is likely to be dynamic; and the notion of standards and vocational qualifications may have limited relevance. Experiential learning, in other words, is a key process in smaller firms.

Smaller firms, then, provide a favourable environment for learning, more especially around 'learning from job context' and 'new occupational skills'. Where they are weakest is in providing for basic occupational learning.

The disadvantages of smaller firms for individual learning

Six kinds of constraint on occupational learning in small firms were evident in our firms – affordability, ownership and control, fear of poaching, limited horizons, pressures of growth, and size. Many of these relate to the scale of the small firm and its related dependency on outside forces.

Affordability

The most striking constraint on individual learning was the widespread absence of training budgets. In six firms, training budgets were nonexistent; in four more firms, training budgets appeared to exist only to claim reimbursement of levies or to justify grants; in Bread Products there had been no training budget until the installation of new equipment necessitated one; and elsewhere the budgeted amounts were trivial. Thus, in fourteen of twenty firms, the commitment to employee learning through formal training budgets was minimal.

Ownership and control

A prominent constraint upon individual learning, whatever the preferences inside the firm, came from outside owners. Both Hotel Tourist and Hotel Heritage reported to a group looking for 'short term profit all the time'. Similarly, outside owners at Clean Air Co., MOD Products and

Bread Products held these firms accountable through tight financial constraints. Visitor Bureau, Convention Bureau and Skills Training had each struggled (largely successfully) with a different kind of constraint, in the form of civil service origins and bureaucratic job definitions.

Poaching and management attitudes

Fear of poaching has been traditionally cited as a reason why small firms don't train, and therefore as an inhibitor to individual learning. Often, though, this turns out to be an alibi, to excuse the fact that a firm would not train anyway (Pettigrew *et al.*, 1989). As such, it invariably stems from the degree of personal commitment which the CEO has towards training. Bread Products was one firm that clearly subscribed to this reasoning.

However, the larger picture was less clear cut. For example, the CEO of Aerospace Engineering acknowledged that 'losing people has a big effect', but that 'we get people back' because of greater satisfaction with 'the higher requirements of the job [at Aerospace Engineering]'. He therefore remained a strong supporter of training. Many of the managers in new firms engaged in 'making the market' for their product or service were also constructive in their approach:

> The name of the game is not to keep salary levels down, but to ensure skill levels increase.

> (production manager, Glass Discs)

The pattern tended to be that in organizations with a professional cadre of managers and external recruitment, support for training was generally widespread, whereas most owner-managers were more frugal. Owner-managers thought that any training, beyond the level necessary for employees to perform their immediate jobs, was a luxury to be provided only when the firm was making large profits. This extended to a lack of interest in training for themselves personally. Making money and 'making ends meet' was often seen as the first priority, and few perceived any correlation between training provision and business success. This attitude, as we shall see, has important implications for management training in the small firm.

Much depends in all this on managers' own career backgrounds and experiences. Those who have *trained professionally* (such as the computer manager at Fibres) value formal education and systematic training, as well as programmatic on-the-job development. Those who have come up through an occupation via a *formal apprenticeship* (such as the CEO at Aerospace Engineering and CEO at Clean Air Co.) value such experience as the foundation stone for others. Those, however, who have established businesses through *entrepreneurial 'flair'* value self-development on-the-job over all else, and imagine everyone else can learn in the same way – even though their own dominance by definition denies others the same latitude to pursue opportunities, take risks, and make mistakes. The relevance of the distinction between 'hierarch/salaried manager', 'craftsman/artisan', and 'opportunist/promoter' (Hornaday, 1990) in this respect is striking.

Limited horizons

A greater constraint than fear of poaching as such, however, may be limited horizons. As Chapters 3 and 4 have shown, firms struggle with the strategic issues of crisis and adaptation, and firms in mature markets may be particularly prone to inhibit new learning. Again, the Bread Products case is illustrative:

> There are few promotion prospects here, so . . . training would generally be a waste of money.
>
> (finance director, Bread Products)

Occasionally, however, firms took the contrary view that it is through investments in individual learning that strategy will evolve. In the Pressings case, in Chapter 3, strategy was informed by an intuitive assessment of employees' present and potential skill levels, while Training International committed 10 per cent of revenue to individual learning in the belief that it would create a stimulating environment for new business ideas.

There is a distinction, then, between those firms which see skill development and training as contributing to strategic opportunities, and those which see skills simply as sustaining strategy. Such horizons may not be unconnected with ownership factors, in so far as many owner-managers have limited ambitions for growth and therefore little need to provide formal training beyond the basic essentials.

Pressures of growth

While growth, as we noted above, can stimulate learning, it can inhibit formal basic training in an occupation or job. The fastest growing firms all had difficulties with this:

> It has become more difficult to manage training as demand has gone up. Experienced people tend to stay on the more difficult jobs, and they put new starters on to the easier jobs. So much is happening that the little things don't happen unless you make them happen. There's been rapid growth, training's not been ordered, and the system of planned training has been diluted.
>
> (production manager, Glass Discs)

The 'pressure of production' in a number of firms, including Fibres,

Glass Discs, and Optics, had resulted in good intentions to provide basic training being put on the back-burner. This gave rise to an interesting pattern, whereby this issue surfaced in renewed form when a business was some seven or so years old and it could no longer live with the variability and unevenness in skill standards. In general, however, even in the most sophisticated of small firms like Fibres, they had come to the conclusion that:

> Training is necessarily reactive . . . to be turned on or off like a tap, and fitted in according to the ups and downs of the business. All you need to have is a broad direction, that's all.
>
> (training advisor, Fibres)

Size

Finally, the greatest obstacle to extended occupational learning in the smaller firm is size itself. New job challenges through promotion opportunities and expanding roles, by definition, are limited in the absence of growth. Attention turns, then, away from the individual firm to progression via job opportunities in the sector. This problem is even more acute in the prevalent climate of large firms downsizing.

THE TAKING OF LEARNING OPPORTUNITIES

The conclusion we might take from the above is that learning in the smaller firm comes about despite those who run them, from informal opportunities afforded by the nature of the small firm. Thus smaller firms' interest in employee learning tended to be informal, and guided by the nature of workplace relationships. How, then, can people go about the task of obtaining the learning that may be available to them? Our evidence suggests opportunities can be taken in three distinct ways, through the demonstration of initiative, interpersonal learning, and learning in teams.

The demonstration of initiative

It was commonplace for the CEO and other managers in these small firms to express support for individuals who demonstrated initiative around their own learning:

- For example, among white-collar employees, the travel and tourism bureaux sought the 'right attitude' toward learning among new recruits (Visitor Bureau), and promoted 'individualized education' responsive to the 'qualities and abilities each person has' (Convention Bureau).
- Likewise, in the flexibility-conscious engineering firms, there was a belief that 'attitude is important' (Aerospace Engineering), an ex-

pectation for 'people to think for themselves' (MOD Products) and a reliance on initiative to substitute for more programmed approaches to employee learning.

Similar statements and expressions could be found for almost every firm in the sample. In many organizations this attitude was reciprocated by employees:

- In many of the newly established service firms (Training International; the Bureaux; Legal Services), there was considerable staff desire to know more about the industry in which they worked, to carve out a clear position for themselves within their firm or industry, and to investigate future career prospects. There was an expectation that they would find their own courses to attend and seek their manager's approval, and in general such requests were approved.

Individual initiative will thus always count for something in development, and many firms could provide 'shining' examples of individuals who had shown promise, and been encouraged to extend themselves. However, it is also often an excuse for a *laissez-faire* approach. For example, training and career progression in the electro-optical industry had traditionally relied on individuals pushing themselves forward:

> I got my own development by shouting loud, to get moved round departments in optical manufacturing. I wish some here would shout louder. I saw that as a quick way of getting skills. That's the way it should work here.
>
> (glass shop manager, Optics)

What happens, though, if employees do not understand this is how they get the opportunity to learn? While a few will always push themselves forward, what happens also to the rest of the employees? Unless there is, as at Glass Discs, Clean Air Co., and Training International, a publicly declared commitment to support people in further training and education, employees will be uncertain about what they can ask for. In many of the newer service small firms, for example, the high degree of informality included uncertainty about what money was available for training and development since CEOs kept the budget to themselves. Declaring that employees should identify courses they want to go on is not enough, therefore. For employees to exercise initiative in their learning, they need the encouragement and guidelines of an explicit policy and evidence in practice of requests for development opportunities being granted.

Similarly, a publicly articulated business strategy allows employees to see the skills which the firm will need, and what skills it will be worth their while acquiring. Thus, at the Convention Bureau, discussion of the future direction of the business had encouraged one of the marketing staff to learn Japanese in advance of a project to develop business there.

Interest in learning requires a learning culture. At Bread Products, attributions of employee disinterest in skill development were part of a low training culture perpetuated by the actions of the firm itself. In contrast, in firms which had traditionally had apprenticeships (Aerospace Engineering; MOD Products), or which required new employees to serve an introductory, probationary period, to gain practical experience after completing their formal studies (Architectural Services), employees had a motivation to continue with their training in order to become fully qualified.

In such cases, the basis for a culture of self-betterment is laid in early developmental experiences and expectations. The demise of a formal apprenticeship system in construction, and of an 'unwritten apprenticeship' in the hotel and catering business, on the other hand, made 'finding a start' difficult and negated the sense of a 'worthwhile career', regardless of people's enthusiasm.

Culture, policy, and sectoral career structures notwithstanding, however, informality around personal and skill development is a fact of life in many small firms. Individual motivation therefore remains a potent factor, and with that the quality of people recruited in the first place. The 'flexible service' firms in the sample tended to attract self-motivated individuals who pushed to secure additional training and development. These included a relatively high proportion of graduates and others with experience of further and higher education.

From the small firm's point of view, the correlation this suggests between higher education and career motivation is, therefore, of special significance: the quality of intake determines the quality of output. From the individual's point of view, it cautions against employees depending on any single firm to support their learning ambitions.

Interpersonal learning

Learning from others on-the-job is a hallmark of the small firm. This may occur on a one-to-one basis, or within teams. In contrast with the *laissez-faire* attitude above, CEOs and other managers tended to have a deliberate and explicit approach to using workplace-based opportunities for basic, remedial, and developmental learning.

- The traditional master–apprentice model still prevailed, for example, in the construction and engineering trades. Elsewhere, in Architectural Services, the partner who was most active in promoting its new design philosophy dedicated about one-third of his time to coaching junior architects in both on-the-job and off-the-job situations. More generally, informants spoke of such things as learning from 'a more experienced member of staff' (Hotel Heritage), and 'valuing older workers as a source of potential knowledge' (MOD Products).

Provision for access to a more experienced coach or role model was thus fundamental to job-centred learning arrangements (as in the traditional way in which an experienced supervisor is tasked to overlook trainees). However, many firms also recognized the possibilities of 'unsupervised' two-way learning, particularly in situations involving technological change.

- For example, a pattern existed in both glass processing (Glass Discs) and skilled engineering (Aerospace Engineering, MOD Products) where older workers were regarded as a source of practical knowledge while younger workers introduced new techniques.

Learning in teams

Two-way learning overlaps with the use of teams. As we will discuss at greater length in Chapter 7, teams were widely supported among the firms in the sample as a vehicle for collective learning, or 'organizational learning'. However, they also provided an opportunity for individual learning, and participation in teams is therefore a source of occupational development the individual can seek out and utilize.

- Exposure to project teams was a traditional route for individual learning leading to supervisory and management positions in construction (House Co., Construction Co., Cable Co.), and for the development of individual skills in architecture (Architectural Services).
- Learning could also stem from 'big events', involving looser team structures, such as international conferences (Visitor Bureau), 'specialization groups' (Legal Services), or the annual business review-cum-training event run by Training International.

As the CEO of Training International, a strong advocate of teamwork, put it in relation to the personal outcomes such events could provide:

People will get better . . . and be more committed if they are involved in the discussions which determine what is done, how, when, and where. This means using any form of development which gets people speaking, communicating and caring.

(CEO, Training International)

Individual learning from participation in teams and coaching relationships is clearly partly dependent on the demonstration of initiative in the first place, or being in the right place at the right time. Coaching and mentoring relationships, for instance, are liable to be selective of those who 'show promise'. The prevalence of natural teams is therefore of critical importance. The scale of smaller firms supposedly makes them more 'team-like'. However, teams are more than just a collection of people in the same place. The organization of the smaller firm and how far teamwork is valued is what matters. We will explore this in detail in the next chapter.

MANAGERIAL LEARNING

Managers as a special group have been largely overlooked in studies of small firms. Paralleling the neglect of the human resource generally, management in small firms has been equated with the owner-manager (or at best with the lead entrepreneur) without regard for those other managers who serve (Curran, 1986; Stanworth and Gray, 1991). In the present context, the learning of managers is relevant from two points of view. First, the development of managers and supervisors as controllers of labour determines the environment for the learning of other employees. Second, the notion of 'free agent careers' is likely to have more immediate application to those, like managers, higher up the organizational hierarchy.

In one sense, managerial learning is a variant of occupational learning. In another sense, it is distinct in its focus on the direction and control over, rather than performance of, productive work. As such, it may also be transferable across industrial sectors, as much management theory broadly assumes.[1] There is a third type of managerial learning, often referred to as 'general management', which transcends occupational function and involves a larger component of strategic decision-making. Since the last of these touches on the strategic direction of the business, the development of management teams, and collective learning, we will hold this over until Chapter 7. Here we will focus on the first and second forms of managerial learning which are essentially to do with individual 'manager' learning.

How do small–medium firms, entrenched in particular industrial sectors, provide for 'manager' learning, and what does this mean for managerial mobility in terms of 'free agent careers'? We consider these questions under five headings:

- the notion of self-management;
- management as a specialist occupation;
- managerial labour markets;
- how managers learn;
- the succession issue in manager development.

Self-management

In an era of 'delayering' and cutting out levels of middle management, we should first consider how far small firms do without managers. Our previous discussion of occupational learning, and in particular learning from job context and work teams, implied that self-management plays a greater role in smaller firms. Many CEOs and managers emphasized the value they put on individuals taking initiative for their own learning. By the same token, they valued initiative in work-based tasks and many stressed the advantage of small firm size in encouraging this.

A second factor, not restricted to small firms, is the trend towards putting more of the responsibility for quality back with the frontline workforce. Thus, several firms (notably in electro-optics) had embraced the total quality management (TQM) philosophy and were promoting quality programmes, and several others intended to do so. As the Glass Shop Manager at Optics put it:

> TQM programmes provide an active means for participation. They are putting problem solving and responsibility for quality back into people's hands, instead of them giving it to management.

Investments in TQM thus provide a growing stimulus towards self-management, in conjunction with the size factor. The more that people, through force of circumstance (small size) or policy (TQM), are able to broaden their perspectives about what they do, or about how their own and other people's jobs interact, therefore, the fewer official 'managers' may be needed.

The issue in small firms, however, is less about reducing managers as the fact that management in many small firms is 'thin' (CEO, Clean Air Co.) – that is, not enough managers and poor managerial talent. It may be that more could be done to develop the workforce to be self-managing (and the role of teams in this respect in small firms is central), but the real problem most commentators address is the negative influence of the lead entrepreneur in inhibiting the development of a management cadre with real management responsibilities (for example, Stanworth and Curran, 1973).

Management as a specialist occupation

Who, then, are the managers? The concept of management as a special occupational group was largely confined to a few firms which were part of larger organizations. These tended to recruit and develop managers as a distinct cohort group, typically with higher levels of education. Thus, Hotel Heritage and Hotel Tourist had a management training programme of job and site rotation operated by head office. Management learning at Glass Discs was also influenced by the parent company from which the original management team was drawn and to which promising managers could return for the next step in their careers.

In other firms, management existed as a group distinguished specifically by status – for instance, at Bread Products, with its classic distinction between 'managers' and 'workers'; or by the requirement for technical qualifications, as in the 'technical process' firms like Fibres.

In most of our small firms, however, (as the skill supply structures in Chapter 5 suggest) the division between management and non-management ranks was more permeable. The expectation in the majority of firms was that people would signal their managerial potential while performing in a direct production or service role. Managers were expected to emerge naturally from their experience as employees. The construction industry (including related businesses like Clean Air Co.) was illustrative of this kind of approach:

> There's a traditional career route out of the trades to site manager, construction manager, then CEO. It's within the developmental possibilities of any individual on site to make staff. All office personnel – surveyor, estimator, marketer, etc., – also have access to CEO opportunities through the overlap in their roles.
>
> (CEO, House Co.)

Few types of business, however, provide such natural skill progression through the various levels of supervision and management to general management as Construction Co., House Co., and Cable Co., where management of labour is the key strategic issue and site management experience is a sound preparation for contract management. In construction, management development then has to add either relevant technical skills to interpersonal skills acquired on-the-job, or to blend these with the technical skills of staff in a top team.

In white-collar occupations, such as in Architectural Services, project management provided a transition from architect to manager. More often, though, people gained new responsibilities and had to learn how to carry these out – often, as at Training International, through periods of rapid growth accompanied by 'crisis promotions' into new management positions.

Managerial labour markets

Although the division between management and non-management ranks may be relatively permeable, therefore, small firms generally lack an internal labour market and career structure to sustain manager development in terms of progression, and management development in terms of learning. Even the career progression described at Construction Co. and House Co. itself embraced frequent career moves between construction firms. At Construction Co., for instance, all six of the most senior managers had worked elsewhere, with periods of employment at Construction Co. varying from two to ten years. At House Co., three of the five senior managers had worked elsewhere, including two who had recruited one another to a series of jobs with different employers over the previous fifteen years. Similar patterns characterized the great majority of our firms, with the phenomenon of managers following one another around between small firms also conspicuous at Optics.

The recent career moves of the twenty CEOs point in the same direction. Table 6.4, for example, indicates that thirteen CEOs (65 per cent of the sample) had changed their employer (including two who had broken away to found their own business); while eleven (or 55 per cent) had come from unrelated businesses, including half of the twelve CEOs in family-owned businesses.

Table 6.5 shows that thirteen (or 65 per cent) of the CEOs had also come from large firms.

The prevalence of such patterns is confirmed in one of the few studies into the operation of managerial labour markets in and between small firms. Using a sample of 49 'fast growth' and a matched sample of 49

Table 6.4 Present CEOs' Backgrounds (by type of business)

	Family-owned/ partnerships		Outside ownership		Total	
	No.	%	No.	%	No.	%
Promoted from within	4	20	3	15	7	35
Broke away to start up own business	2	10	0	.0	2	10
Professional manager in unrelated business	6	30	5	25	11	55
Total	12	60	8	40	20	100

Table 6.5 Present CEOs' Backgrounds (by size of firm)

	Family-owned/ partnerships		Outside ownership		Total	
	No.	%	No.	%	No.	%
From other small firm, or by internal promotion	7	35	0	0	7	35
From large firm	4	20	9	45	13	65
Total	11	55	9	45	20	100

successful but less exceptional firms, and interviewing a total of 107 managers (fifty-five in fast growth, fifty-two in matched firms), Storey found that:

- only 2 per cent of managers in matched firms, and 18 per cent in fast growth firms, had stayed with the same employer in their last three jobs;
- 52 per cent in matched firms, and 42 per cent in fast growth firms had changed employers in each of their last three jobs;
- of those managers joining their current firm direct from an outside firm, 64 per cent of those in fast growth firms came from a 'large' firm employing more than 500 people, as against 34 per cent for matched firms;
- finally, among those changing employers at some stage in their last three jobs, 67 per cent of those in fast growth firms had also changed the sector they work in, compared with 51 per cent of those in matched firms (reported in Stanworth and Gray, 1991: 214–27).

In other words, there is a high degree of mobility among small firm managers generally, demonstrating the extent to which managers need to move between employers to get on. In the more slowly growing firms, this is not entirely surprising given their smaller size (a median figure of 24 employees, compared with a median of 250 employees for the fast growth firms). Managers in these smaller firms are also more likely to move between small firms, whereas those in faster growing small firms are more likely to have a large firm background. Again, this is not entirely surprising, since (a) fast growth implies a need for a rapid increase in specialist expertise (particularly in finance), and (b) fast growth firms are more likely to have ambitions to grow into large firms, and therefore want to develop large firm expertise. In some ways, perhaps the most surprising finding is the extent to which managers moved between sectors, although the portability of financial expertise (which was the major area of perceived weakness in both types of firm, and the area where both most relied on external recruitment) may help to explain this.

Such findings, although limited in terms of sample size, are clear evidence that 'free agent careers' are a reality in the small firm sector. The implications for 'organizational learning' from such moves by senior employees, as well as the dissipation of firm-specific expertise (intellectual capital), are considerable.

How managers learn

How managers say they learn and how CEOs perceive management development taking place is curiously at odds with the above evidence on the extent of mobility between firms. According to those we interviewed, much of their personal development as managers and supervisors arose through promotion as the business had grown. Very little was explicitly attributed to job moves between firms. An individual (they said) gains new responsibilities and has to learn how to carry these out for themself. The development of managers thus appears as a special case of the situation where jobs expand and skills are accrued as new tasks arise: they 'learn by doing' through a more demanding job context.

Perhaps they were simply making no distinction between learning in their present job and previous ones wherever these had been, in which case this may reflect on the approach to management development across British business and industry generally. Nevertheless, in the absence of data on actual mobility, one could be seriously misled about the wider process of management learning in small firms.

Within any one particular firm, however, management development was still largely an 'ad hoc' process. In many of our small firms it was viewed as necessarily self-generated, reflecting the self-made experiences of owners and founders of firms. Such formal management development as occured was largely seen as remedial and keeping up to date in technical aspects, rather than as preparation for a new job or involving fundamental education. The corollary of this was the almost total absence of formal management development programmes.

There were three exceptions to this – (1) studying for professional qualifications (particularly in the construction industry); (2) behavioural skills training related to some important aspect of strategy (as where the CEO of Construction Co. wanted to improve team-working); and (3) the coaching process (or 'interpersonal learning') – the most important of which was the last. Coaching and associated mentoring tended to be on a selective basis, for one of two reasons – to show that key members of staff were valued and to discourage them from leaving, or to remedy or improve some specific area of knowledge or skill.

- The CEOs at MOD Products and Glass Discs, for example, and the personnel manager and manufacturing manager at Fibres, had each engaged individual members of staff in talking over their career plans and devising programmes of action, including external courses and education; while the CEO at Clean Air Co. was actively coaching a number of managers in basic functional knowledge and skills.

Most CEOs were engaged in some such activity with one or two selected employees, but it came nearest to being a public process in those firms which had a cadre of professional managers (MOD Products; Glass Discs; Fibres; and, more recently, Optics).

Without this support, however, most small firm managers have difficulty getting training, even though they see it as vital. They claim not to be able to afford time away to attend courses and so fall back on 'quick-fix' popular management books, or attend occasional one-day seminars and presentations on job-related topics. Such development as they get is focused on the technical skills of their function, whereas the problem is to make the transition into jobs with a more general management focus, or to be able to contribute effectively as part of a general management team. As the CEO of Aerospace Engineering commented: 'In this kind of industry, we don't tend to employ managers. People are employed for their specialist skills, but then you can't get them to go beyond those.' As we will discuss in Chapter 7, this is a critical problem for the strategic development of small firms.

The succession issue in manager development

The issue which tends to unlock management development is succession. The surfacing of succession as an issue is important to management development because it is the point at which the lead entrepreneur has to consider sustaining the viability of the organization beyond themself personally. Until then, he or she will have tended to see the organization as an extension of themself. They may have given some encouragement to personal development, but this is often diffuse. A succession problem – often emerging as a crisis (as Chapter 3 noted) – lends purpose and direction to management development.

The block to focusing the succession issue, however, is the very personal identification the founding or lead entrepreneurs are likely to feel with the business. Having made the business work, devised its strategies, carried the risk, and devoted themselves to its products or service, they often resist handing over their ideas and the day-to-day administrative detail to others – whether through lack of confidence in themselves or in others, or from fear of losing control. They find particular difficulty in devolving responsibility for the more complex activities involving marketing and customer relations which are strategically important.

Because successful small firms are often, as suggested in Chapter 2, operating in new markets and pioneering new products and services, loss of key staff who desert to establish their own competitive business are a particular threat. A number of examples (such as Clean Air Co. and Optics) have been cited of key staff leaving a firm in this way. Training International, Legal Services, Software Products, and the two Bureaux were all prime candidates for similar action by employees. Indeed, the director being groomed to take over from the CEO at the Convention Bureau departed shortly after we completed our study to head up a rival new Bureau in a nearby city. There may then be a hidden reluctance to identify higher job requirements and to make provision for developing subordinates. Larger companies with sounder financial foundations may be more willing in this respect.

As a result, virtually none of the small firms in our sample had any formal programme of succession planning in place. The two notable exceptions were the Visitor and Convention Bureaux, where each CEO had identified someone from within to succeed them, and, in the case of the latter, had put in place a programme of training for his successor and his successor's successor. Once the issue of succession is addressed in this way, it can thus unlock the issue of development for the wider population of managers (as well as for other employees).

A second consequence of making management development more explicit may be to focus the issue of how best managers learn. The theory of entrepreneurship suggests we need to look to the influence of role models in creating entrepreneurial behaviour (Stanworth *et al.*, 1990). From this point of view, lead entrepreneurs can be a potent tool for developing managers in the small firm if they recognize this potential in themselves. Since entrepreneurs have invariably had to learn by doing, they may tend to assume others will learn in the same way. However, they forget they have had the advantage of complete authority, a broader view, and a complete range of tasks. Those who follow are more circumscribed and their opportunities, vision, and power to make things happen are more constrained. The lead entrepreneur needs to make an effort to manufacture such occasions. On the other hand, as Tables 6.4 and 6.5 indicated, breadth and variety of experience also count for a great deal. Creating this in some way must also be critical in developing subordinate managers.

Additionally, the succession issue needs to be continually addressed as a firm continues to grow. At first it is a question of building a broader-based top team, to support the CEO and provide for a successor. Subsequently, exactly the same issues can arise in building a second tier of managers. 'Team entrepreneurs' can be just as neglectful as the single entrepreneur, although the psychological dynamics may be different.

- Thus, at Fibres – in most respects a highly professional organization with a top team of experienced managers in place from the beginning – development of middle managers was largely overlooked until recently. The top team, as the founding cohort, were so immersed in developing the business and working as a group that the next level of managers were not functioning as managers in any real sense. A serious shock to the system of communication and participation which the company valued so highly caused a reappraisal of management development, and a series of initiatives to remedy this neglect.

SUMMARY AND CONCLUSION

The lessons arising from this chapter are several. First, it makes sense to think about individual learning as an investment in an occupation.

However, our thinking need not be constrained by age- or firm-specific assumptions found in traditional models of the occupational career. Also, the four kinds of occupational learning identified – concerned with basic, extended, job-context driven, and new occupational skills – apply across a range of blue-collar and white-collar roles. Of particular interest is how occupational skills originate through firms' entrepreneurial efforts rather than through the educational and training establishment.

Second, patterns of occupational learning tell only part of the story, since in the small–medium firm access to learning opportunities frequently depends on individual initiative. Formal systems appear limited, and learning instead draws heavily on relationships cultivated with bosses, co-workers and team-mates. These relationships provide the bedrock on which individual learning in the smaller firm is founded. The question of whether this provides an adequate basis for developing up-to-date and appropriate skills is another matter, however. The starting point, never-theless, is an appreciation of these processes.

Third, the constraints on individual learning identified – affordability, ownership and control, fear of poaching and management attitudes, limited horizons, pressures of growth, and limited size – say as much about popular misconceptions of learning at work as they do about the limitations of small firms themselves. To measure the opportunity for learning by the existence and size of training budgets is highly misleading. Even when budgets exist, they may be mere accounting entries to reclaim training levies. Most individual learning seems to occur in normal job situations. Limited horizons are a bigger barrier to individual learning than fear of poaching. The experience and ambitions of CEOs themselves are the critical factors.

Fourth, managerial learning in its most basic sense is an extension of occupational learning, involving the person taking on greater respons-ibility and accountability for his or her own job. In most small firms management positions are open to people previously holding occupa-tional roles, rather than to those with special credentials. In turn, the mantle of 'management development' rests heavily on the CEO (and thereafter on other senior managers). Succession planning, if brought into focus, provides a particular opportunity to unlock the issue of manage-ment development more broadly.

Finally, there is strong evidence (even if the quantity of it is limited) that the principle of 'free agent careers' operates widely among small firm managers. This has considerable implications for small firm learning, the maintenance of a unique competence, and for how we view the small firm in its environment. We will pursue these issues in the final two chapters.

NOTE

1 This assumption is, of course, nonsense. It views supervision as a one-way process, whereas it depends on respect. It is also a very partial view of what management and supervision entail. On the contrary, management is rooted in the job context and hence in technical expertise. The same misplaced assumption is what has given us the disembodied practice of portfolio management and rule by accountants at higher levels of management activity.

Chapter 7

Learning and the firm

We often hear that we are entering the era of 'the Learning Society'. Let us hope that this is true.

(E.F. Schumacher, 1973: 21)

INTRODUCTION

Early in the 1980s, Training International was a minor player in the market for personal time management systems, with a product licensed from its Danish sponsor. The Danish firm began consulting to Scandinavian Airline Systems, and this led to Training International being invited to bid for a contract to promote culture change in British Airways. Training International won the contract, launching it on a path that resulted, six years later, in its earning the European Community's vote as 'Europe's leading training organization'.

From the beginning, the CEO believed that business would only develop and expand if all concerned with it could offer input. Levels of management and status difference were resisted in favour of a philosophy of everyone being prepared to contribute and assist one another, irrespective of job designation, seniority, or salary level. This philosophy was applied to Training International and to client organizations alike:

> To continuously change is to continuously learn. You need to reach the heart of everyone in the organization. This is the way all firms have to operate. We told the airline, for example, that they had to paint the insides of their people not just the livery on the planes to make change happen.
>
> (CEO, Training International)

Concurrent with the lack of formalization was an ambivalence about qualifications. People recruited as programme presenters came from diverse backgrounds ranging from postman to deputy head of a large comprehensive school. What was sought was a presenter able to perform before 200 people at any one time, and to do so with conviction. The choice of presenters reflected a philosophy of recruiting 'street-wise people' and resisting the rigidity seen to stem from formal qualifications. The choice of Finance Director was another example:

> (He) is with us today because he failed his final accountancy examinations. I am sure God or Fate sent us this man. He is deep-thinking and a people-first person. This is what we need and what counts . . . He has turned out to be a remarkable financial wizard.
>
> (CEO, Training International)

Training International committed 10 per cent of its turnover to staff training and development, with all members of staff encouraged to spend eleven days each year in external programmes of their own choosing, in addition to the internal programmes the firm arranged for itself and professional courses. As a result, the firm boasted 'home grown' former secretaries, for example, now performing as senior account, production and personnel managers. A profit-sharing plan, and the widespread use of teams, also encouraged employees to adopt a shared interest in the welfare of the firm.

However, a crisis towards 1990 threatened this philosophy of broad employee development, involving two overlapping circumstances: first, a prolonged haemorrhaging of profits to a US subsidiary; second, an excess of personnel as the market shifted away from the 'mass presenter' mode through which the firm had earned its reputation. This led to 'Black Tuesday'[1] when it had to scale back from a peak of 135 down to 65 employees. Training International went into control mode, with strong backing from the CEO's brother now installed as operations director, who began to introduce centralized sales/revenue budgetary targets. But these quickly proved uncomfortable, and the CEO returned from a soul-searching absence from the office to pronounce:

> For a time we lost sight of our direction. I am still not going to run things by numbers and accounts. I'm not an organizer, but a leader with style.
>
> (CEO, Training International)

Meanwhile, the American experience came to be interpreted more as a learning achievement than a financial failure, even by the CEO's brother:

> What was useful . . . is that it has opened our eyes about the training field and what is going to happen in Europe. The Americans have a different marketing concept. Their's is one of 'selling a process' not a stand-alone programme. We learned, albeit painfully, that large organizations want to buy an ongoing relationship over time.
>
> (operations manager, Training International)

At our last contact, Training International remained intent on the broadening of internal knowledge as a key to future success. On the one hand, the CEO signalled diverse skills should be kept in use through his own contribution to stock-in-trade training programmes. On the other hand, he insisted that cultivation of new knowledge was critical:

> What matters is the ability to learn from what is relevant now and for the future. . . . Things of the past are only relevant if they speak to the present. . . . Ongoing learning, and allowing it to happen, is the key to success

(CEO, Training International)

The Training International example takes us, then, beyond the scope of Chapter 5 (skill structures) and of Chapter 6 (individual learning) to contemplate the notion of learning *for the firm as a whole*. How can we conceptualize how firms learn, and what evidence can we draw from our sample data? What particular possibilities do our data suggest for small–medium firms? How can we begin to reconcile the learning of individuals with the learning of firms? These are the kind of questions that the rest of this chapter will explore.

We will begin by reviewing various approaches to understanding how firms learn in general, and their shortcomings in understanding small–medium firms in particular. This will lead us to explore three separate perspectives on sample firms, concerned with aggregate individual learning, the presence of teams, and organizational routines. As our explorations unfold, we will reconnect with previous chapter materials on adaptation and strategic positioning, indicating what is distinctive about the opportunity for learning in smaller firms. Finally, we will point once again outwards from the firm and towards the theme of the final chapter – the extra-organizational dimension of organizational and individual learning, with the prospective tension this creates between the learning of individuals and the learning of firms.

LEARNING AND THE SMALLER FIRM

Learning at the level of the firm – most frequently called 'organizational learning' – is an elusive concept. Some writers emphasize 'the learning of all [an organization's] members' (Pedler *et al.*, 1991); others the organization's 'competitiveness in all functions' (Hayes *et al.*, 1988); and others again the 'functions and skills of business and management' (Lessem, 1991). Beyond these alternative meanings, there is a separate tendency to bracket them all together, or to translate them into a composite theoretical ideal. For example, a 'learning organization' is described as:

> where people continually expand their capacity to create the results they truly desire, where new and expansive patterns of thinking are nurtured, where collective aspiration is set free, and where people are continually learning how to learn together.

(Senge, 1990: 3)

In addition to the question of meaning, few treatments attend to the particular interest of this book, namely learning for the small–medium firm. Specific areas of neglect include intra-organizational phenomena, organizational size, and employee interaction and teamwork, where smaller firms might hold an advantage.

Intra-organizational phenomena

Despite the common disclaimer that 'organizations don't learn, people do', various writers emphasize the organization as a basic unit of analysis. For example, Cyert and March (1963) write about the learning cycle involving 'shocks' to the organizational 'system', precipitating decisions that transform the 'state' of the organization. The problem is compounded by the indiscriminate application of psychological theory to organizations, such as the language of 'stimulus-response' theory. As a result, the subject – that is the organization – stands indivisible into the constituent parts that its people represent (Hedberg, 1981).

Similarly, approaches focusing on organizational culture explore learning based on descriptive, organization-level characteristics through which culture is typically viewed (Hofstede, 1992). Finally, work on 'bureaucratic learning systems' restricts interest inside organizations to one set of variables – the procedures and regulations intended to control the flow of information (Shrivastava, 1983). All of these approaches deflect attention from intra-firm phenomena where the smaller firm may be distinctive.

Size

A related problem in writing on organizational learning is a relative neglect of size. In one review of the literature (Shrivastava, 1983), various 'levels' of learning – unit, plant, organization, industry and society – are noted, but no attempt is made to link these levels to size characteristics. In another review (Fiol and Lyles, 1986), culture, strategy, structure and the environment, but not size, are cited as the principal contextual factors that lie behind organizational learning. A third review (Levitt and March, 1988) emphasizes the learning-by-doing and learning-from-experience themes highlighted in Chapter 6, but again neglects firm size as a contributing variable. Examples prominently cited in recent accounts, such as Royal Dutch Shell and Hanover Insurance, (Hampden–Turner, 1990; Senge, 1990) add to the emphasis on large firm imagery. Meanwhile, the prospective advantages of smaller firms, previewed in Chapter 1 of this book, have received scant attention.

Interaction and teams

Both of the above paragraphs point to a subtler neglect. Emphasis on the organizational level of analysis overlooks interactions inside the firm, and neglect of size overlooks advantages (such as more effective internal communications) that smaller firms may possess. Accordingly, certain popular writers express muted reaction to the widespread downsizing of the 1980s. For example, Senge (1990: 17) worries that 'continual death' of large firms may be 'only a symptom of deeper problems'. Mintzberg (1989: 329) claims '[t]he one thing we must not do is ignore the large, widely held corporation. It is too influential a force in our lives'.

Meanwhile, work teams – which as bigger fish in smaller ponds might be expected to be more influential in the learning of small firms – get mixed treatment. There is no index entry for 'teams' in either of two recent books exploring the 'corporate mind' (Hampden–Turner, 1990) and 'intelligent enterprise' (Quinn, 1992). Teams are similarly neglected in a recent review of organizational learning processes (Huber, 1991). It has been argued that different group interpretations contribute to organizational learning difficulties (Levitt and March, 1988) and that the organizational 'knowledge base' is better advanced through teamwork (Spender, 1991). But both arguments stop short of suggesting work team/firm size interaction effects.

The March and Olsen model

March and Olsen's (1975) model of organizational learning offers a point of departure to address the above difficulties. The model suggests a simple four-stage cycle through which individuals interpret the environment, act upon their interpretation, and through their action precipitate organizational action. The latter in turn responds to the environment, from which the cycle gets repeated (Figure 7.1). The model distinguishes clearly between individual and organizational levels of analysis. While the model

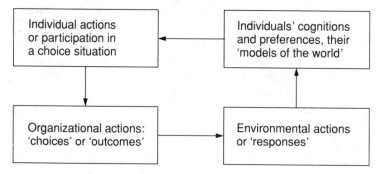

Figure 7.1 A model of organizational learning
Source: March and Olsen, 1975 (147–171)

doesn't indicate firm size or teamwork directly, it allows for their inclusion as moderators between individual and organizational action.

The March and Olsen model suggests three themes that we will explore in the body of this chapter: first, that *aggregate individual learning* is relevant to learning for the firm as a whole; second, that there are processes inside the firm – notably involving *teams* – through which individual action leads to collective action; and third, that the firm functions as an overall *system* in its relations with the environment.

AGGREGATE INDIVIDUAL LEARNING

A recent report by the Royal Society of Arts (Ball, 1991) depicts individual learning occurring in successive foundation, formation and continuation stages. The *foundation* stage is most concerned with a person's basic readiness to learn, the skills needed to do so, and the experiencing of early success and self-confidence through learning activities. The *formation* stage is concerned with broader issues of self-development, the promotion of independent learning, and greater appreciation of role interdependence and teamwork. The *continuation* stage involves emergent self-motivation and independence as a learner, readiness to pursue crucial questions, and a concern with autonomy in both individual and group activities.

A matching frame of reference at the level of the firm can be described as involving dependency, transitional and independency phases. The *dependency* phase seeks to respond to people at the foundation learning stage, by providing formal job training, any necessary remedial or special education, and an introduction to teamwork. The *transitional* phase seeks to respond to people at the formation learning stage, by providing extended industry learning, job rotation and shadowing, and wider opportunities for teamwork and experiential learning. The *independency* phase seeks to respond to the continuation learning stage by promoting linked career planning and educational investments, shared responsibility for production and development goals, and broad commitment to work group autonomy and learning by doing (Jones and Hendry, 1992).

The framework of dependency, transitional, and independency phases suggests a way to think about a firm's relative investment in the aggregate learning of its members. Accordingly, Table 7.1 lists representative activities within each phase, and indicates corresponding investments found within the sample firms. Investments are qualified according to whether they were found to be (a) broadly applied for all job categories, (b) selectively applied for all job categories, or (c) selectively applied for restricted (usually higher status) job categories only.

Table 7.1 Sample firms' investments in aggregate individual learning

	VB	CB	HT	HH	SP	TI	ST	LS	BP	AE	MD	PR	CL	GD	FI	OP	CC	HC	CA	AS
Phase 1: Independency																				
* Formal job training – how to do a specific job	***	***	***	***	***	***	**	**	***	***	***	***	***	***	***	***	**	***	***	***
* Personal remedial/special education		**	**	**	***	***		**		**	**	*	**	**	**	**	**	*	*	**
* Person-centred motivation and skill development	**	***	**	**	**	***	**	**		***	**	**	**	**	**	**	**			**
* Learning and working in groups and teams	***	***	***	***	**	***	**	***	*	**	**	**	***	***	**	**	**	***	***	***
Phase 2: Transitional																				
* Emphasis on team and group involvement	***	***	**	**	**	***		***	*	**	**	*	**	***	**	**	**	**	***	***
* Learning through job rotation and shadowing	**	**	*			**	**	**		***	**		**	***	**	**				**
* Formal training based on individual learning	**	**	*		**	***	**	**	**	**	**	**	**	**	***	**	**			**
* Learning by doing gained through job exposure	***	***	***	***	***	***	**	***	*	***	***	*	**	***	**	***	**	**	**	***
Phase 3: Independency																				
* Support for employee career development	**	**	*	*	**	***		***		***	**	**	*	***	**	**	*	*	*	**
* Work practice exposure to markets and technologies	**	***	*	*	**	***	**	***		**	*	*	*	**	***	***	*		*	***
* Group responsibility for quality improvement	**	**			**	***	**	**		**	**	*	*	***	***	**	**	**	**	**
* Levelling of status in employment situations	**	***				***		**		***	**		**	**	***	**			**	**

Key:

*** broadly applied for all job categories
** selectively applied for all job categories
* selectively applied for restricted job categories

VB Visitor Bureau; CB = Convention Bureau; HT = Hotel Tourist; HH = Hotel Heritage; SP = Software Products; TI = Training International; ST = Skills Training; LS = Legal Services; BP = Bread Products; AE = Architectural Engineering; MD = MOD Products; PR = Pressings; CL = Clean Air Co.; GD = Glass Discs; FI = Fibres; OP = Optics; CC = Construction Co.; HC = House Co.; CA = Cables; AS = Architectural Services

The dependency phase

Much of the evidence for this phase has already been covered in Chapters 5 and 6. Firms had jobs to be done, and invested in basic occupational learning to secure matching employee competence. In addition:

- Firms appearing to invest the least either carried relatively unskilled jobs (Bread Products, Pressings) or recruited ready-skilled people from outside (Skills Centres, House Co.). In cases of high turnover, notably the hotels, the goal was to replace lost skills rather than to promote any aggregate learning effect.

Beyond these basic observations, our interest in the dependency phase rests in its contrasts with subsequent learning phases.

The transitional phase

At this phase, greater differences among sample firms appear.

- Hotel Tourist, Hotel Heritage, Skills Centres, Bread Products, Pressings, House Co. and Cable Co. all made only selective investments in further employee learning.
- There is also greater diversity in the use of teams, with the 'flexible service' firms (both Bureaux, Training International, Software Products) and 'professional service' firms (Legal Services, and Architectural Services), described in Chapter 5, all making broad claims to team involvement.

Clearer distinctions also appear in the promotion of learning through job exposure.

The independency stage

Here, the contrasts among firms appear sharper, and the distinctions in the use of teams and job exposure clearer.

- For teams, the distinction is between those used principally for efficient job performance (for example, Cables), and those used for some higher learning goal (for example, Fibres). Among the latter kind of firm were several manufacturing shops, in both engineering and optical electronics, where the emphasis on teams was linked to recent initiatives in total quality management.
- For job exposure, the distinction is between jobs designed to constrain and jobs designed to promote new learning in conjunction with job performance. Training International, Convention Bureau, MOD Products, Aerospace Engineering, Fibres and Architectural Services were among the most innovative firms in our sample, and the most reliant on expanding job-centred employee learning.

This brief overview of data on aggregate individual learning illustrates the scope of investments in learning that sample firms made. Inspection of Table 7.1 reveals that for many firms the investment was considerable. Different investments by firms across the dependency, transitional and independency phases also suggest different assumptions about employee *readiness* for new learning, as well as firms' market circumstances.

The activities listed in Table 7.1 – such as working in teams, job exposure and shadowing, learning by doing, and group responsibility – also signal the importance of a firm's internal learning processes. How, then, does aggregate individual learning feed into the learning of the firm as a whole? To explore this further, we will next take a more focused look at the functioning of teams.

THE PRESENCE OF TEAMS

Teams provide for the collective learning of their members. Traditional approaches to team learning, in common with traditional approaches to training, have often emphasized off-the-job activities. This concurs with one of two meanings of 'practice', namely as off-site, simulated activity intended to promote changed behaviour back in the workplace. Using this meaning, it has been argued that 'learning teams need "practice fields", ways to practice together so that they can develop their collective learning skills' (Senge, 1990: 258).

However, there is a second meaning of practice – as a complement to theory – that involves the actual *performance* of work activities. Teams from this standpoint are 'communities of practice', drawing learning from 'legitimate peripheral participation' in the work that they do (Lave and Wenger, 1991). An example is documented by Orr (1990), who observed photocopier customer service reps learning that their work was as much about 'repair and maintenance of the social setting' as it was about the technical repairs stressed by their employer. With 'communities of practice', the focus is on 'the ability of people to learn *in situ*' (Brown and Duguid, 1991), rather than away from the context of their jobs. This focus is consistent with our earlier accounts of sample firms' preferences for on-the-job learning.

The notion of the team as community of practice raises the question of how teams are defined. The most significant 'communities of practice' may not be recognizable in formal organizational arrangements. Conversely, formal arrangements may proclaim teams exist despite a lack of collective significance in identified members' work (Brown and Duguid, 1991). Nor, as we noted in Chapter 6, do teams exist simply by virtue of physical proximity. Small firms are not 'team organizations' simply because they comprise relatively few people working closely together. To get beyond these difficulties, it has been suggested we identify teams according to their shared purpose, as either 'discrete units of performance' (Katzenbach and Smith, 1993), or as groups of people connected by 'work flow' and focused on a limited family of subproducts, services or customers (Schonberger, 1990).

Consistent with the above, we adopt a definition of 'team' here as 'a group of people connected by distinctive purpose on behalf of the firm'. What is the usage of such teams in small–medium firms? What purposes are teams set up to serve? And what learning is likely to accrue from team activities?

Inclusive team arrangements

Examination of our sample firm cases shows that the use of teams was widespread. There were recognizable team activities, which can be labelled *inclusive* since they involved most employees, in eighteen of the twenty sample firms. These activities demonstrate three distinct purposes, namely (a) to serve the *customer* directly, (b) to complete a specific *project*, and (c) to pursue improved *quality* (see Table 7.2).

Table 7.2 The uses of teams in sample firms

	Customer Service	Project Delivery	Quality Improvement
Visitor Bureau	X	X	
Convention Bureau	X	X	
Hotel Tourist	X		
Hotel Heritage	X		
Software Products		X	
Training International	X	X	
Skills Training	X		
Legal Services	X	X	
Bread Products			
Aerospace Engineering		X	X
MOD Products		X	X
Pressings			
Clean Air Co.	X	X	
Glass Discs			X
Fibres			X
Optics			X
Construction Co.		X	
House Co.		X	
Cable Co.		X	
Architectural Services		X	

Serving the customer

- The hotels provide a good example of 'communities of practice' defined around customer service, rather than through formal organizational structure. Customers – guests – were broadly visible, and their level of satisfaction reinforced a sense of shared responsibility. Similar 'communities of practice' evolved in the bureaux through staff exposure to 'buyers and members' and involvement in public exhibitions and conferences.
- Most employees at Training International, Skills Training and Legal Services participated directly in the delivery of services, and collectively pursued long-term customer relationships. Clean Air Co.'s installation teams physically performed work at customer premises.

Completing projects

- Projects – 'jobs' – were the traditional focus for teamwork in construction, spanning both blue-collar (Cable Co., Construction Co., House Co.) and white-collar (Construction Co., Architectural Services) roles. The same focus prevailed for the 'packages' developed by Software Products.
- Project activity paralleled the exposure to customers for Clean Air Co. employees. Similarly, projects at Legal Services (cases), Training International and Skills Training (training contracts) and the bureaux (conventions and tourist promotions) complemented the direct customer contact work teams experienced.

Improving quality

- For quality improvement, a common pattern applied in all three opto-electronics firms. Optics reported on a shift from the quality function being 'out on a limb and universally hated' to TQM methods that would 'provide an active means for participation'. Similarly, Fibres flirted with quality as a separate function then 'rationalized' it into a teamwork approach, as the link between employees and the 'end user'. Glass Discs was less advanced, but still viewed its TQM efforts as pursuant of a 'teamwork culture'.
- Progress in the skilled engineering firms followed a parallel course. MOD Products was building quality improvement teams in different product areas, anticipating 'cross fertilization' and 'singular team' benefits for the firm as a whole. Aerospace Engineering was one step behind, but still pursued twin objectives to 'improve total quality' and 'emphasize teamwork'.

The other two manufacturing firms (Bread Products, Pressings) were the only firms in our sample not yet broadly invested in teamwork efforts. However, both of these firms recognized they would soon have to respond to new national and international quality standards. If the experience of other manufacturing firms holds, quality improvement efforts would once more give rise to teamwork, and in turn to teamwork as a vehicle to elicit new learning for the firm.

In summary, Table 7.2 suggests there are distinct mechanisms for team learning according to the industry, or sector, in which a firm operates. In hotels and in the delivery of services through training and legal counsel, the principal mechanism was direct customer contact. In construction and software writing, the mechanism was the specific project the firm had contracted to perform. In manufacturing, the dominant mechanism, filling a gap in traditional teamwork arrangements, was that of quality improvement programmes.

Some service delivery activities combined the customer service and project delivery mechanisms – for example, when clients were served as part of a conference programme, or when a law case was taken as part of an ongoing client relationship. In construction, investments in quality improvement were likely to combine this with the traditional mechanism of project delivery.

Most interestingly, in manufacturing (the opto-electronics and engineering firms) elements of all three mechanisms, intimately related to specific small firm phenomena, combined to create a generalized teamworking culture. A high degree of focus on one or two customers ('dependence') gave rise to a 'customer service' effect in which a visible customer stimulated teamworking. In the same way, a focus on one or two major customers, combined with the batch orientation of small firms supplying industrial users, encouraged a 'project' mentality through specific deadlines for that customer, as where Aerospace Engineering was driven by Rolls-Royce's batch product schedules. In manufacturing firms, overlapping customer service and project influences created an incipient team culture. What quality improvement initiatives tended then to do was to crystallize this into more explicit 'work-flow' based team structures.

- Thus, MOD Products had created a work team to make a new product (an exercise treadmill) for one particular customer, and then built a permanent quality improvement team around it, comprising the production/assembly staff, test engineers, and quality assurance/ inspection, to develop the product, solve problems, and improve work organization.

The dissolution of functional structures in this way anticipates the philosophy of business process re-engineering which is currently attracting much attention among large firms.

Selective team arrangements

While the above arrangements involved many or all employees, there were parallel team arrangements that were more selective and intended to target specific challenges facing firms. These initiatives had a 'strategic' character, in that they were designed to protect, develop and retain some group which possessed a key competence the firm needed:

- At Optics, optical designers were a critical human resource in producing new and customized products. Despite the logistical constraints and costs incurred, designers remained in their preferred location near London, instead of relocating to North Wales. The privileged treatment kept the design team together, and also sustained an opportunity for closer links with the two London area physics departments from which the designers had graduated.
- Fibres paid particular attention to a group of process engineers whose combined qualifications and experience made them difficult to replace. The goal was to continually 'stretch' these people as a way of main- taining loyalty, and prolonging their employment with the company.
- Clean Air Co.'s CEO invested in frequent meetings of sales engineers ostensibly to promote teamwork and new idea generation. However, a broader goal was new learning for the sales engineers in overlapping technical, marketing and presentational skills.

A second kind of selective team development was focused on the management team:

- Software Products had become conscious of the limited management skills associated with a young industry and promotion from within. Aerospace Engineering had the same problem in a more traditional industry. Both saw the solution lying in developing a management team around planning disciplines.
- Both MOD Products and Glass Discs, on the other hand, had relatively mature professional managers, but were concerned to 'build cover' in their management teams, to forestall the possibility of key defections and resultant gaps in internal knowledge and competency.

Business development teams

Finally, certain teams were identifiable whose primary purpose was to promote overall development of the firm's business:

- At Architectural Services, this was focused on the development of a group of younger architects who were seen as most receptive to the new entrepreneurial style required to open up new areas of business and build a specialist reputation. As a result, as we have noted before, the youngest partner was investing considerable time in mentoring and working with this group.

- At Training International, such activity involved a more generalized strategic capability through the development of a company-wide 'teamwork culture'. This culture, secured through long-term employee commitment and continuous learning, was seen as 'part of an ongoing strategic process to enable markets and products to be developed'. The effect of crisis, as we saw in the introduction to this chapter, was to bring about a re-affirmation of this approach.
- At Construction Co., teamworking for business development was focused initially on the top team and was then being spread to other layers. After the retirement of the previous family owner, the new CEO moved decisively toward promoting shared responsibility across a seven-member top management board. A profit sharing plan was introduced and the top team attended off-site team-building and leadership courses, as part of his drive for collective learning and improved firm performance. Members of the executive attended subsequent courses with their own staff.

Team learning as an investment in holistic problem-solving

The distinctions among inclusive, selective and business development team arrangements are reminiscent of Miles and Snow's (1978) distinctions among administrative, engineering and entrepreneurial problems, referred to in Chapters 3 and 4. However, as Deming (1986) cautions, too much can be made of such distinctions 'aimed at the needs of the customer, present and future' (Deming, 1986: 5). Each of the inclusive team arrangements identified has the potential to represent customer needs, either directly or indirectly, to team members. Each arrangement in turn carries an invitation to take a collective interest in the interdependent administrative, engineering, and entrepreneurial problems through which present and future customers get served.

These observations support our earlier contention (Chapter 4) that the Miles and Snow (1978) framework suggests a behavioural rather than a firm typology. Our observations also extend Miles and Snow's thinking beyond seeing the administrative, engineering, and entrepreneurial problems as principally the concern of senior management. Instead, these interdependent problems can be seen as *dimensions* along which collective interest, and in turn learning, can unfold.

This helps us to reconnect with the Jones and Hendry (1992) model adopted earlier in this chapter. Progressive investments from 'dependency' to 'independency', according to that model, were presented as investments in employee readiness for new learning. For individual members, and in turn for teams, the issue of readiness unfolds into the three dimensions noted above. For the firm, the broader issue is one of how readiness is nurtured for overall learning to occur. This issue may be especially critical in times of rapid 'transformation' (Jones and Hendry, 1992) when interdependence among the three components, and the firm's ability to respond, are likely to be highlighted.

How, though, do aggregate individual learning and team-learning actually interact? To explore this question, we need to go beyond discrete team arrangements, to look at the system – in terms of March and Olsen's (1975) model – in which learning takes place. Or rather, we need to dig down inside the organization to look at the processes whereby individual and team-learning are translated into organizational learning.

LEARNING AND 'ROUTINES'

The idea of 'organizational routines' (Nelson and Winter, 1982) offers a reference point to link the different perspectives on firm learning reviewed above. Routines reflect 'what is regular and predictable' (ibid: 15) about a firm's business behaviour, including characteristics of production, employment, customer service and so on that have become embedded in the everyday operations of the firm. Routines are the organizational analogue of individual skills, and – just as the development of skills over time draws upon and modifies individual memory – routines over time draw upon and influence 'organizational memory'. Expressed another way, routines translate collective 'learning by doing' into 'remembering by doing' (ibid: 99).

Routines, like the script to a play, provide roles through which individual skills can contribute to collective performance. Routines also draw heavily on 'tacit knowledge', analogous to the unspoken but mutual understanding on which performance of a play depends. 'Knowing one's job' is dependent on the subtle and continuing messages that give a job meaning, just as 'knowing one's lines' is a mere starting point for a successful play. Like a theatre company's performance style, routines represent the heuristics from which the strategy of a firm is derived (ibid: 133). Routines, in other words, are the 'grammar' or 'deep structure' (Chomsky, 1965), which act as the link between the morphology of individual behaviour and the public language of organizational action.

Thinking about routines helps begin to reconcile our findings on collective learning with the earlier findings on firm adaptation presented in Chapter 4. Routines reflect a firm's use of internal resources, and in particular a trade-off between efficiency and flexibility (Grant, 1991). Thus, a 'limited repertoire of routines can be performed highly efficiently with near-perfect coordination', although the same firm 'may find it extremely difficult to respond to novel situations' (Grant, 1991). The trade-off suggests a distinction between learning efforts directed at simple *maintenance* of existing routines versus *elaboration* of those routines for greater adaptability. Beyond both maintenance and elaboration, there are further possibilities for *building in redundancy* in routines, *changing* routines, and *importing* routines. As the treatment of routines under these headings illustrates, routines exist for the various domains of a business covering engineering, entrepreneurial, and administrative activity (Miles and Snow, 1978). In many instances, also, there are both human and material components to the routine.

Maintenance (and creation) of routines

Four of the five firms for which no mode of adaptation was previously identified – Bread Products, Hotel Tourist, Hotel Heritage, and Skills Training (Glass Discs being the fifth) – made low investments in collective learning.

- Bread Products' intention to maintain its present market strategy and existing routines, and nothing more, underlies that firm's perspective on employee training:

> If you train people too much they'll leave and we not only lose the people we also lose the money we've invested in them. So I see no reason why we should pay for training only for someone else to benefit. In any case, there are few promotion prospects here so people leave anyway. Training would generally be a waste of money.
>
> (finance director, Bread Products)

In the hotels, 'communities of practice' could be discerned around customer service. However, these got little formal recognition, and their function was clearly remedial, to minimize 'memory loss' as experienced employees left and novices took over. Skills Training was too busy trying to salvage itself from existing customer and cash flow crises to address future learning issues. In all three, routines were in decay in the absence of any clear strategic direction. For certain occupational groups in other firms, such as pressworkers in Pressings and cable hands in Cable Co., investments in collective learning emphasized maintenance over any further purpose.

Preceding maintenance, of course, is the creation of routines. Chapter 2's emphasis on the development of skills and systems on the back of a close association with one customer alluded to this; while the challenge in 'capitalizing on environmental beneficence' (see Chapter 4) is to create stable routines quickly to cope with an explosion of activity. This is likely to include a major effort, through training, to replicate skills and adherence to common operational standards.

Glass Discs, 18 months on from start-up and faced with an uncertain market environment, illustrates this early preoccupation with establishing efficient routines. At this point, production remained inefficient – 'a knife and fork operation' in which standards and levels of skill were highly variable. Much effort was therefore being put into defining skills and structured training:

> Part of the next two years is very much establishing company culture, image, and way of operating. We're establishing a completely new way of working, in an area where there's no Group experience. We are making up the rules as we go along, establishing a team culture and blurring the borderlines between marketing, development, and research.
>
> (production manager, Glass Discs)

The importance attached to creating routines is a reminder not to devalue the maintenance of routines. Firms, as social systems, need constantly to reproduce themselves. Maintenance, therefore, need not be associated with inactivity, nor with lack of learning. The reinforcement of routines is an essential part of learning. Arguably, definitions of learning emphasize change in behaviour to the exclusion of all else. If learning is about becoming more effective, that must include recognizing and isolating the effective bits of behaviour and reiterating these – as the concept of 'double loop learning' (Argyris and Schon, 1978) acknowledges.

Fibres provides a prime instance of the creative and energetic maintenance of routines to increase efficiency and effectiveness. It continued to reproduce itself and improve best practice through three mechanisms – its employee commitment system (described in Chapter 2), its quality control system, and a newly installed programme of structured training. Underlying these was the technology-driven nature of the plant, and the proven nature of the technology itself:

> We are very much on a technology-driven productivity curve. Although training does play an important part and employees can play a big part in affecting turnaround times, it is all computer-driven, and depends on technologists to make the plant more effective. Fibres's strength in the marketplace is the consistency of the product. We can achieve technical standards others struggle to meet. But it is not a function of technical people. It is a function of systems, and everyone contributes to that.
>
> (personnel manager, Fibres)

As a result, work routines were grounded in an elaborately documented process management system, in which every stage of the process was recorded and had to be signed off. This had the effect of shifting the emphasis away from individual 'skills', to culture and standards developed in various ways. Various functions acted as custodians and upholders of these standards, although the computing function occupied a special place. However, although the skill requirement among process workers was not great, they had the capacity to undermine the whole operation:

> One of the areas we see a need to concentrate on, to eliminate the 0.001 per cent of faults attributable to careless mistakes, is operators. It is important to maintain their morale and they are seen as the weakest link.
> (personnel manager, Fibres)

The employee commitment system was therefore an important factor in mitigating this. A second factor was the effort being put into developing TQM in 1990. A third was to ensure consistency in standards through training. The rationale and approach to training nicely illustrates the central significance of routines. In fact, successive cohorts of recruits trained to different standards had resulted in 'a very wide range of training preparation', variable understanding of what machines did, and uneven work standards. This had led to a realization that:

> Training is vital. It's the weakest link in the system. Having got the technology and systems right, we've now got to tie that end up.
> (training advisor, Fibres)

The company went about remedying this with customary rigour. First, it appointed a 'production operator training officer', and sent him off on a training officer's course. On return, he trained four operator instructors for each of the four shifts (a total of sixteen instructors), who were then expected to spend a quarter of their time training others. A training checklist was developed from the latest process manual, to inform both training and formally to test all new and existing employees. Subsequently, all employees had to take an annual test on the standards required in their present job, while if anyone was temporarily transferred from their normal job for 60 days or more, they were required to undertake a refresher course of training. As the company training advisor commented:

> They are tying up operator skill more than I have ever come across. They are calibrating the operators in the same way as the machines. It's a real Rolls-Royce system.

Routines in the examples of Fibres and Glass Discs are heavily focused on what Miles and Snow (1978) termed the 'engineering' problem. They are about establishing and maintaining efficient and reliable ways of producing a product. At Fibres, in particular, there is a vast array of production routines which could be minutely described, backed by a learning system for ensuring conformity to these.

Elaboration of routines

In contrast with the maintenance of routines, two of the remaining fifteen firms (Convention Bureau and Visitor Bureau) were principally engaged in what we labelled in Chapter 4 as 'incremental opportunism'. While each looked to information technology to secure themselves a necessary database, each affected low formality in their operations, seeking coherence through the expression of an 'entrepreneurial (or marketing) style' (CEO, Convention Bureau), and constant expansion into new areas of activity:

> For both Bureaux, 'entrepreneurial style' expressed itself in business development through extensive networking (described in Chapter 2), a philosophy for marketing their cities, and a model for managing events which provided a training forum for employees. This model, which both bureaux followed, was – install reliable leaders for 'special events' and through these events provide exposure to multiple facets of the business for less experienced employees. As familiarity increased, so did the capacity of each bureau to take on more work and to promote its own city over national and international rivals.

Routines in this example by contrast, then, have to do with the entrepreneurial task of extending a product-market domain. The Bureaux have a routine for developing the business and a learning routine for familiarizing employees with the overall approach.

Two other patterns of growth described in Chapter 4 – 'developing a related package of services and products', and 'actively searching and targetting additional niches' – also involved the elaboration of routines. Precisely the same pattern can be seen – in a routine for developing the business and a learning routine for training employees. For example:

- Legal Services was clearly organized into, and sought growth around, chosen specialisms such as charity trusts and mortgage repossession. The model for doing so was well established: find a specialist for the initial work; install the specialist as a new or prospective partner; then build an expert team around the specialist through on-the-job learning as casework gets done. To this end, all senior figures in the firm understood the importance of prolonged, case-centred discourse to allow shared learning to take place.

The difference, compared with the Bureaux, was that development tended to be more through externalized elaboration. That is, new bits of business were added on and managed as separate units, with their own operating procedures and routines, either through internal specialization (Legal Services) or in separate companies (Software Products). The Bureaux were relatively unspecialized (although they also separated out some of their newly elaborated activity into, for example, ticket and information centres).

Beyond routines – building in redundancy

Various writers point to exemplary Japanese practices in the promotion of collective learning. Drawing on these, Grant (1991) refers to 'the essential task' that strategy pushes 'beyond the limits of the firm's capabilities at any point in time' so that 'through pursuing its present strategy, a firm develops the expertise required for its future strategy'. However, this perspective calls for a more temporary, and more recursive, view of the established practices that routines represent. Practices become targets as well as triggers for new learning, and the creation of new skills and knowledge assumes a parallel significance to the application of existing skills and knowledge.

An underlying principle in Japanese accounts, which is consistent with cybernetic ideas on 'the brain of the firm' (Beer, 1972; Morgan, 1986), is that of 'redundancy'. Redundancy involves 'the conscious overlapping of company information, business activities, and managerial responsibilities' (Nonaka, 1991: 102). This is distinct from 'organizational slack' (Cyert and March, 1963) which implies under-utilized resources. 'Redundancy' implies enrichment through multiple engagements involving people and information (Galbraith, 1974). Moreover, 'slack' in Cyert and March is represented as a 'stabilizing function', absorbing variability in the firm's environment. 'Redundancy', in this new sense, is geared to innovation and improvement. It is thus more at one with the principles of developmental economics than, for example, with the neo-classical 'economizing' model of the firm (Williamson, 1991).

The principle of redundancy presents a challenge to move beyond old Western connotations of duplication and waste to the new possibilities that surplus, overlapping knowledge provides. Nonaka elaborates on the principle this way:

> Redundancy is important because it encourages frequent dialogue and communication. This helps create a 'common cognitive ground' among employees and thus facilitates the transfer of tacit knowledge. Since members of the organization share overlapping information, they can sense what others are struggling to articulate. Redundancy also spreads new explicit knowledge through the organization so it can be internalized by employees.
>
> (Nonaka, 1991: 102)

The pursuit, creation, and exploitation of redundancy for purposes of business development, continuous improvement, and doing new things, can be seen in our sample firms in three ways – (1) the development of an organization-wide strategic capability, (2) external networking focused on business development teams, and (3) the development of 'team, or corporate, entrepreneurship' in a functioning top team. In each case, there is a coming together of aggregate individual learning and team learning, while the examples in each show a distinctive approach to information-gathering. Finally, they also reflect the need, as we argued in Chapter 4, to develop new human resources (linked through routines) often as a prior condition for creating new lines of business.

Developing organization-wide strategic capability

Training International, which we used to introduce this chapter, made the most explicit investment in knowledge redundancy of all sample firms in order to enhance its strategic capability. It did this through various human resource practices which stimulated sharing.

First, levels of management, formal qualifications, and status differences were resisted in favour of a philosophy of everyone being prepared to contribute and assist one another. This was reinforced by the insistence that 10 per cent of the annual operating budget be dedicated to new learning regardless of the business climate.

Reversals, such as 'Black Tuesday'[1] and the relative failure of the firm's venture into the USA, were then interpreted in a way that reinforced a commitment to continuous learning. The philosophy of 'on-going learning, and allowing it to happen' as the key to success was resilient to changing economic circumstances:

> Only this firm would go into a recession with the CEO and the organization generally handing you a pair of rose coloured spectacles! We are carrying on as if there is no recession. Training budgets have been increased and new products are being developed, with all the expense this incurs.
>
> (credit control manager, Training International)

In particular, the company held an annual 'away-day' to look at the business, which illustrates the pattern of learning and sharing. The 'away-day' each year took different forms, although each one was designed as a learning event. In 1990, it was built round the idea of a French market, with all staff dressed up as French stall-holders, in berets, blue scarves, etc. Each of ten departments or sections in the company had its own stall, and each was asked to list nine things they thought they were good at. Two or three members of all the other departments then went round as 'purchasers', and the stallholders had to sell their own good points, while the other departments could challenge them on these. Every ten minutes a whistle was blown, and the 'buyers' moved on.

Before each whistle, however, the buyer had to make a contract with the seller to remedy those activities or issues they couldn't agree on as 'good points', within a three-month period, and each signed a contract to say they would do something about it. Alan Jones (while researching the company) participated in this, wearing a circus ringmaster's outfit. If there was no agreement by the time the whistle was blown (as happened twice), he listened to the arguments and made a final, binding arbitration. Three months later 'buyers' and 'sellers' met again to review what they had done to fulfil their contracts. Since the business had to be kept going, half the staff from each department attended one day, and the other half at a repeat of the event the following day. This provided a reflection of alternative perspectives within a department, and both sets of contracts were then merged for action within the three months.

As an inter-group exercise, this event was designed to enable people to express the positives and negatives in their view of one other, but in a way, through role-play, that distanced them from real-life. This avoided the expression simply of personal animosities. In addition, it captures, and promoted, a spontaneity in the organization, in that staff were unaware what was in store, but were simply told to bring their costumes along (likewise our researcher). Learning is a regular feature of organizational life, but it is not narrowly routinized. Above all, this particular exercise contributed ideas from the various parts of the organization to improvements all round. In this kind of engagement lies the building of a broad strategic capability throughout an organization, through a kind of internal networking.

External networking focused on business development teams

While enhanced strategic capability can be diffused through an organization, it can also be focused on particular teams. Although Fibres was notable for its operational routines, it also built in systems for 'information redundancy' for purposes of business development.

In a few short years, Fibres had rapidly become the dominant optical fibre maker in Europe, and held ambitions to become number two in the world. It had achieved this position by going beyond its joint-venture founders' belief that 'all they had to build was a carbon copy of [the US founder's], plant and customers would beat a path to our door' (personnel manager, Fibres). One mechanism it made extensive use of was an elaborate external network of experts which it could tap for ideas and advice on a wide range of subjects:

> We have retainers on a lot of specialists (in patents, scientists, etc.) to get their specialist knowledge. We have a large network of 30–40 such outsiders. And that means being able to put teams together, and their being able to suck in outsiders and use their knowledge. It means having employees recognizing the advantages of having contract staff working alongside them.
>
> (CEO, Fibres)

Such a network extends the boundaries of the organization's knowledge. By implication, a department can draw on it routinely, although in practice it is more likely to be activated by project teams set up to address a particular issue. Either way, it represents a learning routine, used to shake attachment to in-bred knowledge and customary problem-solving routines.

The development of team entrepreneurship

Much of the foregoing on routines does not specifically and uniquely touch on small firms. The development of team entrepreneurship, however, as signalled a number of times, is a unique challenge facing the growing small firm. As we argued in Chapter 4, it is the key to accomplishing 'break out' whereby a small firm ceases to be 'customer-dependent' and develops the capacity to act strategically. As the key to small firm growth, it has even been suggested that 'start-ups' should be encouraged which embody teamworking structures and principles (ie. 'team entrepreneurship') from the beginning (Vyakarnam and Jacobs, 1993).

Aerospace Engineering, as we saw in Chapter 4, had invested heavily in new plant and enhanced operational skills in factory and office. It then had to develop a range of higher level skills in order to bring in the business to make effective use of these. Above all, it needed to develop a more integrated management approach – a genuine management team, thinking and acting strategically – to get new business and deliver on it. The problem, as the CEO recognized, was the tendency of organizations like itself, doing jobbing work for industrial companies to their designs, to employ and promote people purely for their specialist technical skills:

> Until the last six months, I always considered manufacturing engineering to be the most important requirement, because we've got to produce funny shapes. As an engineer, I tended to think that was important. But now, when we've got all that, we've got to take a broader approach. The philosophy before I took over was to hold people down because they would want your job. But I take a different view. I want to level people up. But I have inherited people who are not managers. In this kind of industry, we don't tend to employ managers. People are employed for their specialist skills, but then you can't get them to go beyond those.
>
> (CEO, Aerospace Engineering)

The problem small firms like this have is that they may have a group of people who are ostensibly the management team, but this group does not function as a 'community of practice'. That is, they lack a shared perspective and language, and a common orientation to action. Aerospace Engineering had taken the first steps towards creating this through new recruitment. This strengthened the operational base of the organization in certain key areas like quality assurance, computer systems management, and industrial engineering. At the same time, the new recruits brought a wider perspective educationally (as graduates) and through employment experience elsewhere. At the same time, it gave the CEO a more balanced and responsive group of senior managers, and this in turn encouraged him to initiate top team meetings with a wider-ranging strategic agenda.

These meetings were geared to creating a 'planning style' among the management group as a whole, in which there was an emphasis on planning, prioritizing, problem solving, exploring alternatives and ramifications of possible actions, establishing timetables for action, and initiating regular operational reviews. The focus of such discussions was on the requirements for developing the company.

For example, one question the CEO posed was 'what will be required in the machine shop to bring in prototype work?' This represented a more fundamental approach to what had been happening, where the production manager gave such requests limited priority because of resource constraints which others did not acknowledge. This and similar agenda items were intended to create a more dynamic relationship between manufacturing and sales/marketing, and to stimulate a more active market search process.

From one point of view, what Aerospace Engineering was trying to do was develop a strategic planning routine. From another, it was getting functional managers to take responsibility for the organization as a whole. This entailed bringing operational ('engineering') issues to do with basic resourcing into focus with 'entrepreneurial' issues to do with business development. One feature of 'information redundancy', then, is where everyone in a team makes it their responsibility to think about the whole. Sticking to a functional focus may be 'economical', but ends up being ineffective and traps small firms. A second feature is how longer-term issues of business development are addressed while also remedying areas of operational weakness. It solves the conundrum for smaller firms – namely: 'how to satisfy their immediate requirements for economic and financial performance, while creating the conditions for longer-term development and learning'.

'Information redundancy' through team entrepreneurship is the means for a small firm to overcome its limited financial resources and create 'organizational slack'.

A couple of quotations from Fibres show a recognition of precisely the same issue. First, the way the top team had learnt to work exhibits effective 'information redundancy' through team working:

> We have meetings two to three times a week. We live in one another's pockets and no longer meet to a fixed timetable. In building the new

factory, each had to contribute a piece (on the marketing, technology, finance, the building plan, etc.) and put their case through the group of six. It needed little change and I had to do minimal editing. It was testimony to the fact that we had successfully lived in one another's pockets. It was considered by the joint-venture partners to be as good a proposal as they had ever had.

(CEO, Fibres)

But then, below this team, the lessons of team entrepreneurship had to be learnt once again and repeated:

Because we've grown rapidly we have a problem of having recruited experts in their function. That's no longer appropriate, they've got to work in a team, their own job has become more strategic. People like doing what they're good at, so it's hard to stop. We have to build a team below them [the top team] to take over their work.

Changing routines

In other cases, 'break out' from established markets may mean wholesale changes in routines.

As Architectural Services moved from acting as a regional practice to competing for work nationally, it had to adjust its whole way of working. In the regional market, the key operating values were dependability and service. Accordingly, the backbone of the practice was its contracts management system which the firm perfected in the 1960s and which for many years gave it an edge. This served the company well while it concentrated on public sector work, even though its output was 'pretty pedestrian stuff' (partner, Architectural Services).

Entry to the national market, on the other hand, required specialization in design. This happened over a number of years through the kind of projects taken on, which gradually brought a national reputation – first in library design in the late 1960s, then more substantially in leisure centre design in the 1970s. Subsequent specializations developed in transportation and urban redevelopment. In winning these kind of projects, Architectural Services began to play a different kind of game, and the demands of competing in a new arena set up tensions within the business. These eventually resulted in the senior partner being eased out into retirement.

Competing nationally meant broadly being more innovative, projecting a 'house style' (still a point of contention), competing for (and winning) design awards, and seeking a higher proportion of commercial (non-public sector) work:

It means avoiding the grubby image of community architects and claiming the moral high ground through excellence in design, coupled with a strong commercial viewpoint. It means getting alongside developers, not beneath developers.

(partner, Architectural Services)

At the heart of the change was getting away from the 'old professional model of waiting to be called' and, instead, learning to market. The marketing ('entrepreneurial') approach precipitated two kinds of investments – (a) in competitions and speculative proposals, and (b) in the development of external relationships.

For competitions, proposals had to be researched to gain a clearer view of the commercial and market aspects to inform a design, and this meant spending money speculatively. While this involved new entrepreneurial routines (and new attitudes), it also required new management skills because of the higher proportion of non-billable work, longer lead-times to projects, and managing a higher level of risk. Related speculative investments (and networking) went into general image-raising through the media, via journal editors, and mounting exhibitions.

Competitions, meanwhile, were part of the process of developing external relationships, or 'marketing'. This involved prior research on the marketplace, designs, and levels of commercial activity, and 'knowing who are the players in the game'. Other jobs were won through 'the ability to be in the right place, with the right people, at the right time' – for example, by putting together consortia of developers and engineers. In each case, there was a need for political and networking skills neglected in traditional practice:

Positioning for new work calls for networking and political skills that are not a natural part of the architect's education or socialisation. Relationships are of fundamental importance to the complex nature of contracts needed to pull things together.

(partner, Architectural Services)

New business brought about the formation of project teams and job rotation through which learning could be passed on, while the mentoring process in which the design partner engaged with younger colleagues contributed to prior team-building. Such activities, and the simple fact that staff were expected to spend more time out of the office, can be seen as new routines.

Architectural Services thus shows a firm changing its whole orientation – through changes in image and reputation, prospecting activity and the effort put into networking, new design expertise through new kinds of project, as well as in the decay (through overload) of its contracts management system. Underlying these changes was the development of many new routines. Such a shift inevitably involves a clash with an existing culture and values, which is often only resolved through crisis (as in the case of succession).

FIRM SIZE, LEARNING AND STRATEGIC POSITIONING

At the start of this chapter we noted how the literature on organizational learning has neglected size, and its associated intra-organizational effects. Certain writers on teams have acknowledged the benefits that limited size can bring. For example, Lawler (1986) has claimed team-centred 'high commitment' work systems are better achieved in units of no more than 500. More recently Reich (1991), in writing about 'creative teams', has pointed to the direct barrier to learning that large size can represent:

> At each point of connection [in a network] are a relatively small number of people – depending on the task from a dozen to several hundred. If a group was any larger it could not engage in rapid and informal learning.

According to these views, teams provide a learning advantage in small–medium firm situations which larger firms cannot so easily create.

Teams also facilitate information redundancy, 'because they provide a shared context where individuals can interact with each other' and 'dialogue and discussion' emerge, and where people can 'integrate their diverse individual perspectives into a new collective perspective' (Nonaka, 1991). An indirect argument can therefore be made that redundancy is also better served, because of greater team effectiveness, in the smaller firm.

Further support for the learning advantage of smaller firms can be drawn from Nonaka's comments on middle managers:

> Middle managers are working at the intersection of the vertical and horizontal flows of information in the company. They are seen as a bridge between the visionary ideals of the top and the often chaotic market reality of those on the front line of the business.
>
> (Nonaka, 1991: 104)

Nonaka does not address the number of levels of middle management, but in large firms this would predictably be higher, and the visibility of the lead entrepreneur lower. In such circumstances the structural and political barriers to information flow, and therefore to information redundancy, would be typically greater in larger as compared with smaller firms. Many of our firms implicitly recognized this in their determination to stay small – for example, 'seventy people [was] a nice sized business' (CEO, Aerospace Engineering) and 'we don't want to grow beyond 400 employees . . . to preserve the feeling of family and enterprise' (CEO, Fibres). Architectural Services was determined to restrict growth to an upper limit of 100 employees, while Training International's CEO wanted to keep employee numbers under 250 'to retain the family spirit'. Both Fibres and Training International expressed an intention to split their firms into two rather than face growth beyond the numbers indicated.

The above helps us reconnect with the emphasis placed on the lead entrepreneur in Chapter 2. The suggestion here is that the founding or lead entrepreneur has a distinct opportunity, grounded in greater personal visibility and a simpler infrastructure, to promote firm learning. For those who identify with that opportunity, the three themes of strategic positioning identified in Chapter 2 take on broader meaning. The cultivation of niche markets and network relations can promote competitive advantage from internal learning activities, while the creation of employee identification and commitment can promote shared dedication to new learning and the persistence of tacit knowledge, which in turn may reinforce loyalty.

As we saw in Chapter 3, however, the lead entrepreneur can be an obstacle to a small firm's development. We must therefore be careful in generalizing about leadership and learning. Among the examples in this chapter, the most personalized leadership style occurred in Aerospace Engineering and Training International, where the lead entrepreneur was also the principal owner. The greater 'baggage' of external ownership (Fibres) or of older partners and a conservative tradition (Architectural Services) may have influenced the adoption of a more formalized leadership style in other firms. All, however, demonstrated an engagement with learning. This suggests little can be gleaned from the study of leadership, or the relationship between leadership and firm learning, in the absence of other variables. Instead, our evidence suggests that the cultivation of new learning needs to take into account a range of historical and contextual factors playing upon the firm.

The issue of loyalty is equally problematic. As we saw in Chapter 7, much individual learning responds to occupational forces, and is concerned with building a presence in the occupational labour market. Moreover, there is growing evidence that greater learning occurs in industrial sectors characterized by high inter-firm flows of information (Camagni, 1991, Porter, 1990). Movement of people between firms is one way to promote information flows, as well as to elevate the level of learning – and so of human capital, and competitiveness – in the sector as a whole (Saxenian, 1990). In other words, '*organizational* learning' represents too narrow a perspective.

This can be seen in product innovation which often comes about by importing expertise and routines from outside the firm. '*Importing and combining routines*' is a further way, then, of looking at routines. Pressings and MOD Products, for instance, both developed innovations by importing people, technologies, and routines. As the CEO of Pressings put it:

What you've had is a bloke come in from outside both disciplines [shell pressing and roller manufacture], who knew nothing – who had a totally fresh outlook.

Because I made it my business to sell the pressing to every major conveyor and roller manufacturer in the UK, I have physically been to every single one of them, and have seen most of their shopfloors, and manufacturing set-ups, I have talked to most of their technical design people, their applications engineers, and even guys on the shopfloor physically on the machines. If you take that degree of information input on a national basis, from small companies up to great big ones, you've got a lot of information and you sift it. You sift it for what's worthwhile, and then build your own improvements in on what you've seen. Latterly, I'm having the same kind of information input from the USA. I'm now going all over the US, looking at their factories. So you can see how they've developed.

I say then how it [the design concept] should go together; we talk about it; and then Brian [recruited as a presswork expert] makes an input in terms of how it is physically done within the confines of our plant, equipment, and skill levels here.

Given the role in innovation of imported routines, organizational learning needs, then, to be supplemented by inter-organizational (or 'extra-organizational') learning. We will return to this issue in the final chapter.

SUMMARY AND CONCLUSION

In contrast with the preceding chapter, this chapter has focused on learning at the level of the firm. Using the March and Olsen (1975) model as a point of departure, we have explored themes concerned with aggregate individual learning, the role of teams, and the firm as a learning system. Exploring aggregate individual learning illustrated the scope of investments made, as well as suggesting different assumptions about employee readiness to join in shared learning efforts. Inclusive team arrangements were distinguished according to direct customer service, project completion, or quality improvement goals. Further distinctions across inclusive, selective, and business development teams extended our previous interpretation of Miles and Snow's (1978) work. Accordingly, the administrative, engineering and entrepreneurial problems emerged as dimensions along which team learning can occur.

Thinking about the firm as a system then led us to look at the role of routines as the means by which individual and team learning are trans-lated into organizational learning. Interpreting firm adaptation in the light of the management of routines deepens our understanding of what adaptation means for the use of human resources. To this end, we distinguished maintenance, elaboration, redundancy, and changing rou-tines, as well as a further conceptual possibility, importing and combining routines. Among other things, these highlighted varying degrees of pervasiveness in the development of strategic capability – organization-wide, focused on business development teams, and top team entrepreneurship.

This kind of analysis around the under-developed concept of 'routines' is, however, relatively new. There is a need therefore for more fine-grained description and analysis to build on what we have been able to elicit from our own cases.

Finally, we connected ideas about information redundancy and teams to claim a distinct learning opportunity for small–medium firms. In these firms, the greater visibility of the lead entrepreneur affords a link between strategic positioning and new learning, including tacit learning, for the firm as a whole.

This chapter concludes a shift in emphasis in our findings from the firm (Chapters 2–4), toward the person (Chapters 6 and 7), and back again to the firm (Chapter 8). However, all of our findings affect both firms and people. Moreover, both firms and people are dependent for their livelihood on the industrial sectors (and regions) in which they are located. A composite picture of how 'Strategy through People' comes about therefore calls for firms, people, sectors, and locality to be considered simultaneously. That will be the task of our concluding chapter.

NOTE

1   In the UK, tragic events are still popularly prefaced by the label 'Black' without regard for racial undertones.

Chapter 8

Towards a 'new science of organization'

> When it comes to action, we obviously need small units, because action
> is a highly personal affair, and one cannot be in touch with more than
> a very limited number of persons at any one time.
>
> (E.F. Schumacher, 1973: 65)

In the closing weeks of 1991, IBM chairman John Akers announced a
sweeping reorganization to convert his company into 'a federation of
flexible and competing subsidiaries' (*The Economist*, 1991). Each would be
empowered to determine its own agenda, sourcing and staffing requirements, and to cultivate its own alliances both within and outside IBM. This
was Akers' second major reorganization during his five years in office. The
first, which had sought to protect IBM's core bureaucracy but make it more
sensitive to customer needs, was judged not to have gone far enough. What
about the second reorganization? Could this erstwhile 'excellent' company
(Peters and Waterman, 1982) now re-invigorate itself? Had it learned
enough so that 'out of one big blue, many little blues' (*Business Week*, 1991)
could now be made?

The world didn't wait long for an answer. On December 16, 1992, Akers
reported a further 'precipitous' decline, and the company took a $6 billion
charge against asset write-offs and a 25,000 person workforce reduction.
Credit rating agencies downgraded IBM's debt, and critics claimed
'Byzantine bureaucracies' still ruled (*Wall Street Journal*, 1992). An
announced break-out of disc drive and printer units, but not of work-
stations, was judged half-hearted: 'There isn't a single example of cross-
industry success among the major computer makers. And there isn't likely
to be one.' (Stahlman, 1992). On January 26, 1993, Akers resigned, soon to
be replaced by an outsider to both IBM and its industry, but an insider to
corporate restructuring (*Business Week*, 1993a).[1]

At the time of Akers' 1991 announcement, the ink was drying on
Oliver Williamson's latest manuscript. Williamson's (1975, 1985) theory
of 'transaction costs' across organizational boundaries, and within it his
treatment of 'vertical coordination' had in the past been used to bolster

the advantages of the large integrated firm idealized by the old IBM. Now he was saying that past fascination with such firms was misplaced. Specifically, the fascination with 'market power', as projected on to the likes of IBM, had 'played a role in the recent business strategy literature that belies its relative importance' (Williamson, 1991). The great majority of firms operate without control over the marketplace, and face uncertainty as best they can through opportunism and voluntary association. For Williamson, a 'new science of organization' in the 1990s is called for, to challenge old assumptions about size in particular, but also about governance and the organization of labour inside the firm.

THE STORY SO FAR

With Williamson's call in mind, let us recap the main points of our analysis as it has unfolded in Chapters 2 through 7.

Strategic positioning: The strategic positioning of the successful small firm unfolds through the pursuit of niche markets, building network relations, and creating employee identification. Niche markets, frequently stemming from single market leads or customer relationships, can be exploited to accumulate discrete market power and returns to niche specialization. Networking complements niche marketing and leverages a firm's network as a capital resource. Creating employee identification seeks in turn to leverage human resources for strategic ends, either normatively or instrumentally through rewards of various kinds.

Crisis: Most firms occasionally face and must manage their way through watershed events. These span a range of external market causes and internal management causes. Crises of customer dependence and crises of control are prominent, and the evidence points more toward cyclical, rather than life-stage, models of firm development. Upheaval, namely the compound effect of crisis and renewal, involves the breaking of old strategic recipes, the introduction of a new configuration of roles, and a new reference point in 'organizational memory'. A previously neglected, but constructive, side to crisis involves the establishment of new systems and competencies.

Adaptation: Despite purists' arguments to the contrary, adaptation, and in particular its entrepreneurial component, is prominently linked to the existing domain of the firm. Seven recognizable modes of adaptation fall into distinct customer-pull and capacity-push subgroups. The modes of adaptation reflect overlapping strategic, behavioural, and developmental themes about a firm and its actors. Adaptation in turn stimulates concomitant activities of building the firm's human resource base, searching for new market opportunities, and developing broader networks.

Adaptation implicates the importance of internal factors in ongoing strategy formation, prominently among them the capacity to process new information.

Skill supply: Strategic positioning, crisis management and adaptation become reflected, implicitly or explicitly, in skill supply activity which draws to a varying extent on sector and locality. At the same time, smaller firms are exposed to a wide range of influences in their labour markets, and the realization of their business strategies is contingent upon developments in their labour market. The result is distinct patterns of skill supply, involving recruitment, training, and the development of commitment. On occasions (perhaps surprisingly often in our sample) the small firm can influence external supply, as in the case of Cable Co. over occupational qualifications for cable hands. Aggregate strategies of skill supply also have repercussions for the labour market from which individual firms draw. Above all, however, business strategy is constrained by the resource dependencies the firm experiences in respect of its internal and external labour supply. Labour markets, skill supply, and strategic positioning are thus intertwined in the long-term development of the smaller firm.

Individual learning: A focus on individual learning, in place of the narrower focus on training, highlights the 'free agency' of a worker's career – especially among the managers of small firms, who in our sample and in other studies have been shown to be highly mobile. Individual learning is anchored in an occupation, and involves both established and new occupational skills components. Learning new occupational skills relies on participation in entrepreneurial activities that are often not yet reflected in industry training arrangements. More generally, learners draw heavily on relationships and teamwork, and are introduced to 'managerial learning' as new responsibilities are undertaken. Claimed constraints on individual learning, notably limited budgets, may be less significant than a firm's inability to foresee the need for new learning to occur.

Firm learning: Learning at the level of the firm can be viewed from several standpoints. Investments in aggregate individual learning signal a firm's overall readiness for new learning. The make-up of teams – 'communities of practice' – signals how learning can stem from shared experiences focused on customer service goals, project completion goals, or quality improvement goals. In turn, the firm's administrative, engineering and entrepreneurial 'problems' can be re-interpreted as dimensions for shared learning activity. New learning can involve elaboration of a firm's existing routines, or, more fundamentally, building redundancy into the firm's routines. A combined commitment to information redundancy and limited size can bring a learning advantage to smaller firms – if the lead entrepreneur is willing to take advantage of it.

Taken as a whole, Chapters 2–7 show how the strategy of the small–medium firm is dependent on, and is the vehicle for, the development of people. This is an important perspective for strategic management to take on board – hence the title of this book, 'Strategy Through People'. Chapters 5 through 7 also, however, put this relationship between people and firms in a wider context. That is to say, people and firms occupy overlapping worlds made up of competing and cooperating firms interacting with people in labour markets.

Labour market economists are accustomed to describing this interface in terms of the price of labour derived from comparative bargaining power – much as the Porterian approach to strategy emphasizes market power. In contrast, we have interpreted this interface, in keeping with a resource-based, learning perspective, in terms of the conflict individuals and firms face between learning and skill development in and for the firm and learning and skill development for individual occupational advancement. Thus, any single firm faces a strategic dilemma between contributing to learning and retaining ownership of it.

There is a further dimension to this. Firms draw upon a stock of knowledge, which is located in the sector and locality at large, while people depend on the general health of sector and locality for the level of skills they can acquire. The strategic possibilities for the smaller firm need to be seen in the light of patterns of industrial organization, including relationships with larger firms, which have consequences for skills development.

The major part of this final chapter is concerned with this issue, through a review of the evolving modern industrial economy and the place of small firms within it. This will mostly take us beyond the scope of our data and the design of our research, and raise more questions than it gives answers. We shall nevertheless conclude by suggesting some guidelines for practice within a 'new science of organization' (Williamson, 1991) which accommodate the different levels of analysis our study has encompassed.

A WORLD OF FLEXIBLE SMALL FIRMS?

In the early 1970s the long-run decline in small firms in the USA and UK halted, and their number and share of employment have since then steadily climbed. From the early 1980s, also, large firms increasingly decentralized their operations to smaller establishments. Evidence of increasingly severe recessions, in 1974–76 and again in 1979–82, led a

number of writers from different perspectives to connect these developments to the disintegration of 'mass' markets – the 'crisis' of 'Fordism' –
and the need for more flexible means of production (Aglietta, 1979; Piore
and Sabel, 1984). These trends gave rise to a view of a future dominated
by smaller production units.

At the same time, we have seen a reassertion of the importance of the
large international firm, with Dicken (1992), for instance, calling transnational corporations (TNCs) 'the single most important force in the
modern world economy'. In the USA and Japan more than 50 per cent of
total trade (exports and imports) is carried out within TNCs, and possibly
as much as 80 per cent of the UK's manufactured exports are from either
UK-owned or UK-based foreign multinationals (Dicken, 1992: 49). In total,
it is reckoned that one-fifth to one-quarter of world production in the
world's market economies is performed by transnationals, dominated by
a core group of 600 such firms (United Nations Centre on Transnational
Corporations, 1988).

How do we reconcile these competing claims ostensibly between small
and large firms? There are some points of contact – in, for instance, the
view that TNCs need to be increasingly flexible to cope with localized
patterns of consumption. Otherwise, however, their claims seem to point
in diametrically opposite directions.

The answer lies in whether flexibility is seen as a strategy of
'fragmentation' led by large corporations (Aglietta, 1979), or as 'flexible
specialization' which uniquely advantages the smaller firm (Piore and
Sabel, 1984). Aglietta argued that large firms were creating or sponsoring
small *units* as a way of regaining control over the labour process (including
wage costs and the ability of organized labour to restrict management
control). Piore and Sabel, on the other hand, laid more stress on the
inadequacy of mass production techniques themselves, and the need for
a flexible, skilled labour force (rather than a cheap one) to respond to
market conditions. The 'second industrial divide' (Piore and Sabel, 1984)
is thus one where the formerly 'secondary' sector of smaller firms regains
the advantage over the 'primary' sector of large firms which previously
dominated through economies of scale (Pollert, 1988):

> In short, the flexible specialization model elevates the smaller business
> into a central position in the economy while the fragmentation model
> tends to give it a more peripheral role, in a dualistic industrial structure.
> (Stanworth and Gray, 1991: 232)

Understanding these two processes and which one truly reflects
what is going on is obviously critical to the future of the small–medium
firm.

Flexible specialization

As Stanworth and Gray (1991) comment, the bulk of the evidence for the flexible specialization model derives from the industrial districts of Emilia–Romagna in Italy (Brusco and Sabel, 1981; Goodman *et al.*, 1989), and even this evidence has come into question (Amin, 1989). They also suggest there is little evidence of flexible specialization in the UK.

One reason for this may be a confusion between flexible specialization *per se* and the idea of the 'industrial district' which has been linked to it. Sustaining the position of the small firm under flexible specialization is thus supposedly a system of interconnected small firms drawing upon certain common facilities (such as information technology) and a pool of skilled workers immersed in craft traditions. The absence of such conditions, however, does not necessarily invalidate flexible specialization as a technology-led process, although the industrial district may be valuable in sustaining it.

More pertinent to flexible specialization as a technology-led process supposedly favouring small firms is the cost of the new flexible technology of advanced CNC (computer numerically controlled) machines (Pollert, 1988; Morris and Imrie, 1992). Larger companies are obviously better placed to make such investments (although with the aid of grants and loans small firms like Aerospace Engineering can do so, and in certain areas, like PCs for manufacturing control, the cost of new technology has fallen rapidly). New computer-based technologies enable production to be carried out in smaller units, but these may still belong to large firms.

In a detailed statistical survey of manufacturing in the USA (with special emphasis on metal working), however, Carlsson (1989) has shown that not only did average plant size become smaller between 1972–82 (a finding compatible with the continuing dominance of large firms), but also that the number of establishments and firms increased. Thus, the number of companies increased in 81 out of 106 industries. A similar decline in plant size accompanied by increases in the number of establishments occurred in many other countries, including the UK and Japan. Such data support a flexible specialization thesis of small firms.

Firm size on its own, however, is an inadequate indicator of flexible specialization. More pertinent is batch size. This reflects the ability of a firm (its flexibility) to respond to lower volume, more specialized, non-mass markets. Unfortunately, we are not aware of any systematic data on trends in batch size, uncontaminated by the peaks and troughs of the business cycle (or equally of systematic evidence on the break-down of mass markets).

Moreover, as Carlsson acknowledges, the decline in unit size is compatible with a parallel process of large firms hiving off non-core activities (that is, with the fragmentation thesis). It is highly possible, then, that flexible specialization and fragmentation are complementary processes occurring simultaneously.

The case for a technology-based flexible specialization is thus unproven. Even if it were proven, however, a specialized and flexible technology does not in itself guarantee primacy and security for the smaller firm. It may just as likely be a servant of large firms. We have to look beyond flexible specialization as a technology-led process to the economic and social organization in which small firms are embedded. In this respect, theorists are right to link flexible specialization to the idea of the industrial district, with its supportive relationships among networks of small firms and quasi-public infrastructure servicing and regulating these.

Fragmentation and the Japanese system

The key process under 'fragmentation' is sub contracting. In sub-contracting, smaller production units, which may be nominally independent firms or establishments of large corporations, are dominated by the larger firm. This process is thus entirely compatible with the dominance of transnationals. Indeed, in the 'new international division of labour' whereby manufacturing is sub contracted to low wage locations in the Third World – as in the case of the American semi-conductor industry (Florida and Kenney, 1991) – TNCs play a leading role.

Sub contracting is a well-established pattern of industrial organization, although there is some evidence that it is less developed in the UK than in other parts of Western Europe (Lorenz, 1989) and compared with Japan (Trevor and Christie, 1988). Earlier, we cited evidence that 50 per cent of small firms in the Cambridge SBRC (1992) survey carried out sub contract work, and that among these firms sub contracting accounted for 43 per cent of their turnover.

In recent years, however, interest has turned from the extent of sub-contracting to the nature of the power relationship and what passes between customer and supplier. There are very different implications for small firm viability and the development of skills from (a) large firms dual-sourcing from a host of small firm suppliers with price a prime consideration (the traditional model); (b) large firms externalizing labour-intensive, non-core activities to reduce fixed costs and improve administrative efficiency (the 'fragmentation' model); and (c) large firms seeking a close relationship with a limited number of preferred suppliers in the interests of enhanced reliability, continuous quality and product improvements, and shorter developmental lead times (the Japanese system).

The last of these clearly departs some way from the 'fragmentation' system as conceived by Aglietta (1979). Although it appears to leave the large company firmly in the driving seat, it is unlike the US and UK systems dominated by large corporations ('Big Business') in the extent to which community and collective institutions mitigate naked price competition (Best, 1990). Equally, it is a far cry from a network of small firm *primary* producers, implied in the flexible specialization model, even though there is a stimulus to specialization in the smaller firm. We may think of the Japanese system of sub contracting, then, as a distinctive 'third way'.

The question then is how far, if at all, has the Japanese system of 'obligational' or 'relational' contracting (Dore, 1983) displaced the 'adversarial' or 'arms-length' approach that has hitherto characterized UK and US large firm-small firm relationships? In the UK, the Japanese system appears to be largely confined to two sectors (motor vehicles and electronics) where there has been a direct influence from Japanese transplants (Morris and Imrie, 1992). In these sectors, there have been real changes in buyer-supplier relationships involving new methods of collaboration, increased personnel, technical and management assistance, increased information exchange, and more rigorous vetting procedures in the interests of quality. On the other hand, there is uneven development of such practices. In a study of ninety three units in one locality, Rainnie (1991) found little change from the customary adversarial relationship emphasizing price, and even Morris and Imrie (1992: 170) in their study of leading-edge companies concluded that:

> while it is argued that the new relationships indicate a new era of cooperation between businesses, it is clear from our research that the evolving systems of supplying are more to do with enhancing corporate control and competitiveness, perhaps heralding a new phase of corporate reorganization and growth. In this sense, they are part of the evolving global, corporate economy.

A prime instance of this is the expectation that the Single European Market will produce, first, a process of rationalization among large firms, followed by these new larger firms rationalizing their supply networks containing myriad small–medium firms. We have already begun to see the first stage of this, before recession and high interest rates curtailed the process of acquisition and merger (Peat Marwick McLintock, 1991).

What tendencies are evident in our firms?

For present purposes, evidence of flexible specialization and subcontracting among our own sample of firms is of less consequence than what is happening in the wider environment from which they draw their skills. Nevertheless, we can make some observations on how far the processes identified above were discernible among our firms.

Evidence for flexible specialization

The evidence of our firms securing themselves in niche markets would suggest the flexible specialization thesis has some merit. Most of those that were able to had specialized in some way. A few – Aerospace Engineering, MOD Products, and Optics – competed on their ability to deal with small production runs and responded to requests for customized products. This, however, may reflect nothing more than a traditional role for small firms, within a defence and aerospace industry characterized by elaborate tiers of primary, secondary and tertiary contractors.

As to relationships between small firms, there were a number, as we noted in Chapter 2, who worked through an elaborate network of suppliers for whom they were themselves customers (Construction Co. and House Co.), or whom they organized within the local economy (Visitor Bureau, and Convention Bureau). These also had a distinctive local or regional flavour. On the other hand, it was notable how far all the manufacturing firms were oriented to suppliers and customers outside their locality. Aerospace Engineering, for instance, had only one of its twelve customers within a 25-mile radius. In the case of the three opto-electronics firms who were selected for their proximity in a potential industrial district, this was even more marked. None of their customers were in the immediate locality and all exported, while much of their supplies came from abroad. Glass Discs purchased from its parent company in Germany and Finland, as well as locally in the UK; Fibres dual-sourced from the UK and abroad; and Optics purchased glass 'blanks' locally, but also from Germany and Japan.

Industrial districts were equally underdeveloped in terms of infra-structure relationships. While the Visitor Bureau and Convention Bureau, as quasi-public organizations themselves, perforce worked with the public (as well as private) sector, relationships for all other organizations were almost exclusively oriented to sector rather than locality. The only exception was in the use of the local further education system by staff working for higher qualifications, usually sponsored by the companies. For advice on training, the three biggest users of the system – the opto-electronics firms – relied on the sectoral training organization (although admittedly the new system of locally-based Training and Enterprise Councils had not yet bedded down).

Evidence for fragmentation

The fragmentation thesis is supported by the example of the two 'spin-offs' – Fibres, as a joint venture, and Glass Discs as a subsidiary – which were established as independent ventures (on greenfield sites) to get away from the relatively bureaucratic cultures and adversarial labour relations of their parent companies. The privatization of Skills Training could also be interpreted in this way, as could the setting up of the Visitor Bureau and Convention Bureau on an arms-length basis from local government.

Evidence for Japanese-style sub-contracting

On sub-contracting and customer relations more broadly, there was a diversity of experience. Some – like Aerospace Engineering and MOD Products – had sought preferred supplier status, secured through audited quality standards; engaged in technical cooperation over product design; but still found their major customer primarily interested in driving down price. Aerospace Engineering, in particular, complained about the way its main customer treated its suppliers, and was interested in getting suppliers to set up an association to defend their interests.

Bread Products, likewise, felt it was being driven by unreasonable and arbitrary demands by its principal supermarket customer. Others, like Fibres and Pressings, while involved in technical collaboration with their immediate customers, had gone beyond these to engage, on their own initiative, with final users – in the case of Pressings, meeting with some disapproval.

Accommodating diversity

These brief observations indicate a diversity of economic relationships and tendencies. It is possible also that this diversity goes further even than the three models we have outlined. For example, on the face of it, flexible specialization and Japanese-style sub-contracting provide a poor reflection of the way service firms fit into the economy. As Stanworth and Gray (1991: 234) observe, nine out of ten firms who employ between 1 and 24 people are in the services and construction sectors. Flexible specialization and sub contracting models, in contrast, are heavily oriented to manufacturing (as for example in Carlsson's (1989) data).

Many services, however – specifically producer services – can be accommodated within the manufacturing model. Thus, Training International, Skills Training, and Software Products performed specialized services for other firms, while Clean Air Co., Cable Co., and Architectural Services provided services broadly related to the construction industry.

This still leaves, however, a multitude of consumer services, represented in our study by Legal Services and the two hotels, and at large by retailing, education, health, sports and leisure, personal finance, catering, and many other major sectors. In a number of these, such as retailing and catering, small firms or establishments are major suppliers.

In the short-run development of these consumer services, the driving force is organizational as much as technological, even though technology can transform the delivery of a service (as in fast food) and in the long-run may displace it (as in the invention of household gadgets displacing bought-in services). The growth of franchising, for instance, is as much an organizational innovation as it is technology-driven. As a form of control by one organization over others through a standard business format, franchising has elements, therefore, of sub contracting that conform to Aglietta's (1979) model. Small units are sponsored by larger wealthy or more innovative organizations, so that they carry fewer financial risks, lower management costs, and less exposure to organized labour.

From this point of view, the three models outlined above may be sufficient after all to describe the variety of organizational forms and relationships in the new economic order.

It is important to keep these three alternative models in mind in thinking about labour markets and firms' access to, development of, and retention of skills because of the very different implications they carry. This is particularly necessary in order not to be seduced by the idea of flexible specialization and its accompanying image of industrial districts. We say this in the knowledge that our own discussion of small firms tends in this direction. As Carney (1991: 471) observes, there has been an over-emphasis on this model:

> Flexible specialization is ultimately a model in the economic theory tradition of the firm as a production function and as such is ill equipped to analyse elements of business enterprise that are essentially organizational.

That is, the flexible specialization thesis ignores a large part of economic structure and alternative tendencies in the modern economy.

In the next section, we will develop the specific implications for people and skills of flexible specialization-with-industrial districts and relational sub contracting, and reflect on how our representation of firms' strategizing fits with these.

BEYOND THE FIRM

Our discussion of small–medium firms throughout this book has been largely posited upon smaller firms as independent entities, making their own strategy in niche markets. Such a perspective implicitly assumes an economy of flexible specialization. We then looked on the mobility of their human resource as an issue in their ability to sustain a unique competence through opportunities to import organizational learning, on the one hand, and being able to hold on to tacit skills, on the other.

In pointing, however, to trends in labour flexibility, including (and perhaps especially) the mobility of managerial and technical strata, we identified a conflict. Mobility of labour in the interests of entrepreneurship and economic dynamism promotes the dissolution of skills and embedded tacit knowledge. The paradox is that firms may promote flexible labour market strategies which undermine their own capacity to retain and develop skills. In turn, this threatens the strategic management paradigm in which the firm is the dominant actor, marshalling resources. In practical terms, this means looking at ways of mitigating the effects of an economy of atomistic firms and atomistic individuals (or, as one might say, perfect markets). Meanwhile, for the purpose of theorizing about the firm, it means incorporating the sectoral and regional dimensions of labour markets which lie beyond the individual firm.

Industrial districts and labour markets

These concerns lead to the argument for industrial districts as a factor which can mitigate against firms' vulnerability to market competition for their human resources. The fascination with industrial districts is a recognition of the benefits which flow from a concentration of related activities in close proximity. This recognition is partly based on what has gone (a nostalgia even), partly on new sunrise industries, and partly on discovering the persistence of the form in traditional industries. In the process, the work of Marshall (1911), Beccatini (1978), Brusco (1982), Piore and Sabel (1984), and Goodman et al., (1989) have contributed a language of description and analysis.

A notable feature of the early 1980s was the decline and break-up of large industrial sites. In the UK, sites like IMI at Whitton, GEC at Trafford Park, and Pilkington throughout St Helens are now shells of their former selves. In their day, these agglomerations of common and related activities provided an internal labour market of skills, along with a company loyalty and culture. At the same time, whole districts, such as spinning and weaving on the Pennines between Lancashire and Yorkshire, have been denuded through mass closures and redundancies. Here, the labour market operated more externally, with more inter-company movement and 'spot' recruitment. But the basic principles of a sector rooted in a local community were common to both, with the community playing an important role in maintaining and mobilizing supplies of labour (with skills handed down 'from father to son', and whole families recruiting one another to the same workplace). As they declined, however, these benefits were submerged in the perception of rigid skill definitions and labour attitudes, and constraints on mobility, which contributed to their demise.

Meanwhile, new patterns of industrial concentration arose, notably in Silicon Valley (Saxenian, 1990) and Boston's Route 128 (Dorfman, 1983). Their particular contribution was a model of innovation through business start-ups spun-off from the R&D labs of larger corporations (Silicon Valley) or university research centres (Route 128) via departing scientific and technical staff. The elements of this model were (a) a mobile scientific labour force, (b) closely networked with one another, (c) motivated by a team-based, creative work environment and the opportunity for substantial shared rewards, and (d) the development of a venture capital industry prepared to risk large sums on entrepreneurs with an idea (Florida and Kenney, 1991). It was thus essentially a social model of innovation, combining people and investment facilities in 'social structures of innovation' (Florida and Kenney, 1988). The success of this model in incubating high tech-based growth industries has spawned world-wide attempts at replication through science parks.

The third case was the discovery of the industrial districts of Europe, in the 'Third Italy' and Germany, in traditional industries like textiles, footwear, and machine tools. This led to a reassessment of the competitive prospects for small firms in traditional sectors and identified the role of public and quasi-public institutions in fostering local development. Subsequently, Porter (1990) has documented similar complexes around the world, and many other examples of previously unregarded industrial districts have been described (see, for example, Storper and Scott, 1990). The concentration of related production activity in these examples ensures a pool of specialized skilled labour. What the industrial district does, which the company often fails to do, is to manage it flexibly:

> the recourse to increased flexibility in the modern economy has been marked by a decisive reagglomeration of production and resurgence of the specialized industrial district.
>
> In such environments the local labour market becomes an important analytical category. It is mainly in dense local labour markets that external flexibility of labour tends to rise, and in such situations the contradictory role of the local community as a source of flexibility and as a shackle on it is thrown into strong relief.
>
> (Storper and Scott, 1990: 581)

In other words, the local labour market allows sectoral skills to circulate, while the force of attraction of community keeps these available for local firms – especially for small firms which have greater difficulty recruiting outside their locality:

> The net result, *ceteris paribus*, will be greater flexibility in job-holding and tenure patterns in larger, as opposed to smaller, local labour markets.
>
> (Storper and Scott, 1990: 582)

Finally, it brings benefits for people:

> the speed of rotation of workers through the local job system is likely to correlate positively with the size of the local labour market, and periods

of unemployment in larger centres are likely to be relatively frequent but relatively short. This proposition would seem to apply particularly to those categories of upper-tier workers whose skills are more sector- and agglomeration-specific than firm-specific.

(Storper and Scott, 1990: 582)

The result is benefits in terms of job security and/or employment security (for the individual), and labour market security (a pool of workers for the firm to draw on). These comments, however, need qualifying in two principal ways, in relation to the type of sector and types of skill.

Which sectors, which skills?

First, labour markets work differently in different types of industrial district, and secondly, they work differently for different groups of workers.

Scott and Storper (1990), for example, identify three types of industrial district – involving craft industries (this would include the traditional sectors in Europe referred to above), high technology manufacturing (such as Silicon Valley), and business and commercial services (to be found in all big cities – Wall Street and the City of London would be examples). At the same time, each is segmented into a number of different skill groups, from relatively unskilled clerical and assembly workers to highly qualified technical and professional grades. Job security, employment security, and labour market security vary for different skills and types of district. Thus, Florida and Kenney (1991) argue that the high technology industrial district, far from being a source of stability, exhibits hyper-entrepreneurialism as key scientific and technical staff hop between firms and constantly start-up new ones.

Industrial districts as linked firms performing complementary activities

It is necessary, therefore, to have regard, not just to the fact that a number of firms may be concentrated in one place, but to consider also the basis on which they compete and the relations between them. In effect, we have to recognize two models of the industrial district – or alternatively, apply the term in a narrower sense (as most theorists have tended to do) to describe linked firms carrying out complementary activities. Thus:

Sectors in which firms specialize by activity will have a different dynamic from sectors composed of identical firms engaging in the same activities.

(Best, 1990: 132)

Districts comprising many similar producers will compete with one another largely on the basis of price and develop a similar set of skills that are mobile within a labour market operating on the same principle of bidding down price. This reflects the neo-classical model of competition, and the way many traditional indigenous sectors have competed.

In contrast, networks of firms may develop on the basis of specialization in complementary (externalized) activities, with each firm in the production chain developing a distinctive capability through increased firm-specific experience. The basis of competition is the ability of a firm to develop a distinctive capability through learning, and the returns to the firm derive from its capacity to engage in continuous improvement in products and processes (in other words, by achieving both efficiency and innovation). In the same way, key employees are valued for their in-firm experience or 'learned' competence (in effect, firms compete for them by bidding up their price). This reflects the view of competition and the firm set out by Penrose (1959) and Richardson (1972), and increasingly the nature of competition in the modern world (Best, 1990).

The critical factor is how exposed a market is to outside competition:

> A sector in which firms are coordinated by the market alone can persist even though firms have not specialized by activity as long as the sector is insulated from competition. But market-coordinated districts will come under competitive pressure from collaboratively coordinated districts once the barriers to trade are relaxed. It follows that a specific industrial district can be outcompeted in the international marketplace, even though individual firms within it have organized themselves according to minimum transaction costs.
>
> (Best, 1990: 132)

If competition resides, then, in the capacity for learning through specialization, the sector-region becomes the unit of competitiveness and of analysis. The similarity/complementarity distinction therefore leads to a reconceptualization of the boundaries of the firm and of the notion of a sector (Best, 1990: 131). This requires, in turn, institutions to moderate the tendency of independent firms and people to behave as if they are each 'atomistic' actors.

Alternatives to industrial districts

The theory of industrial districts in its full form, as developed above, involves firms cooperating in some sense. As Best (1990: 17) observes:

> We are left with images of a sector as more than a collection of autonomous firms, and of inter-firm relations as involving more than price competition. . . . From this viewpoint, firms not only compete, but

they can also cooperate to provide common services, to shape the 'rules of the market game', and to shape complementary investment strategies.

There is, however, an alternative model of linkage, cooperation, and mutual regulation – the Japanese system of subcontract relations. Best's book is an extended debate on the merits of each which recognizes their fundamental similarities. At the heart of this is a view of competition involving constellations of firms. In the case of Japan, government early on recognized that the development of the firm involves the development of the sector as a whole. As Best (1990: 241) notes, back in 1963 Japan's Small and Medium Enterprise Modernization Promotion Law observed that:

> The modernization of small and medium enterprises implies a concept of a very comprehensive nature. It . . . extends to the modernization of a small and medium enterprise as an entire system, which includes modernization of relationships between individual enterprises as well as different industries.
>
> (Small and Medium Enterprise Agency, 1986: 8)

The difference between the Japanese sub contracting system and industrial districts is that in the former it is large corporations which promote modernization, stimulate specialization, and organize cooperation in the sub-contract system – not least through spin-offs (Gerlach, in press). Thus, 50 per cent of Japanese large firm capital is commonly invested in smaller firms that have been spun-off.

In principle, preferred supplier relationships offer greater security, scope for the small firm to sustain higher levels of pay, and discourage labour mobility. Close relationships on product design and improving process efficiencies and quality stimulate company specialization and enhance employee skills. This may extend to direct customer pressure on, and support for, training. Before its abolition, the UK's National Economic Development Office (NEDO) saw the possibilities in this and was trying to encourage training down the 'supply-chain' (NEDO, 1990).

Stability and development through sub contract relationships is thus sectorally based, although large firm lead manufacturers (*kaisha*) may seek to organize smaller firms in proximity to themselves wherever they operate.

'STRATEGY THROUGH PEOPLE': THREE CORNERSTONES FOR POLICY AND ACTION

This chapter has sought to locate our findings on small–medium firms within the theoretical debate on the 'new economic order' and the 'new competition'. In doing so, we have confirmed the need for analysing small firm strategy at a number of connected levels. In conclusion, we will draw together the key elements of our 'strategy through people' perspective covering the three levels of analysis, and suggest some guidelines for practice and action. These three levels can be expressed in the following terms as: the multifunctional nature of jobs; the catalysis of teams; and the interpenetration of sectors and labour markets. In addition, routines and the firm as an employment system act as a bridge across these levels, and provide the 'glue' as it were to the idea of the firm as a functioning entity. Taken together, these provide a set of analytical categories to support a learning theory of the firm.

The multifunctional nature of jobs

The 'tragedy of the commons' analogy – whereby the threat of one farmer's overgrazing leads to pre-emptive grazing by others – has recently been used to urge shared understanding on to competing firms (Best, 1990: 239). However, we would extend the analogy to the relationship between employer and employee, where there is often a temptation to take out ('graze') rather than to recognize mutual benefits from a shared investment in job experience.

For the firm, multiple functions sought from a job begin with the most basic, as a source of production, and extend through expectations about team performance and flexibility. In other cases, the firm is concerned that a job supplies up-to-date skills and knowledge, or is a resource for quality improvement. The job may also be viewed as a base for gathering new information, or more broadly as a 'brain cell' behind the intelligence of the firm.

For the person, a contrasting set of job functions begins with a means to a livelihood and a basis for direct learning. The job also serves as a platform for interpersonal learning and formal learning, and affords a place in the broader labour market. A presence in the labour market in turn provides a lever for career development and use of the job as a source of personal reputation. The job also provides direct or indirect access to external networks, and serves as a medium for individual enterprise, through enactment of an 'entrepreneurial career'.

Figure 8.1 illustrates the interconnected functions of the job, for both the firm and the individual jobholder. Our listing of the first item on each side – 'a source of production' for the firm, and 'a means to a livelihood' for the person – is intentional. These functions capture the traditional assumptions about jobs underlying Taylorism or 'Fordism', upon which much modern management theory has been built. However, the representation of multiple other functions of the job, in contributing to the firm's strategy on the one hand, and the person's unfolding career on the other hand, illustrates the incompleteness of those once dominant, and still influential, views about the running of the firm.

Functions for the **firm**

Functions for the **person**

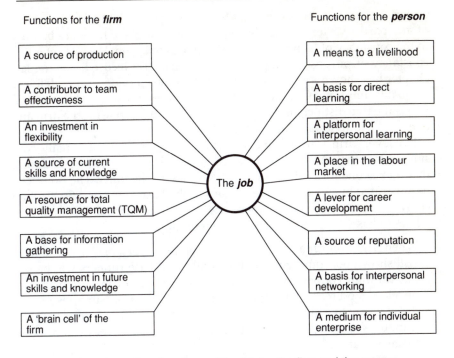

Functions for the firm		Functions for the person

A source of production

A means to a livelihood

A contributor to team effectiveness

A basis for direct learning

An investment in flexibility

A platform for interpersonal learning

A source of current skills and knowledge

A place in the labour market

The *job*

A resource for total quality management (TQM)

A lever for career development

A base for information gathering

A source of reputation

An investment in future skills and knowledge

A basis for interpersonal networking

A 'brain cell' of the firm

A medium for individual enterprise

Figure 8.1 Interdependent functions of the job for the firm and the person

Since our research took place at a time when a shared discomfort with static assumptions was giving way to debate about how more dynamic employment arrangements could be achieved, the elemental unit of employment – the job – assumes new significance, and provides a focus in which the implications for firms and people can be simultaneously considered. Recognition of the diverse functions jobs fulfil lends depth to the picture of an organization, and so to the possibilities for new job arrangements.

The dual sets of functions served by the job lead on to their implications for learning. As Chapter 7 has illustrated, firm learning draws on but is not a simple aggregate of individual learning, while opportunities for individual learning benefit from the activities of the firm. The force which binds individual learning into the firm is the routines which become established either intentionally or otherwise in the firm. Routines, in their various forms, in turn are developed and transmitted largely through team-based activity.

The catalysis of teams

We refer here to the catalysis of teams in a particular way. Catalysis involves a substance that without changing itself promotes change in other bodies. We are not suggesting that the make-up, capability or functioning of any particular team remains constant. Instead, we refer more broadly to the constancy of teams within the activities of a firm. We also refer to a constancy of purpose during any team's existence, focused – as the last chapter has shown – on one or more of customer service, project delivery or quality improvement outcomes. A continuing presence of teams promotes the two distinct kinds of learning noted above, one for the firm and one for the individual team member.

However, firm learning and individual learning are not usually considered together. And when they are, it is most often from a standpoint that makes one form of learning subordinate to the other. The point can be illustrated by two recent uses of the 'baseball team' analogy. First, Ohno (1984), in writing about Japanese 'right on time' production methods, relates to baseball as 'the essence of cooperation':

> When 'right on time' has been implemented, every player in the field will show good timing in catching balls, and base runners will be put out through cooperative teamwork. Each section can systematically develop good team play. Again to use baseball terms, supervisors and directors are like hitting, fielding, and running coaches. A good baseball team uses system plays, perfecting their teamwork so they can respond to any situation.

The above is in contrast to Sonnenfeld's (1989: 215) use of the same point of comparison. For him, baseball teams exemplify a form of career system that 'rel(ies) upon skilled, individual performers with transferable talents that can be taken by other teams':

> baseball teams [exist] where innovation is at a premium, the lack of employment security heightens the pressure for creativity. The pool of risk takers is not limited to the internal labour market but can also involve midcareer hires of expert or celebrity status. The spirit in the baseball team is upbeat where employees see themselves as minor celebrities hoping for a shot to be a true star.

The contrast between these two disparate uses of the same sports team analogy can be addressed as follows. Ohno is concerned with the industrial sector, and the success of the firm within it, while Sonnenfeld is concerned with the labour market, and the success of individuals. Ohno looks at jobs for how they benefit the firm, Sonnenfeld for how they benefit individuals.[2] Bringing both pictures together supports claims about the interdependence of sectors and labour markets, and about the multifunctional nature of jobs.

There remains, however, a clear contrast in the two authors' views of the team, namely as a vehicle for collective learning, and as a vehicle for individual learning, respectively. Equally successful teams can be based in teamwork or on individual stars. At the level of the sector, both views of the team are important. The firm can learn better to compete with other firms, the individual can learn better to compete with other individuals. The composite result can be a healthier, more competitive industry sector as a whole. To extend the baseball team analogy, standards of play in the league can be raised, and the league as a whole can offer greater value to the public, its prospective customers.

Differences in the approach to teamwork, in the extent to which it is 'inclusive' or 'exclusive' (to use the language of Chapter 7), may be fundamental, however, to economic success. Thus, Florida and Kenney (1991) have argued that Japanese firms perform better at diffusion and the task of turning innovations into a continuous stream of mass-produced products, and hence capitalizing on inventions, because they are function-ally integrated systems of production *and* R&D, and teamwork runs through the whole. That is, they pursue inclusive teamwork. In this respect, service firms, which provide the best examples of 'inclusive teams' in our study, may be the model for the future.

Moreover, although teams provide 'communities of practice' joined in the pursuit of customer service, project completion, or quality improve-ment objectives, not all team members are directly in contact with the customers they serve. As a result, the quality of learning may be critically dependent on certain people, who act as 'boundary spanners' between the team and its wider environment. Few of Aerospace Engineering's techni-cians met directly with Rolls-Royce representatives; few construction workers met directly with the developer or main contractor for whom they worked; the young architects at Architectural Services had limited direct exposure to the kinds of clients they sought to win.

In these and many other situations, the quality of the team's (or 'community's') practice is dependent on its links through networking activity. These links are illustrated in Figure 8.2. From this point of view, 'communities of practice' may transcend individual firms (Hendry *et al.*, 1994). A second implication is that groups who need to learn but whose members lack direct personal contact with external stimuli rely on 'learn-ing routines' to absorb new lessons and to transfer learning.

The interpenetration of sectors and labour markets

Strategy unfolds within the industry sector in which a firm operates. For small–medium firms, strategy – and the networks associated with it – may also have a regional flavour (although this was far from being generally the case among our firms). At the same time, as Porter (1990) emphasizes, labour market factors – comprising human resources, know-ledge resources, and the training and education infrastructure – are an important part of the overall factor endowment underlying industrial

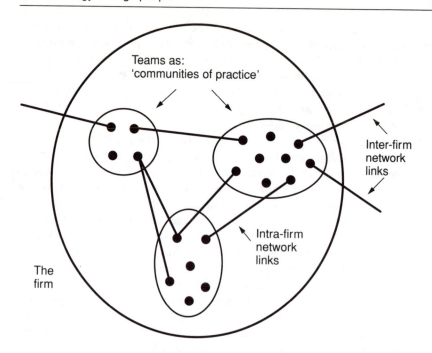

Figure 8.2 Teams, networks, and the firm

competitiveness. This has a regional and national dimension, and firms participate in a variety of labour markets (although occasionally even small firms also engage in an international one, as in the market for hotel chefs).

Networking, either to serve the strategic interests of firms, or to serve people's careers, is the thread that holds industrial sectors and labour markets together. Moreover, both purposes are often served simultaneously. The point is obvious for owner-managers or lead entrepreneurs whose personal success is tightly linked to the success of the firm, although other instances of dual-purpose networking also occur where managers keep their contacts and options open through links with competitors and affiliated firms, and where, as in the construction industry, employees are constantly on the look-out for the next job.

Our findings therefore modify and extend the recent literature on industrial regions. We did not find pure examples, such as those portrayed for Modena, Italy (Brusco, 1986), or Silicon Valley, California (Saxenian, 1990), where regions embraced both firm strategic and individual career activities. Instead, we found industrial sectors and labour markets to overlap in a shared geographical space, consistent with Ratti's (1991) idea of the 'supporting space' that defines a firm and the synergies it enjoys.

To start from a concern for the interpenetration of industrial sectors and

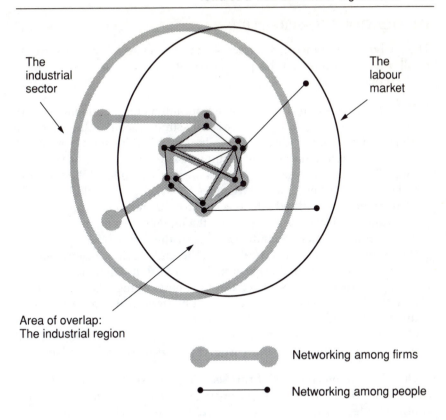

The
industrial
sector

The
labour
market

Area of overlap:
The industrial region

Networking among firms

Networking among people

Figure 8.3 Interpenetration between the industrial sector and the labour market

labour markets, as shown in Figure 8.3, allows for analysis of a broader range of situations, while retaining the opportunity for industrial regions to be brought into focus. Meanwhile, the firm as an employment system in the eye of these forces struggles to retain control of people's skills and their commitment.

In summary, then, the multifunctional nature of jobs promotes both firm and individual learning (through teams), while being directed by the strategic interests of the firm and the career interests of the person. In turn, these trace back to distinct sectoral and labour market contexts. The greater the overlap of these contexts, the greater the apparent opportunity for synergy in learning efforts. In other words, one might predict that a high degree of interdependence between individual, firm, sectoral and local contexts would stimulate innovation and development in the firm alongside personal development and fulfilment in the individual; while low interdependence would produce stasis, dislocation, and all sorts of other negative effects.

IMPLICATIONS FOR PRACTICE

The analytical framework we have set out serves to identify a series of implications for action. At this point, we will simply list some of the more obvious ones.

1 The basis of modern competition is continuous improvement in products and processes (in other words, the simultaneous achievement of both efficiency and innovation). Flexible specialization within industrial districts and relational sub contracting are alternative ways of achieving this. What assuredly does not do so is the Fordist model of Big Business, as Best (1990) terms it, which assumes a market of semi-skilled people who can be readily fitted into jobs, and for that reason are presumed to be economically mobile without attachments to community. As a description of American industrial life at the turn of the last century, this is probably not inaccurate. For the end of the present century, however, for America, Europe, and the Far East, it will no longer do.

2 Entrepreneurship takes effect through networking efforts. It is the quality of networking, however, which matters, at whom or what it is directed. Smaller firms would seem to have a choice between pursuing close sub-contract relations with larger firms, or networked relations with smaller firms, as the route to strength, security, and excellence.

Our observations on small firms securing themselves initially through dependence on a limited number of customers are indicative of the subcontract route – an association confirmed in Rainnie's (1991) study of subcontractors where he found a limited customer base, usually of two to four customers, was a common factor. On the other hand, our observations on small firms securing themselves in niche markets and generally aspiring to independent strategic action point in the other direction, towards networked relationships. What is far from clear, however, is that small firms see localized networked relations as a *necessary* basis for independence, and work at creating them.

The approach to networking among smaller UK firms is generally sectorally focused, half-hearted and defensive – focused, for example, on efforts to regulate pay or, less often, to sustain training structures. Examples include Cable Co.'s role in organizing a trade association of cable-laying firms to establish a grade and wages structure; and, among larger firms, the lobbying in the construction industry for the retention of an industrial training board when all others had been abolished. Significantly, this was because large firms saw themselves vulnerable to labour poaching and the free-loading that is rampant in the sector.

The best example of active networking is perhaps a mixed pattern, where sub contract relationships are established on a regional basis (again in construction) to create an extended internal labour market for the larger firm with relative stability for a small group of favoured suppliers. This suggests a localized network structure may need larger firms to focus it.

In turn, this suggests that 'cooperative' relationships in local product and labour markets will vary between extremes of dependence and independence, permanance and impermanance (Pyke, 1988) – much as strategic alliances do (Lorange, 1986) – according to whether vertical (customer-led relationships) or horizontal relationships predominate.

3 Because they equate the firm with themselves, owner-managers of small firms tend to have a limited perception of the relationships in which they are engaged. Figure 5.1 (p. 110) anticipated this theme of inter-connection which has dominated Chapters 5–8. Such relationships pull the firm in different directions, but also represent a potential which is insufficiently exploited. Consequently, small firms tend to rely excess-ively on the 'primary' networks of the founding or lead entrepreneur, and neglect the 'secondary' networks of knowledge and skills which other employees have to offer. Consequently, the tendency after start-up is to fasten down on customers and skills and lose the innovative potential which these secondary networks can supply.

4 The sequence of development in the small firm, from customer de-pendence to a more broad-based independence, suggests cooperative strategies may become more salient, not less salient, as a firm grows. Equally, as a sector moves from relative insularity (where firms trade primarily on price) to become more exposed to world-wide competition, it too may need to change its character, with firms becoming more cooperative. Strategic alliances among transnationals would seem to bear this out. The policy implications of this for sectors characterized by mainly small–medium firms, however, have been slow to take root. This seems especially relevant to new high tech sectors where innovation may initially be highly localized.

5 The absence in our study of examples of inter-firm cooperation and institutions of governance to protect and promote cooperation may not be an accident. They may simply not exist in a well-developed form in the UK, in the way they do, for example, in Germany and in federal states like Baden-Wurttemberg in particular. The lack of infrastructure on UK science parks, other than landscaping, is a sign of this in-difference. Small firms on science parks, nevertheless, have scope for joint action in areas like management development where their prob-lems, by virtue of being start-ups going through parallel life cycles, are very similar. In the UK, a number of firms on Aston Science Park, Birmingham, have joined forces to meet their needs for training and development. This would appear to be a unique venture, however.

6 As firms increasingly fragment through decentralization, networks for management and organizational development become an important

option for many medium-sized firms and establishments. Wherever internal labour markets are not large enough to sustain management development in-house, firms need to look at options for cooperation outside. This may range from simple visits to friendly firms to see best practice elsewhere – to 'action learning' exchanges and short secondments.

7 National labour markets behave in different ways according to well-entrenched norms. In the UK and USA, managerial labour markets are relatively fluid and inter-firm mobility is the path to career progression (Crockett and Elias, 1984). This fits with the observation of high levels of top management mobility in our study and the findings from David Storey's research cited in Chapter 6.

Suprisingly, this is not matched by levels of voluntary turnover among other grades of staff. With the exception of Bread Products and the two hotels where turnover was acute, and small pockets in, for example, Architectural Services, voluntary labour turnover was almost everywhere in the range 2–3 per cent per annum. This goes against the conventional assumption that labour instability is high in smaller firms and a problem (Curran and Stanworth, 1979b). Most managers in our study confirmed that this was not the case. For one reason, voluntary turnover in an era of high unemployment is likely to be generally lower; for another, when large firms have been shedding labour rapidly, small firms have become comparatively secure places of employment (as the CEO of Aerospace Engineering observed). The result may be a desirable combination of stable skills and mobile entrpreneurship. As the training advisor for Fibres commented:

> Most companies have now got a very stable workforce, with a lot of experience. That is not fully appreciated when compared with the 1970s, when 30–50 per cent turnover was not unusual.

The behaviour of labour markets, however, is not static and is susceptible to many factors. Given that small businesses tend to employ a higher proportion of younger, less qualified, and female staff (Storey and Johnson, 1987), the changing demography of age and gender will affect who enters the small firm labour force. Likewise, there is the considerable issue, which we have not considered, of who forms new firms and why, and how recession affects the propensity to do so. Such phenomena need to be regularly monitored. They are clearly relevant to concepts of entrepreneurship, innovativeness, and 'free agent careers'.

SUMMARY AND CONCLUSION

In *Strategy through People*, we emphasize the inseparability of strategic and human resource activities. We see our findings as a contribution to the greater interchange between managerial and economics perspectives we envisioned in Chapter 1. Fragmentation of theory has contributed to the problems of Western industrial organization, and reconnection of previously disparate ideas is necessary. This will involve new theory that spans old disciplinary boundaries.

There is a practical side to our findings, for governments, firms, and the people who participate in industrial society. In practice, as in theory, there are risks of fragmentation: of the hand of government on firms, or the hand of firms on people, or the hand of people – through political action – on government, acting without concern for their interdependence. A shared agenda calls for a focus on the competitiveness of industrial sectors, and the inter-firm and interpersonal processes that contribute to it.

In sum, we suggest three features – the interpenetration of sectors and labour markets, the multifunctional nature of jobs, and the catalysis of teams – as cornerstones of a 'strategy through people' perspective. We offer these as heuristics for theoretical analysis, policy, and practice. How well do the policies and practices of governments and firms match up to the call for sectors and labour markets to be considered simultaneously? How well do policy and practice accommodate the multiple functions served by jobs? How well do policy and practice incorporate the learning opportunities inherent in work and through teamwork in particular? These questions embrace both strategic and human resource issues.

When all of the above questions can be answered in the affirmative, it points towards a markedly different interface between strategic and human resource activity. This would be an interface free of static assumptions about firms, status, people, employment, market power, or knowledge. It would be an interface open to new possibilities for discovery, adaptation and learning, based on dynamic relationships between firms' strategies and people's careers.

The findings revealed in this book – covering strategic positioning, crisis, and adaptation, investment in and responsiveness to outside networking, pursuit of flexible specialization, and reluctance over formal planning and formal training – are all evidence of the dynamic, uncertain world in which the smaller firm operates. We should be beyond seeing such patterns as evidence that small firms are 'underdeveloped', or lacking in comprehensive management systems, or that the small firm is behaving as an awkward outsider to an 'industrial state' of mature large firms (Galbraith, 1971). Instead, our data support what a growing number of observers are coming to appreciate, namely that the above patterns signal the underlying relevance of smaller firms in modern-day competition, their occasional superiority, and essential complementarity to large firms.

Smaller firms are critical to the health of the sectors in which they participate. It is instructive that all four of Porter's (1990) principal examples of national competitive advantage – the German printing press,

US patient monitoring equipment, Italian ceramic tile, and Japanese robotics industries – have flourished from intensive competition among small firms rather than dominance by a few large ones. These, though, are mere samples of a trend incorporating – as we saw in the opening chapter of this book – broad US, European, and East Asian patterns in the overall organization of industry.

The message has not been lost on large firms, who in the 1980s began to reverse the old ideal 'to get as big as possible' towards a new ideal resting in 'how small an organization can be and still get the job done' (Kanter, 1989: 352). This trend extends even to successful large firms who are now increasingly organized into autonomous business units. The relatively isolated voice of Schumacher (1973: 245) twenty years before rings prophetic:

> The large organization will consist of many semi-autonomous units, which we may call quasi-firms. Each of them will have a large amount of freedom, to give the greatest possible chance to creativity and entrepreneurship.

Accordingly, the findings here embrace both independent firms and high autonomy business units, and thus the great majority of firms and employment in the industrial world.

In closing, we return to Williamson's call for a 'new science of organization', and within it a view of 'incomplete contracting', or in our terms, dynamic relationships. This view should be concerned with 'how to effect adaptation to changing circumstances, whence uncertainty is a key feature' (Williamson, 1991). Our findings in this book emphasize the multiple connections among sector, community, firms, and people to which the 'new science' must respond. We have suggested a view concerned with the interpenetration of industrial sectors and labour markets, the parallel firm-centred and person-centred functions of a job, and the catalysis of teams for new learning. These emerge as the cornerstones of a 'strategy through people' perspective.

NOTES

1 At the time of going to press, there is a postscript to this story. Incoming CEO, Lou Gerstner, although declaring 'at heart I'm a decentralizer', subsequently reversed Akers' break-up plans (*Business Week*, 1993b). More recently, he determined a principal 'strategic theme' for the future would be to 'leverage IBM's size and scale' (*Business Week*, 1994). Time will tell whether this reversion to a market power mentality will be successful. It may defer IBM's short-term collapse, but deflect from long-term corporate competitiveness.

2 The above need not be taken as any direct comparison of Japanese versus Western cultures, although it is – perhaps misleadingly – illustrative of how these cultures have been popularly represented (Arthur, 1992b).

Appendix A: Researching 'Strategy through people'

> Great damage to human dignity has resulted from the misguided attempt of the social sciences to adopt and imitate the methods of the natural sciences.
>
> (E.F. Schumacher, 1973: 239)

The data in this book derive from a broad-based study of strategic change and human resource development in twenty UK-based small–medium firms, which we carried out for the UK Department of Employment during 1989–91. Whereas much of the literature on small firms until then had been preoccupied with new firms in their start-up phase, we were concerned with the broader strategic issue of how small firms consolidate and grow. We therefore focused on firms having more than twenty-five employees to reflect those that had already undergone some significant growth, and provisionally set our upper limit at 500 employees, in line with the European definition of the small–medium enterprise.

In keeping with the traditionally limited focus on small firm development, the human resource dimension, including the training of employees, had also been largely neglected (Curran, 1986) – aside from a preoccupation with the skills and motivations of owner-managers at start-up and during early growth. The study was therefore designed also to redress this second shortcoming.

Preliminary literature review

Before embarking on fieldwork, we carried out a literature review to develop a theoretical framework; identify themes, debates, and hypotheses; and map what was known about human resource management (HRM) and human resource development (HRD) in SMEs (Arthur and Hendry, 1990). This identified a number of key topics and variables which we focused on in the construction of our fieldwork sample and in our data collection. However, we did not aim to test specific hypotheses and thereby constrain the data unnecessarily (Eisenhardt, 1989), but sought to capture the key processes and events affecting small firm development with their human resource implications. The intended outcome for the sponsor was a series of typologies and taxonomies that might assist policy-makers formulate appropriate support to smaller firms.

In such circumstances, the virtue of the case study is its ability, if properly conducted, to capture the context and process of organizational development and change (Pettigrew, 1990), while its limitations can be minimized by multiple case approaches (Yin, 1989) and validation through on-site follow-up to expose new and unexpected findings (Kirk and Miller, 1986). Multiple case studies, systematically searched, can thereby begin to remedy the a-theoretical, pragmatic character of small firm studies (Romano, 1989; Cromie, 1990; Gibb and Davies, 1990; Keasey and Watson, 1991).

The research protocol

With these objectives and requirements for carrying out case studies in mind, we proceeded as follows. First, we constructed a detailed research protocol under six broad headings:

1 Business strategy (including the firm's history and competitive environment).
2 HRM (covering such issues as pay, management style, and ways of developing commitment).
3 Skill structure and skill requirements, skill availability, and skill supply strategy.
4 The role of training and approaches to training within the skill supply strategy.
5 The role of less formalized and long-term approaches through HRD (including team-working and career progression).
6 Finally, 'critical incidents' of how each firm had dealt with major changes in its skill requirements in recent years.

In relation to business strategy, we collected data on organizational history, ownership, business and markets, customer and supplier relationships, competitive situation, performance and growth, the evolution of business strategies, future plans and planning processes, ambitions for growth, strategic challenges facing the firm, and management structure and backgrounds. Against this, we were then able to juxtapose the requirements for and approach to employee resourcing. In this way we were able to build up a detailed picture of the strategic history of each firm and its developing resource needs over the most recent ten-year period, with particular attention to major developments in that time.

Meanwhile, critical incidents are a useful supplement to (or substitute for) real time study in getting at context and process issues in organizational change. They highlight significant dramas which disrupt routines, thereby rendering them transparent (Pettigrew, 1979; Curran et al., 1991).

Sampling design

The sample of firms was constructed around five major parameters likely to affect the needs and resourcing of smaller enterprises – namely, stage of development, size, ownership, local labour market, and sector.

To allow for comparisons under various headings, we aimed at core groupings of three to four enterprises in the same sector, overlapping with similar groupings in distinct local labour markets. In addition, other pairs of firms and some one-off 'outliers' allowed for greater variety and the unexpected. Similarly, we aimed at an even breakdown between manufacturing and services, and a distribution of firms within four broad categories of size by numbers of employees (25–50, 51–100, 101–200, and 201–500). In this way, within the limits of sample size (determined by funding and timescale for the project) we tried to get a balance between 'sameness' and 'difference'. Or to put this another way, in 'grounded theory' terms we sought to maximize the opportunities for 'saturation' of, and differentiation between, concepts (Glaser and Strauss, 1967).

It will be apparent from this that we were not aiming at a 'representative' sample in any statistical sense. For instance, while we wanted to give more weight to the service sector than has been common in small business research (Burrows and Curran, 1989), a 50: 50 split still does not reflect the balance between manufacturing and services in the UK economy, while representativeness according to size would involve a heavy preponderance of very small enterprises. Our objective instead was 'theoretical sampling' (Glaser and Strauss, 1967) around issues of growth and development. Very small firms, for instance, provide limited insight into sustainable growth.

We then approached firms on the basis of knowledge gleaned from a variety of sources to ensure coverage of the five major parameters. In doing so, we developed the sample in two stages. This enabled us to target organizations to firm up on emerging themes and to redress the sample in various ways to provide additional contrasts (Yin, 1989). For example, early on we decided to limit the number of firms at the top end of the size range as soon as we found large firm phenomena beginning to recur.

Data collection and analysis

The fieldwork was carried out by the three authors throughout 1990. Between six and ten people per firm were typically interviewed in each case, although, to limit the demands on people's time, only two or three in one or two very small firms. These interviews were conducted with the aid of the detailed research protocol which was gradually filled out through successive interviews to build up a picture of the firm. In every case, the managing director or equivalent was interviewed (often more than once), along with a cross-section of people by function and organization level, to cross-check on data and intepretations in critical areas. In addition, we drew on archival material and published secondary sources, both on the enterprise and sector, to achieve some triangulation of data. The resulting cases were typed up using the headings from the research protocol to allow for ready comparison and systematic searching across cases. Varying in length from 35–70 pages, they provided a substantial, in-depth picture of each company.

Issues from the research were then fed back to the individual companies, to provide opportunity for further data collection and corroboration, especially of the emerging patterns in the sample as a whole. This took place at anything between one and six months after the initial data collection. This also allowed for a measure of 'real-time' data collection of intervening developments, especially on how they were coping with problems and challenges already identified. These developments were either incorporated in the case or in an appendix to it.

As the cases were written, the authors discussed them for emerging themes, and at the halfway stage a preliminary analysis was systematically conducted (Eisenhardt, 1989). The final twenty cases were then examined independently and then jointly by all three researchers to take advantage of multiple perspectives and to reconcile interpretations (Miles and Huberman, 1984; Pettigrew, 1990). The resulting findings were developed in a report to the funding agency, the UK Department of Employment (Hendry *et al.*, 1991).

These findings and the original cases have since been progressively revisited in the light of specific areas of the literature on which our themes bear (Eisenhardt, 1989). This book is the result of this deepening analysis. In the process, we have developed the representativeness of our findings in one important way. That is, in writing this book and exploring particular themes, we have been able to draw on a major survey of 2,028 small enterprises in the UK since undertaken (Cambridge SBRC, 1992), as well as various smaller-scale focused studies, and to match our sample and findings against these. To a lesser extent we have also made use of the annual Reports of the President (for example, 1990) on the State of Small Business in the USA. These provide a larger quantitative dimension to our qualitative data and enhance its reliability in particular areas, by providing a more 'objectivist' check on the case studies (Eisenhardt, 1991; Eisenhardt and Bourgeois, 1988) (notwithstanding the criticism that research modelled from the outset in this way can fall between two stools (Borch and Arthur, 1994)).

Appendix B: Summary of the cases

TRAVEL, TOURISM, AND LEISURE

The Visitor Bureau

The Visitor Bureau, located in the West Midlands, traces its origins back to 1980 when the City decided to close its information centre and at the same time promote the city as a major centre for business meetings, travel and tourism. The idea of a Bureau was also being pushed by a group of local private businessmen. The Visitor Bureau came into existence initially under the auspices of the City Council and to this day the local public sector influence remains with both major political parties being represented on the Bureau's Board of Directors. The chairmanship of the Board alternates between the two main political party representatives. The remaining Board members are made up of local businessmen and hotel managers who are elected to serve on a two-yearly basis. The Bureau has grown dramatically and has been responsible for helping to change the face of the City. Starting with a handful of employees, the Bureau now employs forty-four people (full and part-time), has a turnover of £4 million per annum, and is in a profit making position.

The Bureau's Chief Executive has been the key figure in generating Bureau business and development, and it was he who spearheaded the drive for an International Convention Centre in Birmingham and the new Hyatt Regency Hotel to complement it. The Centre will open in 1991 and will be one of the world's premier conference/convention facilities. The Bureau and its organization and systems have become a model for other newly emerging convention bureaux. The Visitor Bureau now markets itself internationally and has impacted on the way in which other local businesses and organizations (e.g. hotels, tour operators, taxi firms, restaurants, etc.) provide customer service to incoming visitors to the City.

The Convention Bureau

The Convention Bureau, located in West Scotland, in many ways mirrors the work of the Visitor Bureau. It has a shorter life-span but has developed an enviable pedigree in its short existence (started 1984). Having initially started with the backing of the City Council and several neighbouring regional councils, the Bureau has now more or less severed all links with its public sector background. It employs fifty-five people on a full and part-time basis. Having initially attempted to address the convention, travel and tourism business in general, the Bureau now engages in niche marketing by targetting professional associations on a world-wide basis. Destination marketing is the key activity of the Bureau and it is successful. In 1982, 700,000 people visited the City as against 2.3 million in 1989. The amount spent on marketing – £400,000 – has produced an estimated £56 million revenue into the City from 1986–1996. The lead role of the Chief Executive has been of major importance in the Bureau's development.

Hotel Tourist

Hotel Tourist is located in the South East. It maintains a basic full-time staff of around forty people and retains the services of part-time staff, as and when required, for large functions. The hotel is one of many hotels making up a large UK hotel chain. In addition to offering accommodation to business people visiting the City, tourists are also a major source of revenue. The hotel, as it is today, has its origins back in 1946. The current annual turnover is approximately £1 million, with a profit of £250,000. The hotel is facing major problems in that the opening of the Channel Tunnel threatens to make the City a 'backwater'. Most visitors stay there overnight on their way down to get the boat for a Channel crossing. The opening of the tunnel is likely to see people making the journey to the Continent in one day. The hotel is suffering from a lack of refurbishment/investment. High room rate charges are resulting in disillusioned and complaining guests. In turn these factors are influencing staff morale and motivation resulting in a massive annual staff turnover.

Hotel Heritage

Hotel Heritage is located in the West Midlands in a medium-size market town. The hotel dates back to the thirteenth century and is part of the same hotel chain as Hotel Tourist. Hitherto, Hotel Heritage has been privately owned and recognized around the world as a place of excellence, both in terms of accommodation and the quality of the food available in its elegant silver-service restaurant. The hotel has been the scene of many social and fashionable events and has attracted an international array of people.

Today, the hotel is a shadow of its former state and although its reputation generally remains intact, it is now in need of a major face-lift and much needed refurbishment, given the charges made for rooms and the limited facilities available in them. The hotel employs forty-three people and has recently been taken over by a major UK hotel chain, the latter now seeking to impose more business-like systems of management and audit. The emphasis is on cost-cutting linked to higher revenues. The hotel's market is also changing with a need to attract more conference visitors to the hotel in addition to the general tourist. The hotel is situated in a delightful part of the West Midlands with a strong historical flavour to the area.

COMPUTER SOFTWARE

Software Products

Software Products is an independent company located in the West Midlands and employing 130 people. This company, recently formed in 1979, has undergone massive growth in the past two or three years as it has found a niche market providing specialist software packages for insurance companies. A very high proportion of insurance policies normally have to be returned to the potential client. The software devised by Software Products seeks to offer a more or less flawless system to ensure a high and rapid turnaround of policy acceptance. The firm was established by three people who had previous experience in the field. The company now has major backing from two international insurance houses and will soon begin entering the international market through its acquisition of a Boston (USA) based company. There has been a rapid growth in terms of numbers of employees recruited. The directors and senior managers, who have grown with the company, are now having to organize the firm without themselves having the experience of more junior levels of management. The firm is in a state of financial transition, with aims to create more profit from its rapidly increased sales.

TRAINING CONSULTANCY

Training International

Training International is based in the West Midlands. Started in 1980, the company was voted the leading training company in Europe by the EC in 1989. The firm has 130 employees and is engaged in getting other firms to go through culture change programmes. Training International has grown dramatically in the last six years or so with its major break being a contract to take all 36,000 British Airways staff world-wide through a 'People First' programme. Initially, Training International was involved in time-management training. The company is privately owned by two brothers, with one acting as Chief Executive and the other as Managing Director. The organization is itself now at a point of transition in that its own products/services need to be transformed to meet the changing nature of training and development needs in potential client companies and organizations. The company turnover is approximately £14 million at the present time, with a high rate of profit on that.

Skills Training

Skills Training was formed in May 1990 as a result of the Government selling off its skill training centres. These were formed throughout the UK just after the Second World War to train people rapidly in practical skills, such as building, painting and decorating, and carpentry. The three people who purchased Skills Training acquired four centres at various locations around the country at little cost. A deal was struck with the Government that it would provide continued funding for one year in return for the new purchasers taking over the centres. The new owners are now trying to utilize the various premises to create profit centres. Such training as will be provided will be reduced, and facilities used for other purposes, such as small business start-up space letting. Local companies in all areas are experiencing a recession and therefore not readily willing to pay for apprentices and others to attend the various courses provided at the new Skills Training centres. Overall the company employs sixty people but these numbers will be reduced over the next twelve months as the new owners/managers complete an audit of the business.

PROFESSIONAL SERVICES

Legal Services

Legal Services is based in the West Midlands. It is an independent solicitor's practice with thirty-five employees. The firm started in 1981 with one sole owner/partner and one secretary, and has grown in recent years to become the third largest practice in the town. The firm is now owned by three partners and revenue is increasing each year. In 1989 the gross income was £800,000 with a profit of £195,000. The firm has identified specific market niches which it has developed. To resource the various activities the firm has attracted staff with experience in matrimonial law, civil and criminal law, and property conveyancing and mortgage repossession. The firm is one of only three recognized specialist firms outside London which has an expertise in charitable trust work. The firm continues to grow but will have to face the challenge as to whether additional continued work and growth will produce significant revenue to warrant further expansion.

FOOD AND DRINK MANUFACTURE

Bread Products

Bread Products is located in the West Midlands. It is one of only a small remaining number of independent bakers in the country. With 350 employees, the firm actually goes back many years but the present company has its origins back in 1962. The firm makes bread and specialist morning/breakfast products (e.g. fruit loaves, teacakes) which it sells to small shops, small supermarket outlets, and to major supermarket chains such as Tesco. The firm is privately owned by a holding company which, in turn, is owned by an old established flour-milling family. Current annual income is £15 million with a profit of £750,00. This profit level is regarded as good in the industry. Presently the firm has a £5 million loan to repay. The money was used to purchase new production equipment but the new managing director believes the company was wrongly advised as to which machinery should be purchased and where it should be located in the factory. The production of bread is now totally computerized. The company experienced a major fire some years ago which proved to be financially traumatic. The industry is rapidly shrinking as more and more large supermarket chains turn to making their bread in-house. Bread is a 'loss leader' in most stores, and shops and bread producers, such as Bread Products, are constantly faced with a price war from competitors. The risk is that this will reach a stage where it becomes unprofitable for the firm to remain in business.

MECHANICAL/ELECTRICAL ENGINEERING

Aerospace Engineering

Aerospace Engineering is an independent company located in the West Midlands conurbation. It was established approximately thirty years ago as a family-run business. It was then bought out in 1985 by a number of people and subsequently the new managing director purchased the whole company with a venture capital loan and with money of his own. The firm produces components for fuel systems in the aerospace industry, as well as for hydraulic applications, in a range of specialist and more common metals. The company currently employs 61 people with a present annual turnover of £2 million. Recent returns have fluctuated from a profit of £137,000 in 1987, to a small loss in 1988, and back into profit in 1989, with good prospects for 1990. In 1988–89, it suffered a lull in orders while its major customer destocked following its own privatization. The company experienced a major lack of investment under its previous owners, but since 1986 has undergone a major three-year re-investment of £900,000 under its new owner.

MOD Products

MOD Products is located in the West Midlands, having been originally founded in 1832 outside Glasgow to serve the shipbuilding and associated industries. Initially, the firm specialized in lighting for ships, and designed and manufactured other ship fittings, and then by extension supplied lighting for railway carriages and industrial buildings. At an early stage in its existence, it opened a manufacturing plant in the West Midlands to serve the railways there. By 1980 this business was significantly into supplying the defence industry, in the form of light fittings for the Royal Navy, but had become established also in aerospace through a range of 'connectors' and radar 'slip rings'.

By the early 1980s, MOD Products was still a private company, family-owned. In 1982 it was acquired by a holding company operating in electrical support systems and connectors, and the business has developed with investment from the holding company, in addition to maintaining a close relationship with the Glasgow based business of MOD Products.

The firm's major customer is the Ministry of Defence and in 1990 the company employed 100 people and had a £4.2 million revenue, with an approximate profitability of £100,000. In recent years annual profits have been dropping from around £300,000, to the 1990 figures which they hope to maintain.

Pressings

Pressings is an independent company with its origins back in 1826 when the firm originally made gilt toys. Today the firm, located in a largely residential area of the West Midlands, makes primarily heavy duty industrial conveyor components. The typical product is now a pressed steel bearing housing. The father of the present owner acquired majority control of the company from the original family owners in 1979. Following his death in 1983, his son acquired the remaining shares in 1987. Pressings now employs forty-three people with a revenue of approximately £1.5 million. It was losing money even though turnover has increased each year since 1985, but is now making a profit. The company hitherto lacked business and organizational discipline, and also faced the threat of losing its main customers. Under the present managing director, its sales position has been made more secure, the manufacturing system has been over-hauled, and business and administrative controls introduced.

Clean Air Co.

Clean Air Co has thirty-nine employees and is based in the North Midlands. The firm is located on a modern, mixed industrial estate. Formed in 1964, the company was previously located at Stoke-on-Trent and was in the business of importing hydraulic tools as an agent for an American manufacturer. A new sales director joined in 1969 but he fell out with the owner. The sales director then acquired the main shareholding and began moving the business into fume-extraction equipment, relocating it to its present site in the mid-1970s. The new owner died in 1977, and after some protracted management difficulties and restructuring, the business went through a traumatic period which did not completely end until 1986. Behind the company control issue lay other matters to do with alleged fraud and theft (of ideas and business). Revenue has risen steadily since 1984 to a figure currently approaching £3 million. In 1984 profits were approximately £84,000, with a dip in 1988 into loss. The financial difficulties in the mid-80s were overcome by tighter control and making staff redundant. More recently, under a new managing director, sales are rapidly increasing with good profit prospects. The wife of the previous owner retains the bulk of the shares, and relies on the business for income.

ELECTRO-OPTICAL

Glass Discs

Glass Discs was formed in March 1989 as a subsidiary of a major glass producing company. It has sixty-two employees and is located on a modern industrial park in North Wales. The company is concerned with electro-optics (a convergence of electronic and optical technologies). Electro-optics uses glass as the medium for transmitting wave forms (light and magnetism), both as an operating medium (telecommunications and avionics displays) and as a storage medium (compact discs and discs for computer records). Glass Discs has products of both kinds, with 95 per cent of the disc production going to one customer. It aims to increase turnover and numbers of employees rapidly, but is still very much in a start-up phase, with major uncertainties in its markets and with production inefficiencies to be ironed out.

Fibres

Fibres employs 350 people, also on a modern industrial estate in North Wales. The firm is a joint venture owned 50: 50 by two other companies. These came together to produce optical wave guides (i.e. optical fibre cables) for international telecommunications systems. The firm was established in the late 1970s but did not commence business until early 1983. Turnover has changed little in the past four years and has averaged between £35-£40 million. It is profitable. The company has gained 65 per cent of the market share in the UK and now sees itself developing its markets on a world-wide basis.

Optics

Optics is located on three sites, principally in North Wales, but also in North London and the West Country. Headquarters is based at the (smaller) North London site. The firm is engaged in the optical lens polishing business and in optical-electronics in general. The North Wales business was started in 1982 by three former employees of another glass firm. This expanded too rapidly and in 1987, after various buy-outs, the business became part of the present larger group. The firm now employs ninety-three people and in 1989 had total revenue of £3.9 million, with a small profit. In recent years the firm has suffered major traumas: in 1984 when the firm became insolvent after too rapid an expansion, and was taken over; and in 1987 when certain other manufacturing facilities were transferred from London to North Wales. Major management changes occurred in late 1989, while further transfer of facilities from the other two sites to North Wales and automation of polishing lines are now in prospect.

CONSTRUCTION

Construction Co.

Construction Co. is based in the North East. It employs between 270–330, depending on the state of projects. Founded in 1907, the company is a subsidiary of a family business engaged in general construction work, with the business 97 per cent family-owned. Projects vary greatly, spanning both new building and reconstruction. Annual turnover is at present increasing, although profits have fluctuated considerably. In 1989 the firm's turnover was £19.5 million. Although increased turnover represents growth, the wild fluctuations in profit serve to highlight the cyclical nature of the construction industry. The company has been through 'every kind of "up and down" imaginable in the past ten years' (MD).

House Co.

House Co. is a subsidiary of Construction Co., also based in the North East. The division grew from uncertain beginnings within the Construction Co.

that involved partnership deals in the 1970s with the City of Newcastle to develop low cost housing on council land. A dramatic downturn in the construction market caused Construction Co.'s management to turn to homes building as an alternative source of business, beginning around 1981. Construction Co. almost went bankrupt and after this event a separate division was established (House Co). The company presently employs between 57–81 people depending on the state of business, with the Group handling certain administrative tasks such as wages and personnel.

Cable Co.

Cable Co. is located in the North East. It was established in 1968 when cable laying was emerging as a significant activity within the construction industry. Using physically able gangs of unskilled labour under the supervision of a qualified electrician, the gangs are able to lay cable at a much faster pace (and more cheaply) than a group of qualified electricians. The firm was started by a time-served electrician, and is now the largest of its kind in the country with an annual turnover of around £6.0 million. The company recently lost its independence when it became part of a consortium group of companies headed by a major insurance company. Customers include the large national construction companies and businesses located throughout the UK, including the London Underground. Cable Co. employed 95 people in 1985 but employee numbers have since grown to 247. Senior management believe the 'tight ship' operation they run has enabled the company to outrun the competition both in terms of operation and profitability. Profits doubled in 1990 to £538,000.

Architectural Services

Architectural Services is an independent architectural practice formed from the merger of two smaller practices in 1962. It is located in the North East. It is owned by four partners and seeks to offer a full range of architectural services on a national basis. The firm has a number of particular specialities including the design of leisure centres and libraries. Employee numbers have grown from thirty-eight in 1980 to eighty-one in 1989. The firm had a revenue of £2.4 million in 1989, producing a profit of £406,000. 1986 was a watershed year when the partners pressed for the remaining founder partner to retire. This has allowed a shift in business focus and a more aggressive approach to marketing. The company is increasingly moving from the fee-bid arena to the commercial sector where there are non-financial criteria for selecting an architect.

References

Acs, Z.J. and Audretsch, D.B. (1987), 'Innovation, market structure and firm size', *Review of Economics and Statistics*, 69, pp. 567–574.

Advisory Council on Science and Technology (ACOST) (1990). *The Enterprise Challenge: Overcoming Barriers to Growth in Small Firms*. London: HMSO.

Aglietta, M. (1979). *A Theory of Capitalist Regulation: The US Experience*. London: New Left Books.

Aitkenhead, M., Liff, S. and Reeves, D. (1992), 'Personnel issues in small businesses in the 1990s', unpublished paper, University of Warwick.

Aldrich, H. and Zimmer, C. (1986), 'Entrepreneurship through social networks', in D. Sexton and R. Smilor (eds) *The Art and Science of Entrepreneurship*, Cambridge, Mass.: Ballinger.

Amin, A. (1989), 'Flexible specialization and small firms in Italy: myths and realities', *Antipode*, 21, 1, pp. 13–34.

Amit, R., Glasten, L. Muller. (1990), 'Does venture foster the most promising entrepeneurial firm?' *California Management Review*, 32, 3, pp. 102–111.

Anderson, C.R. and Zeithamal, C.P. (1984), 'Stage of the product life cycle, business strategy and business performance', *Academy of Management Journal*, 27, 1, pp. 5–24.

Antonelli, C. (ed.) (1988). *New Information Technology and Industrial Change: The Italian Case*. Dordrecht/Boston/London: Kluwer Academic Publishers.

Aoki, M., Gustavson, B. and Williamson, O.E. (1990). *The Firm as a Nexus of Treaties*. London: Sage.

Argenti, J. (1976). *Corporate Collapse: The Cause and the Symptoms*. Maidenhead: McGraw-Hill.

Argyris, C. and Schon, D.A. (1978). *Organisational Learning: A Theory in Action Perspective*. Reading, Mass.: Addison Wesley.

Arthur, M.B. (1992a), 'Career theory in a dynamic context', in D.H. Montross and C.J. Shinkman (eds) *Career Development: Theory and Practice*, Springfield, IL: Charles C. Thomas, pp. 65–84.

Arthur, M.B. (1992b), 'East meets West again: Some thoughts about careers, cultures and competitiveness', Address to the Academy of Management, Careers Division, Las Vegas.

Arthur, M.B. and Hendry, C. (1990), 'Human resource management and the emergent strategy of small-to-medium-sized business units', *International Journal of Human Resource Management*, 1, 3, pp. 233–250.

Arthur, M.B. and Kram, K.E. (1989), 'Reciprocity at work: the separate, yet inseparable possibilities for individual and organizational development', in M.B. Arthur, D.T. Hall and B.S. Lawrence (eds) *Handbook of Career Theory*, New York: Cambridge University Press, pp. 292–312.

Arthur, M.B., Hall, D.T. and Lawrence, B.S. (eds) (1989). *Handbook of Career Theory.* Cambridge: Cambridge University Press.

Aston Business School/Cousins Stephens Associates (1991). *Constraints on the Growth of Small Firms.* London: HMSO.

Atkinson, J. and Meager, N. (1986). *Changing Patterns of Work: How Companies Introduce Flexibility to Meet Changing Needs.* Falmer, Sussex: Institute for Manpower Studies.

Aydalot, P. (1988), 'The role of small and medium-sized enterprises in regional development: Conclusions drawn from recent surveys', in M. Giaoutzi, P. Nijkamp and D.J. Storey (eds) *Small and Medium Size Enterprises and Regional Development,* London: Routledge.

Axelrod, R. (1984), *The Evolution of Cooperation.* New York: Basic Books.

Ball, C. (1991). *Learning Pays: The Role of Post-Compulsory Education and Training.* London: Royal Society of Arts.

Bannock, G. and Daly, M. (1990), 'Size distribution of UK firms', *Employment Gazette,* May, pp. 255–258.

Bannock and Partners (1990). *Enterprises in the European Community,* Brussels/Luxembourg: Commission of the European Communities.

Bannock, G. and Peacock, A. (1990), *Governments and Small Business,* London: Paul Chapman.

Barber, J., Metcalfe, J.S. and Porteous, M. (eds) (1989), *Barriers to Growth in Small Firms,* London and New York: Routledge.

Batstone, S. (1991), 'Entrepreneurial reputation and social capital', working paper, University of Warwick.

Beccatini, G. (1978), 'The development of light industry in Tuscany: an interpretation', *Economic Notes,* vols 2–3, pp. 107–23.

Beer, S. (1972). *The Brain of the Firm.* Harmondsworth: Allen Lane, Penguin.

Beer, M. Spector, B., Lawrence, P. R., Mills, D. Q., and Walton, R. E. (1984). *Managing Human Assets.* New York: Free Press.

Belbin, M. (1981). *Management Teams: why they succeed or fail.* London: Butterworth-Heinemann.

Benner, P. (1982), 'From novice to expert', *American Journal of Nursing,* 82, 3, pp. 402–7.

Bennis, W. and Nanus, B. (1985). *Leaders: The Strategies for Taking Charge.* New York: Harper & Row.

Berryman, J. (1983), 'Small business failure and bankruptcy: a survey of the literature, *International Small Business Journal,* 1, 1, pp. 17–59.

Bessant, J. (1993), 'Towards Factory 2000: designing organizations for computer-integrated technologies', in J. Clark (ed.) *Human Resource Management and Technical Change,* London/Newbury Park/New Delhi: Sage.

Best, M.H. (1990), *The New Competition,* Cambridge, Mass.: Harvard University Press.

Birch, D.L. (1987). *Job Creation in America,* New York: Free Press.

Birch, D.L. (1979), 'The job generation process', MIT Program on Neighborhood and Regional Change, Cambridge, Mass.

Birley, S. (1985), 'The role of networks in the entrepreneurial process', *Journal of Business Venturing,* 1, pp. 107–117.

Birley, S., Cromie, S. and Myers, A. (1990), 'Entrepreneurial networks: their emergence in Ireland and overseas', *International Small Business Journal,* 9, 4, pp. 56–74.

Birley, S. and Westhead, P. (1990), 'Growth and performance contrasts between 'types' of small firms', *Strategic Management Journal,* 11, 7, pp. 535–557.

Boeker, W. (1989), 'Strategic change: The effects of founding and history', *Academy of Management Journal*, 32, 3, pp. 489–515.

Bolton Report (The), *Small Firms, Report of the Committee of Inquiry on Small Firms*, HMSO, London, Cmnd 4811, 1971.

Borch, O.J. and Arthur, M.B. (1994), 'Strategic networks among small firms: implications for strategy research methodology', unpublished paper, Nordland Research Institute, 8002 Bodo, Norway.

Bowen, D. E., Chase, R.B., Cummings, T.G. and Associates (1990), *Service Management Effectiveness*, San Francisco: Jossey Bass.

Bowen, D.E. and Schneider, B. (1988), 'Services marketing and management: Implications for organization behavior', in B.M. Staw and L.L. Cummings (eds) *Research in Organizational Behaviour, Volume 10*, Greenwich, CT: JAI Press, pp. 43–80.

Bracker, J.S. and Pearson, J.N. (1986), 'Planning and financial performance of small, mature firms', *Strategic Management Journal*, 7, 6, pp. 503–522.

Brock, W.A. and Evans, D.S. (1989), 'Small business economics', *Small Business Economics*, 1, pp. 7–20.

Brown, J.S. and Duguid, P. (1991), ' Organizational learning and communities of practice: toward a unified view of working, learning and innovation', *Organization Science*, 2, 1, pp. 40–57.

Brusco, S. (1982), 'The Emilian model', *Cambridge Journal of Economics*, 6, pp. 167–84.

Brusco, S. (1986), 'Small firms and industrial districts: the experience of Italy', in D. Keeble and E. Wever (eds) *New Firms and Regional Development in Europe*, London: Croom Helm, pp. 184–202.

Brusco, S. and Sabel, C. (1981), 'Artisan production and economic wealth', in F. Wilkinson (ed.) *The Dynamics of Labour Market Segmentation*, London and New York: Academic Press.

Bryman, A., Bresnen, M., Beardsworth, A.D., Ford, J., and Keil, E.T. (1987), 'The concept of the temporary system: the case of the construction project', in S.B. Bacharach and N. DiTomaso (eds) *Research in the Sociology of Organisations, Volume 5*, JAI Press, pp. 253–283.

Buchanan, D. and Boddy, D. (1983), *Organisations in the Computer Age*, London: Gower.

Burgleman, R.A. (1983), 'A process model of internal corporate venturing in a major diversified firm', *Administrative Science Quarterly*, 30, pp. 350–372.

Burgleman, R.A. and Sayles, L.R. (1985). *Inside Corporate Innovation*. New York: Free Press.

Burke, J.W. (1989). *Competency Based Education and Training*. London: Falmer Press.

Burns, P. (1989), 'Strategies for success and routes to failure', in P. Burns and J. Dewhurst (eds), *Small Business and Entrepreneurship*, London: Macmillan.

Burrows, R. and Curran, J. (1989), 'Sociological research on service sector small businesses: some conceptual considerations', *Work, Employment and Society*, 3, 4, pp. 527–539.

Business Week (1991), 'Out of one big blue, many little blues', 9 December, p. 33.

Business Week (1993a), 'IBM's new boss: Faith in a stranger', 5 April, pp. 18–21.

Business Week (1993b), 'Rethinking IBM', 4 October, pp. 86–97.

Business Week (1994), 'Lou Gerstner unveils his battle plan', 4 April, pp. 96–98.

Camagni, R. (ed.) (1991). *Innovation Networks*. London: Bellhaven.

Cambridge Small Business Research Centre (SBRC) (1992), *The State of British Enterprise*, University of Cambridge.

Cannon, T. (1985), 'Innovation, creativity and small firm organisation', *International Small Business Journal*, 4, 1, pp. 33–41.

Carlsson, B. (1984), The development and use of machine tools in historical perspective', *Journal of Economic Behavior and Organization*, 5, pp. 91–114.

Carlsson, B. (1989), 'The evolution of manufacturing technology and its impact on industrial structure: an international study', *Small Business Economics*, 1, pp. 21–37.

Carney, M. (1991), 'Book Review', *Work, Employment and Society*, 5, 3, pp. 469–471.

Casson, M.C. (1982), *The Entrepreneur: An Economic Theory*, Oxford: Martin Robertson.

Chaganti, R. (1987), 'Small Business Strategies in Different Industry Growth Environments', *Journal of Small Business Management*, 25, July, pp. 61–68.

Chakravarthy, B.F. (1986), 'Measuring strategic performance', *Strategic Management Journal*, 7, 5, pp. 437–458.

Chalmers, N.J. (1989), *Industrial Relations in Japan: The Peripheral Workforce*, London: Routledge.

Child, J. (1977). *Organization: A Guide to Problems and Practice*. London: Harper and Row.

Chomsky, N. (1965). *Aspects of the theory of syntax*. Cambridge, MA: MIT Press.

Christensen, C.R., Andrews, K.R., Bower, J.L., Hamermesh, R.H. and Porter, M.E. (1987) *Business Policy: Text and Cases*, Homewood, IL: Irwin.

Churchill, N.C. and Lewis, V.L. (1983), 'The five stages of small business growth', *Harvard Business Review*, 61, May-June, pp. 30–50.

Clark, R. (1979), *The Japanese Company*, London: Yale University Press.

Clarke, K.J. (1989), 'Technological change and strategic management: technological transilience and the British automotive components sector', in R. Mansfield (ed.) *Frontiers of Management*, London and New York: Routledge, pp. 109–126.

Clifford, M., Nilakant, V. and Hamilton, R.T. (1990), 'Management succession and the stages of small business growth', *International Small Business Journal*, 9, 4, pp. 43–55.

Coleman, J.S. (1988), 'Social Capital in the Creation of Human Capital', *American Journal of Sociology*, 94, 1, pp. 95–120.

Coleman, J.S. (1990), *Foundations of Social Theory*, London: Belknap Harvard.

Collins, O.F., Moore, D.G. and Unwalla, D.B. (1964), *The Enterprising Man*, East Lansing: Graduate School of Business, Michigan State University.

Cooper, A.C., Willard, G.E. and Woo, C.Y. (1986), 'Strategies of high-performing new and small firms: a re-examination of the niche concept', *Journal of Business Venturing*, 1, pp. 247–260.

Covin, J.G., Slevin, D.P. and Covin, T.J. (1990), 'Content and performance of growth-seeking strategies: a comparison of small firms in high- and low-technology industries', *Journal of Business Venturing*, 5, pp. 391–412.

Crockett, G. and Elias, P. (1984), 'British managers: a study of their education, training, mobility and earnings', *British Journal of Industrial Relations*, xxii, 1, pp. 34–46.

Cromie, S. (1990), 'The problems experienced by young firms', *International Journal of Small Business*, 9, 3, pp. 43–61.

Curran, J. (1986), *Bolton Fifteen Years On: A Review and Analysis of Small Business Research in Britain 1971–1986*, London: Small Business Research Trust.

Curran, J., Blackburn, R.A. and Woods, A. (1991). *Profiles of the Small Enterprise in the Service Sector*, Small Business Research Centre, Kingston Polytechnic.

Curran, J. and Stanworth, J. (1979a), 'Worker involvement and social relations in the small firm', *Sociological Review*, 27, 2, pp. 317–342.

Curran, J. and Stanworth, J. (1979b), 'Self-selection and the small firm worker: a critique and an alternative view', *Sociology*, 13, 3, pp. 427–444.

Curran, J., Jarvis, R., Blackburn, R.A. and Black, S. (1991). *Small Firms and Networks: Constructs, Methodological Strategies and Preliminary Findings*. Small Business Research Centre, Kingston Polytechnic.

Curtain, R. (1987), 'Skill formation and the enterprise', *Labour and Industry*, 1, 1, pp. 8–38.

Cyert, R.M. and March, J.G. (1963), *A Behavioural Theory of the Firm*, Englewood Cliffs, NJ: Prentice-Hall.

Daft, R.L. and Weick, K.E. (1984), 'Toward a model of organizations as interpretations systems', *Academy of Management Review*, 9, 2, pp. 284–295.

Dalton, G.W. (1989), 'Developmental views of careers in organizations', in M.B. Arthur, D.T. Hall and B.S. Lawrence (eds) *Handbook of Career Theory*, New York: Cambridge University Press, pp. 89–109.

Dalton, G.W. and Thompson, P.H. (1986), *Novations: Strategies for Career Management*, Glenview, IL: Scott Foresman.

Davis, C.D., Hills, G.E. and LaForge, R.W. (1984), 'The marketing/small enterprise paradox: a research agenda', *International Small Business Journal*, 3, 3, pp. 31–42.

Dawitt, K. (1983), 'Myths of small business failure', *The CPA Journal*, 53, September, pp. 73–74.

Deming, W.E. (1986). *Out of the Crisis*. Cambridge, Mass.: Centre for Advanced Engineering Study, Massachusetts Institute of Technology.

Dicken, P. (1992). *Global Shift*. 2nd edition, London: Paul Chapman.

Doeringer, P.B. and Piore, M.J. (1971), *Internal Labour Markets and Manpower Analysis*, Lexington, Mass: Heath.

Doctor, J., Van der Haorst, R. and Stokman, C. (1989), 'Innovation processes in small- and medium-sized companies', *Entrepreneurship and Regional Development*, 1, 1, pp. 33–53.

Dodge, H.R. and Robbins, J.E. (1992), 'An empirical investigation of the organizational life cycle model for small business development and survival', *Journal of Small Business Management*, 30, January, pp. 27–37.

Dore, R. (1983), 'Goodwill and the Spirit of Market Capitalism', *The British Journal of Sociology*, 34, 4, pp. 459–482.

Dore, R. and Sako, M. (1987), 'Vocational education and training in Japan', in R. Dore (ed.) *Taking Japan Seriously*, London: Athlone.

Dorfman, N (1983), 'The development of a regional high technology economy', *Research Policy*, 12, pp. 299–316.

Doyle, J. and Gallagher, C. (1988), 'Size-distribution, growth potential, and job generation contribution of UK firms', *International Small Business Journal*, 6, 1, pp. 31–56.

Drazon, R. and Kazanjian, R.K. (1990), 'A reanalysis of Miller and Friesen's life cycle data', *Strategic Management Journal*, 11, pp. 319–324.

Dreyfus, H.L. and Dreyfus, S.E. (1984), 'Putting computers in their proper place: Analysis versus intuition in the classroom', in D. Sloan (ed.) *The Computer in Education: A Critical Perspective*, New York: Columbia Teachers College Press.

Drucker, P.F. (1985), *Innovation and Entrepreneurship*, London: Heinemann.

Dubini, P. and Aldrich, H. (1991), 'Personal and extended networks are central to the entrepreneurial process', *Journal of Business Venturing*, 6, pp. 305–313.

Dunning, J.H. (1988), 'The eclectic paradigm of international production: a restatement and some possible extensions', *Journal of International Business Studies*, XIX, 1, pp. 1–31.

Economist (The) (1991), 'Scenting extinction', 14 December, pp. 69–70.

Eisenhardt, K.M. (1989), 'Building theories from case study research', *Academy of Management Review*, 14, 4, pp. 532–550.

Eisenhardt, K.M. (1991), 'Better stories and better constructs: the case for rigor and comparative logic', *Academy of Management Review*, 16, 3, pp. 620–627.

Eisenhardt, K.M. and Bourgeois, L.J. (1988), 'Politics of strategic decision making in high-velocity environments: towards a mid-range theory', *Academy of Manage-*

ment Journal, 31, 4, pp. 737–770.

Eisenhardt, K.M. and Schoonhaven, C.B. (1990), 'Organizational growth: Linking founding team, strategy, environment and growth among US semiconductor ventures', *Administrative Science Quarterly,* 35, pp. 504–529.

Employment Department (1992), *Labour Market and Skill Trends 1991/92: Planning for a Changing Labour Market,* Sheffield: Employment Department Group.

Fiegenbaum, A. and Karnani, A. (1991), 'Output flexibility – A competitive advantage for small firms', *Strategic Management Journal,* 12, 2, pp. 101–114.

Finley, D. (1980), 'How small businesses can profit from demographics', *American Demographics,* May, pp. 16–19.

Fiol, C.M. and Lyles, M.A. (1985), 'Organizational learning', *Academy of Management Review,* 10, 4, pp. 803–813.

Firnstahl, T.W. (1986), 'Growing concerns: letting go', *Harvard Business Review,* 64, September/October, pp. 14–18.

Fitzroy, F.R. (1989), 'Firm Size, Efficiency and Employment: A Review Article', *Small Business Economics,* 1, pp. 75–80.

Flamhotz, E.G. (1986). *How to Make the Transition from Entrepreneurship to a Professionally Managed Firm.* San Francisco: Jossey-Bass.

Florida, R. and Kenney, M. (1991), 'Organizational factors and technology-intensive industry: the US and Japan', *New Technology, Work and Employment,* 6, 1, pp. 28–42.

Flynn, P.M. (1988), *Facilitating Technological Change: the Human Resource Challenge.* Cambridge, Mass.: Ballinger.

Ford, J. (1982), 'Who breaks the rules?' the responses of small business to external regulation', *Industrial Relations Journal,* 13, 3, pp. 40–49.

Fourcade, C. (1984), 'The demarriage of firms: international comparisons', *International Small Business Journal,* 3, 2, pp. 46–55.

Furino, A. (ed.) (1988) *Cooperation and Competition in the Global Economy: Issues and Strategies.* Cambridge, Mass.: Ballinger.

Galbraith, J.K. (1971). *The New Industrial State.* Boston: Houghton Mifflin.

Galbraith, J.R. (1974), 'Organization Design: An Information Processing View', *Interfaces,* 4, pp. 28–36.

Ganguly, P. (1985), *UK Small Business Statistics and International Comparisons,* London: Paul Chapman Publishing.

Gardner, D.M. (1983), 'The marketing concept: its dimensions for the 'big' small firm', in G.E. Hills, D.J. Barnaby, and L.R. Duffus (eds) *Marketing and Small Business Entrepreneurship,* Washington, D.C.: International Council for Small Business.

Gerlach, M.L. (1992), *Alliance Capitalism: the Social Organization of Japanese Business,* Berkeley: University of California Press.

Gersick, C.J.G. (1991), 'Revolutionary change theories: a multilevel exploration of the punctuated equilibrium paradigm', *Academy of Management Review,* 16, 1, pp. 10–36.

Ghemawat, P. (1991). *Commitment: The Dynamic Of Strategy.* New York: Free Press.

Gibb, A. (1984), 'The small business challenge to management', *Journal of European Training,* 7, pp. 3–41.

Gibb, A. and Davies, L. (1990), 'In pursuit of frameworks for the development of growth models of the small business', *International Small Business Journal,* 10, 1, pp. 15–31.

Giddens, A. (1979), *Central Problems in Social Theory,* London: Macmillan.

Giles, E. and Starkey, K. (1988), 'The Japanisation of Xerox', *New Technology, Work and Employment,* 3, 2, pp. 125–142.

Glaser, B. and Strauss, A. (1967). *The Discovery of Grounded Theory: Strategies of Qualitative Research.* London: Weidenfeld and Nicholson.

Glueck, W.F. (1980), *Business Policy and Strategic Management*, Tokyo: McGraw-Hill.

Goffee, R. and Scase, R. (1985), *Women in Charge: The Experience of Female Entrepreneurs*, London: Allen & Unwin.

Goffman, E. (1968), *Asylums*, Harmondsworth: Penguin.

Goodman, E., Bamford, J. and Saynor, P. (eds) (1989), *Small Firms and Industrial Districts in Italy*, London and New York: Routledge.

Goss, D. (1991), *Small Business and Society*, London: Routledge.

Gow, I. (1987), 'Management education, training and development in Japan', in C. Handy, I. Gow, C. Gordon, C. Randlesome and M. Moloney *The Making of Managers: a Report on Management Education, Training and Development in the United States, West Germany, France, Japan, and the UK*, London: National Economic Development Office.

Granovetter, M. (1984), 'Small is bountiful: Labor markets and establishment size', *American Sociological Review*, 49, pp. 323–334.

Grant, R.M. (1991), 'The resource-based theory of competitive advantage: Implications for strategy formulation', *California Management Review*, 53, 3, pp. 114–135.

Gray, B. and Ariss, S.S. (1985), 'Politics and strategic change across organizational life cycles', *Academy of Management Review*, 10, 4, pp. 707–723.

Greiner, L.E. (1972), 'Evolution and revolution as organizations grow', *Harvard Business Review*, 50, July/August, pp. 37–46.

Gunnigle, P. and Brady, T. (1984), 'The management of industrial relations in the small firm', *Employee Relations*, 6, 5, pp. 21–24.

Gupta, A.K. (1984), 'Contingency linkages between strategy and general manager characteristics: a conceptual examination', *Academy of Management Review*, 9, 4, pp. 399–412.

Guth, W.D. and A. Ginsberg (1990), 'Guest editors' introduction: corporate entrepreneurship', *Strategic Management Journal*, 11(S), pp. 5–15.

Hakim, A. (1987), 'Trends in the flexible workforce', *Employment Gazette*, 95, 11, pp. 549–560.

Hall, D.T. (1976). *Careers in Organizations*. Santa Monica, Calif.: Goodyear.

Hambrick, D. and MacMillan, I. (1984), 'Asset parsimony – managing assets to manage profits', *Sloan Management Review*, 25, Winter, pp. 67–74.

Hampden-Turner, (1990). *Charting the Corporate Mind*. New York: Free Press.

Handler, W.C. (1990), 'Succession in family firms: a mutual role adjustment between entrepreneur and new generation family members', *Entrepreneurship: Theory and Practice*, 15, 1, pp. 37–51.

Hayes, R. H., Wheelwright, S. C., and Clark, K. B. (1988). *Dynamic Manufacturing: Creating the Learning Organization*. New York: Free Press.

Hebert, R.F. and Link, A.N. (1989), 'In search of the meaning of entrepreneurship', *Small Business Economics*, 1, pp. 39–49.

Hedberg, B. (1981), 'How organizations learn and unlearn', in P.C. Nystrom and W.H. Starbuck (eds) *Handbook of Organizational Design, Vol. 1*, Oxford: Oxford University Press, pp. 8–27.

Hedberg, B. and Jonsson, S. (1977), 'Strategy making as a discontinuous process', *International Studies of Management and Organisation*, VII, pp. 89–109.

Hellgren, B. and Stjernberg, T. (1987), 'Networks: an analytical tool for understanding complex decision processes', *International Studies of Management and Organization*, 17, 1, pp. 81–102.

Hendry, C. (1990), 'The corporate management of human resources under conditions of decentralisation', *British Journal of Management*, 1, 2, pp. 91–103.

Hendry, C. (1991), 'International comparisons of human resource management: putting the firm in the frame', *International Journal of Human Resource Management*, 2, 3, pp. 415–439.

Hendry, C. (1993), 'Personnel leadership in technical and human resource change', in J. Clark (ed.), *Human Resource Management and Technical Change*, London/Newbury Park/New Delhi: Sage.

Hendry, C. (1994), *Human Resource Strategies for International Growth*, London and New York: Routledge.

Hendry, C. (1995), *Human Resource Management: A Strategic Approach to Employment*, London: Butterworth–Heinemann.

Hendry, C., Arthur, M.B. and Jones, A.M. (1991a), 'Learning from doing: adaptation and resource management in the smaller firm', 11th Annual International Conference of the Strategic Management Society, Toronto, October.

Hendry, C., Arthur, M.B. and Jones, A.M. (1991b), 'Entrepreneurship and the creation of new momentum in the small–medium firm', unpublished paper, University of Warwick.

Hendry, C., Jones, A.M. and Arthur, M.B. (1991c), 'Skill supply, training and development in the small–medium enterprise', *International Small Business Journal*, 10, 1, pp. 68–72.

Hendry, C., Jones, A.M., Arthur, M.B. and Pettigrew, A. (1991), *Human Resource Development in Small-to-Medium-Sized Enterprises*, Research Report No. 88. Sheffield: Employment Department.

Hendry, C., Jones, A.M. and Cooper, N. (1994). *Creating a Learning Organisation: Strategies for Change*. Sutton Coldfield: Man-made Fibres Industry Training Organisation.

Henslin, J.M. (1981), 'What makes for trust?' in J.M. Henslin (ed.) *Down to Earth Sociology*, 3rd edition, New York: Free Press.

Hirsch, P. (1987). *Pack Your Own Parachute*. Reading, Mass.: Addison-Wesley.

Hjern, R., Hull, C., Finlayson, D., Gillespie, A. and Goddard, M. (1980), *Helping Small Firms Grow*, International Institute of Management, Discussion Paper Series, Berlin.

Hodgson, G.M. (1988), *Economics and Institutions*, Cambridge: Polity Press.

Hofer, C.W. and Schendel, D. (1978), *Strategy Formulation: Analytic Concepts*, St Paul, Minn.: West Publishing.

Hofstede, G. (1992), 'Cultural dimensions in people management: the socialization perspective', in V. Pucik, N.M. Tichy and C.K. Barnett (eds) *Globalizing Management: Creating and Leading the Competitive Organization*, New York: Wiley.

Holmes, S., Kelly, G. and Cunningham, R. (1991), 'The small firm information cycle: a reappraisal', *International Small Business Journal*, 9, 2, pp. 41–53.

Hornaday, R.W (1990), 'Dropping the E-words from small business research', *Journal of Small Business Management*, 28, 4, pp. 22–33.

Hrebiniak, L.G. and Joyce, W.F. (1985), 'Organizational adaptation: Strategic choice and environmental determinism', *Administrative Science Quarterly*, 30, pp. 336–349.

Huber, G.P. (1991), 'Organizational learning: the contributing processes and literatures', *Organization Science*, 2, 1, pp. 88–115.

Hudson, J. (1987), 'The age, regional and industrial structure of company liquidations', *Journal of Business Finance and Accounting*, 14, 2, pp. 199–213.

Imrie, R.F. (1986), 'Work decentralisation from large to small firms: a preliminary analysis of subcontracting', *Environment and Planning*, 18, pp. 949–965.

Ingham, G. (1970). *Size of Industrial Organisation and Worker Behaviour*. Cambridge: Cambridge University Press.

Jackson, S.E. and Dutton, J.E. (1988), 'Discerning threats and opportunities', *Administrative Science Quarterly*, 33, pp. 370–387.

Jarillo, J.C. (1988), 'On strategic networks', *Strategic Management Journal*, 9, 1, pp. 31–41.

Jarillo, J.C. (1989), 'Entrepreneurship and growth: the strategic use of external resources', *Journal of Business Venturing*, 4, pp. 133–147.

Jelinek, M. (1979). *Institutionalising innovation*. New York: Praeger.

Johannisson, B. (1988), 'Business formation – a network approach', *Scandinavian Journal of Management*, 4, 3/4, pp. 83–99.

Johannisson, B. (1991), 'Economies of overview – guiding the external growth of small firms', *International Small Business Journal*, 10, 1, pp. 32–44.

Johanson, J. and Mattsson, L-G. (1988), 'Internationalization in industrial systems – a network approach', in N. Hood and J-E, Vahlne (eds) *Strategies in Global Competition*, London: Croom Helm.

Jones, A.M. and Hendry, C. (1992). *The Learning Organization: A Review of Literature and Practice*. London: The Human Resource Development Partnership

Judkins, P., West, D. and Drew, J. (1985). *Networking in Organizations: The Rank Xerox Experiment*. Aldershot: Gower.

Kanter, R.M. (1989). *When Giants Learn to Dance*. London: Routledge.

Katzenbach, J.R. and Smith, D.K. (1993). *The Wisdom of Teams*. Boston: Harvard Business School Press.

Keasey, K. and Watson, R. (1987a), 'The prediction of small company failure: some behavioural evidence for the UK', *Accounting and Business Research*, 65, Winter, pp. 49–58.

Keasey, K. and Watson, R. (1987b), 'Non-financial symptoms and the prediction of small company failure: a test of the Argenti hypothesis', *Journal of Business, Finance and Accounting*, 14, 3, pp. 335–354.

Keasey, K. and Watson, R. (1991), 'The state of the art of small firm failure prediction: achievements and prognosis', *International Journal of Small Business*, 9, 4, pp. 11–29.

Keep, E. (1989), 'Corporate training strategies: The vital component?' in J. Storey (ed.) *New Perspectives on Human Resource Management*, London: Routledge, pp. 109–125.

Kerr, C. (1954), 'The Balkinisation of labor markets', in E.W. Bakke (ed.) *Labor Mobility and Economic Opportunity*, Cambridge, Mass.: MIT Press, pp. 92–110.

Kirk, J. and Miller, M.L. (1986). *Reliability and Validity in Qualitative Research*. Newbury Park, Calif.: Sage.

Kirkpatrick, D. (1988), 'Smart ways to use new temps', *Fortune*, 117, 4, pp. 110–116.

Kirzner, I.M. (1985). *Discovery and the Capitalist Process*. Chicago: University of Chicago Press.

Koike, K. (1988). *Understanding Industrial Relations in Modern Japan*. New York: St. Martin's Press.

Kroeger, C.V. (1974), 'Managerial development in the small firm', *California Management Review*, 17, Fall, pp. 41–47.

Kudla, R.J. (1980), 'The effects of strategic planning on common stock returns', *Academy of Management Journal*, 23, 1, pp. 5–20.

Lave, J. and Wenger, E. (1991). *Situated Learning: Legitimate Peripheral Participation*. New York: Cambridge University Press.

Lavoie, D. and Culbert, S.A. (1978). 'Stages of organization and environment', *Human Relations*, 31, pp. 417–438.

Lawler, E.E. III (1986). *High Involvement Management*. San Francisco: Jossey-Bass.

Lawler, E.E. III (1992). *The Ultimate Advantage: Creating the High-Involvement Organization*. San Francisco: Jossey-Bass.

Lawrence, P. (1985), 'The history of human resource management in American industry', in R.E. Walton and P.R. Lawrence (eds) *HRM Trends and Challenges*, Boston: Harvard Business School Press, pp. 15–34.

Lawrence, R.Z. and Saxonhouse, G.R. (1991), 'Efficient or exclusionist? The behavior of Japanese corporate groups', *Brookings Papers on Economic Activities*, 1, pp. 311–341.

Lazarson, M.H. (1988), 'Organisational growth of small firms: an outcome of markets and hierarchies?', *American Sociological Review*, 53, pp. 330–342.

Lee, D.J. (1981), 'Skill, craft, and class: a theoretical critique and a critical case', *Sociology*, 15, 1, pp. 56–78.

Legge, K. (1989), 'Human resource management: A critical analysis', in J. Storey (ed.) *New Perspectives on Human Resource Management*, London: Routledge, pp. 19–40.

Legge, K. and Gowler, D. (1989), 'Rhetoric in bureaucratic careers: managing the meaning of management success', in M.B. Arthur, D.T. Hall and B.S. Lawrence (eds) *Handbook of Career Theory*, New York: Cambridge University Press, pp. 437–453.

Lessem, R. (1991). *Total Quality Learning: Creating a Learning Organisation*. Oxford: Blackwell.

Levitt, T. (1972), 'Production line approach to service', *Harvard Business Review*, September/October, pp. 41–52.

Levitt, B. and March, J.G. (1988), 'Organizational learning', *Annual Review of Sociology*, 14, pp. 319–340.

Lippman, S.A. and Rumelt, R.P. (1982), 'Uncertain imitability: an analysis of interfirm differences in efficiency under competition', *Bell Journal of Economics*, 13, pp. 418–438.

Loasby, B.J. (1992). *Equilibrium and Evolution*. Manchester: Manchester University Press.

Lorange, P. (1986), 'Human resource management in multinational cooperative ventures', *Human Resource Management*, 25, 1, pp. 133–148.

Lorenz, E.H. (1989), 'The search for flexibility: subcontracting networks in French and British engineering', in P. Hirst and J. Zeitlin (eds) *Reversing Industrial Decline? Industrial Structure and Industrial Policy in Britain and Her Competitors*, Oxford: Berg.

Lounamaa, P.H. and March, J.G. (1987), 'Adaptive coordination of a learning team', *Management Science*, 33, pp. 107–123.

Lovering, J. (1990), 'A perfunctory sort of post-fordism: economic restructuring and labour market segmentation in Britain in the 1980s', *Work, Employment and Society*, May, pp. 9–28.

Lydall, H.F. (1958), 'Aspects of competition in manufacturing industry', *Bulletin of Oxford Institute of Economics and Statistics*, 20, 4, pp. 319–337.

Macmillan, I.C., L. Zeman, and P.N. Subbanarasimha (1987), 'Criteria distinguishing successful from unsuccessful ventures in the venture screening process', *Journal of Business Venturing*, 2, 2, pp. 177–191.

Mahoney, J.T. and Pandian, J.R. (1992), 'The resource-based view within the conversation of strategic management', *Strategic Management Journal*, 13, pp. 363–380.

Mainiero, L.A. (1986), 'Early career factors that differentiate technical management careers from technical professional careers', *Journal of Management*, 12, pp. 561–75.

March, J.G. and Olsen, J.P. (1975), 'The uncertainty of the past: organizational learning under ambiguity', *European Journal of Political Research*, 3, pp. 147–171.

March, J.G. and Simon, H.A. (1958). *Organisations*. New York: Wiley.

Marlow, S. and Patton, D. (1993), 'Employment relations, human resource management strategies, and the smaller firm', unpublished paper, De Montfort University.

Marshall, A. (1911). *Industry and Trade*. London: Macmillan.

McClelland, D.C. (1961). *The Achieving Society.* Princeton, NJ: Van Nostrand.

McGann, A. (1993), 'The UK enterprise population 1979–1991', *NatWest Review of Small Business Trends*, 3, 1, pp. 5–13.

McGee, J. (1989), 'Barriers to growth: the effects of market structure', in Barber, J., Metcalfe, J.S. and Porteous, M. (eds) *Barriers to Growth in Small Firms*, London and New York: Routledge.

McKiernan, P. and Morris, C. (1992), 'Strategic planning and financial performance in the UK SMEs: does formality matter?', unpublished paper, University of Warwick.

Melin, L. (1987), 'The field of force metaphor: A study in industrial change', *International Studies of Management and Organisation*, XVII, 1, pp. 24–33.

Miles, M.B. and Huberman, A.M. (1984). *Qualitative Data Analysis: A Sourcebook of New Methods.* Newbury Park, Calif.: Sage.

Miles, R.E. and Snow, C.C. (1978). *Organisational Strategy, Structure, and Process.* Kogakusha: McGraw Hill.

Miles, R.E. and Snow, C.C. (1986), 'Organizations: new concepts and forms', *California Management Review*, 28, 3, pp. 62–73.

Miller, D.C. and Form, W.H. (1951). *Industrial Sociology.* New York: Harper and Row.

Miller, D. and Friesen, P.H. (1980), 'Momentum and revolution in organisational adaptation', *Academy of Management Journal*, 23, 4, pp. 591–614.

Miller, D. and Friesen P.H. (1980). *Organizations: A Quantum View.* Englewood Cliffs, NJ: Prentice Hall.

Miller, D. and Friesen, P.H. (1984), 'A longitudinal study of the corporate life cycle', *Management Science*, 30, pp. 1161–1183.

Milne, T. and Thompson, M. (1982), 'The infant business development process', Management Studies Working Paper No. 2, University of Glasgow.

Mintzberg, H. (1978), 'Patterns in strategy formation', *Management Science*, May, pp. 934–948.

Mintzberg, H. (1979). *The Structuring of Organisations.* Englewood Cliffs, NY: Prentice Hall.

Mintzberg, H. (1987), 'Crafting strategy', *Harvard Business Review*, 65, July/August, pp. 66–75.

Mintzberg, H. (1989). *Mintzberg on Management.* New York: Free Press.

Mintzberg, H. (1990), 'The design school: reconsidering the basic premises of strategic management', *Strategic Management Journal*, 11, 3, pp. 171–195.

Mitchell, D.J.B. (1990), Employee benefits and the new economy: a proposal for reform', *California Management Review*, 33, 1, pp. 113–130.

Mody, A. (1989), 'Firm strategies for costly engineering learning', *Management Science*, 35, pp. 496–512.

Moore, W.L. and Tushman, M.L. (1982), 'Managing innovation over the product life cycle', in M.L. Tushman and W.L. Moore (eds.) *Reading in the Management of Innovation*, Boston: Pitman Press.

Morgan, G (1986). *Images of Organization.* Newbury Park, Calif.: Sage.

Morris, J. and Imrie, R. (1992). *Transforming Buyer-Supplier Relations: Japanese-Style Industrial Practices in a Western Context.* London: Macmillan.

National Economic Development Council (1990). *Developing Suppliers in Engineering.* London: National Economic Development Office.

Nelson, R.R. (1991), 'Why do firms differ, and how does it matter?', *Strategic Management Journal*, 12, pp. 61–74.

Nelson, R.R. and Winter, S.G. (1982). *An Evolutionary Theory of Economic Change.* Cambridge, Mass.: Belknap.

Neustadt, R.E. and May, E.R. (1986). *Thinking in time: The uses of history for decision makers.* New York: Free Press.

New York Times (The) (1992), 'Harvard Business Review cancels an article on IBM', 21 December, 1992.

Nonaka, I. (1991), 'The knowledge-creating company', *Harvard Business Review*, November/December, pp. 96–104.

Nystrom, P.C. and Starbuck, W.H. (1984), To avoid organizational crises, unlearn', *Organizational Dynamics*, 12, Spring, pp. 53–65.

O'Neill, H.M., Saunders, C.B. and Hoffman, A.N. (1987), 'Beyond the entrepreneur: planning as the organization grows', *Business Forum*, 12, pp. 38–40.

Ohno, T. (1984), 'How the Toyota production system was created', in K. Sato and Y. Hoshino (eds) *The Anatomy of Japanese Business*, London: Croom-Helm.

Orr, J. (1990), 'Sharing knowledge, celebrating identity: war stories and community memory in a service culture', in D.S. Middleton and D. Edwards (eds) *Collective Remembering: Memory in Society*, Beverly Hills, Calif.: Sage.

Orton, J.D. and Weick, K.E. (1990), 'Loosely coupled systems: a reconceptualization', *Academy of Management Review*, 15, 2, pp. 203–223.

Osterman, P. (1987), 'Choice of employment systems in internal labor markets', *Industrial Relations*, 26, 1, pp. 46–67.

Ouchi, W.G (1981) *Theory Z*. Reading, Mass.: Addison-Wesley.

Pavitt, K., Robson, M. and Townsend, J. (1989), 'A fresh look at the size distribution of innovating firms', in F. Arcangeli *et al.* (eds) *Frontiers of Innovation Diffusion*, Oxford: Oxford University Press.

Peat Marwick McLintock (1991), 'UK Business Expansion Falls Behind Other Major EC Countries', London, 3 June.

Peck, J.A. (1989), 'Labour market segmentation theory', *Labour and Industry*, 2, 1, pp. 119–144.

Pedler, M, Burgoyne, J. and Boydell, T. (1991). *The Learning Company*. London: McGraw-Hill.

Penrose, E. (1959). *The Theory of the Growth of the Firm*. Oxford: Basil Blackwell.

Perry, C. (1985), 'Stage theories of small business growth', *Management Forum*, December, pp. 190–203.

Perry, C. (1987), 'Growth strategies for small firms: principles and case studies', *International Small Business Journal*, 5, 2, pp. 17–25.

Peters, T. (1991), 'Competitive strategies and cooperation', Address to the Strategic Management Society Annual Conference, Toronto, October.

Peters, T.J. and Waterman, R.H. (1982). *In Search of Excellence*. New York: Harper and Row.

Pettigrew, A.M. (1979), 'On studying organizational cultures', *Administrative Science Quarterly*, 24, pp. 570–581.

Pettigrew, A.M. (1985). *The Awakening Giant*. Oxford: Basil Blackwell.

Pettigrew, A.M. (1990), 'Longitudinal field research on change: Theory and practice', *Organisation Science*, 1, pp. 267–292.

Pettigrew, A.M., Arthur, M.B. and Hendry, C. (1990). *Training and Human Resource Management in Small-to-Medium-Sized Enterprises: A Critical Review of the Literature and a Model for Future Research*. Sheffield: Training Agency.

Pettigrew, A., Hendry, C., and Sparrow, P. (1989). *Training in Britain: Employers' Perspectives on Human Resources*. London: HMSO.

Pettigrew, A.M. and Whipp, R. (1991). *Managing Change for Competitive Success*. Oxford: Basil Blackwell.

Pfeffer, J. (1983), 'Organizational demography', in L.L. Cummings and B.M. Shaw (eds.) *Research in Organizational behaviour, vol. 5*, Greenwich, CT: JAI Press.

Pfeffer, J. and Baron, J.N. (1988), 'Taking the workers back out: recent trends in the structuring of employment', in B. Staw (ed.) *Research in Organizational Behaviour, Volume 10*, JAI Press, pp. 257–303.

Piore, M. and Sabel, C. (1984). *The Second Industrial Divide: Possibilities for Prosperity.* New York: Basic Books.

Pitt, M. (1989), 'Corporate birth, crisis and rebirth: the emergence of four small UK service firms', in R. Mansfield (ed.) *Frontiers of Management,* London and New York: Routledge, pp. 262–277.

Pollert, A. (1988), The flexible firm: fixation or fact?', *Work, Employment and Society,* 2, 3, pp. 281–316.

Porter, M.E. (1980). *Competitive strategy.* New York: Free Press.

Porter, M.E. (1987), 'From competitive advantage to corporate strategy', *Harvard Business Review,* May-June, pp. 43–59.

Porter, M.E. (1990). *The Competitive Advantage of Nations.* London: Macmillan.

Prahalad, C.K. and Hamel, G. (1990), 'The core competence of the corporation', *Harvard Business Review,* 68, May/June, pp. 79–91.

Pucik, V. (1988), 'Strategic alliances, organizational learning, and competitive advantage: the HRM agenda', *Human Resource Management,* 27, 1, pp. 77–93.

Pyke, F. (1988), 'Co-operative practices among small and medium-sized establishments', *Work, Employment and Society,* 2, 3, pp. 352–365.

Quinn, J.B. (1992). *Intelligent Enterprise.* New York: Free Press.

Quinn, J.B. (1977), Strategic goals: process and politics', *Sloan Management Review,* 19, 1, pp. 21–37.

Quinn, J.B. (1991), 'Strategies for change', in H. Mintzberg and J.B. Quinn (eds) *The Strategy Process: Concepts, Contexts, Cases,* Englewood Cliffs, NJ: Prentice Hall International.

Quinn, R.E. and Cameron, K. (1983), 'Organizational life cycles and shifting criteria of effectiveness: some preliminary evidence', *Management Science,* 29, 1, pp. 33–51.

Rainnie, A. (1989). *Industrial Relations in Small Firms, Small Isn't Beautiful.* London: Routledge.

Rainnie, A. (1991), 'Flexibility and small firms: prospects for the 1990s', Hatfield Polytechnic Business School Working Paper 1991/2.

Ratti, R. (1991), 'Small and medium-size enterprises, local synergies and spatial cycles of innovation', in R. Camagni (ed.) *Innovation Networks: Spatial Perspectives,* London: Belhaven.

Redding, S.G. (1990). *The Spirit of Chinese Capitalism.* New York: de Gruyter.

Reddy, N.M. and Rao, M.V.H. (1990), 'The industrial market as an interfirm organization', *Journal of Management Studies,* 27, 1, pp. 43–59.

Reich, R.B. (1991). *The Work of Nations.* New York: Knopf.

Reich, R.B. (1987), 'Entrepreneurship reconsidered: the team as hero', *Harvard Business Review,* May-June, pp. 77–83.

Report of the President (1990). *The State of Small Business.* Washington: United States Government Printing Office.

Richardson, G.B. (1972), 'The organization of industry', *Economic Journal,* 82, pp. 883–96.

Roberts, I.P. (1986), 'Industrial Relations in Small Firms: In Search of a Framework', Ninth International Small Firms Policy and Research Conference, Gleneagles.

Robinson, R.B. (1983), 'Measures of small firm effectiveness', *Journal of Small Business,* 21, 2.

Robinson, R.B. and Pearce, J.A. (1983), 'The impact of formalised strategic planning on financial performance in small organisations', *Strategic Management Journal,* 4, 3, pp. 197–207.

Robinson, T. (1990). *Partners in Delivering the Goods: the changing relationship between large companies and their small suppliers.* Mimeo, 3i, London.

Romanelli, E. (1989), 'Environments and strategies of organisation start-up: effects on early survival', *Administrative Science Quarterly,* 34, pp. 369–387.

Romano, C.A. (1989), 'Research strategies for small business: a case study approach', *International Small Business Journal*, 7, 4, pp. 35–43.

Rosen, C. and Young, K.M. (1991). *Understanding Employee Ownership*. Ithica, NY: ILR Press.

Rothwell, R. (1986), 'The role of small firms in technological innovation', in J. Curran, J. Stanworth and D. Watkins (eds) *The Survival of the Small Firm, Volume 2: Employment, Growth, Technology and Politics*, Aldershot: Gower.

Rothwell, R. (1989), 'Small firms, innovation and industrial change, *Small Business Economics*, 1, pp. 51–64.

Rumelt, R.P. (1979), 'Evaluation of strategy: theory and models', in D. Schendel and C.W. Hofer *Strategic Management*, Boston: Little, Brown.

Rumelt, R.P., Schendel, D. and Teece, D.J. (1991), 'Strategic management and economics', *Strategic Management Journal*, 12(S), pp. 5–30.

Rumelt, R.P. (1984), 'Towards a strategic theory of the firm', in Lamb, R.B. (ed.) *Competitive Strategic Management*, Englewood Cliffs, N.J.: Prentice Hall, pp. 556–570.

Sandberg, W.R. (1992), 'Strategic management's potential contribution to a theory of entrepreneurship', *Entrepreneurship Theory and Practice*, Spring, pp. 73–90.

Sato, Y. (1989), 'Small business in Japan: A historical perspective', *Small Business Economics*, 1, pp. 121–128.

Saxenian, A. (1990), 'Regional networks and the resurgence of Silicon Valley', *California Management Review*, 33, 1, pp. 89–112.

SBRT (1991), *Small Business Research Trust Quarterly Survey of Small Business in Britain*.

Schein, E.H. (1978). *Career Dynamics, Matching Individual and Organizational Needs*. Reading, Mass.: Addison-Wesley.

Schein, E.H. (1983), 'The role of the founder in creating organizational culture', *Organizational Dynamics*, 11, Summer, pp. 13–28.

Schein, E.H. (1990), 'Reassessing the "divine rights" of managers', *Sloan Management Review*, 30, 3, pp. 63–68.

Schonberger, R.J. (1990). *Building a Chain of Customers*. New York: Free Press.

Schumacher, E.F. (1973). *Small is Beautiful*. New York: Harper and Row.

Schumpeter, J.A. (1934). *The Theory of Economic Development*. Cambridge, Mass.: Harvard University Press.

Schumpeter, J.A. (1949). *Change and the Entrepreneur*. Harvard University: Research Centre in Entrepreneurial History.

Scott, M., Roberts, I., Holroyd, G. and Sawbridge, D. (1989). *Management and Industrial Relations in Small Firms*, Research Paper No. 70. London: Department of Employment.

Senge, P.M. (1990). *The Fifth Discipline: The Art of Organizational Learning Systems*. New York: Doubleday.

Sengenberger, W., Loveman, G. and Piore, M.J. (1990). *The Re-Emergence of Small Enterprises: Industrial Restructuring in Industrial Countries*. Geneva: International Institute for Labour Studies.

Shamir, B., House, R.J. and Arthur, M.B. (1993), 'The transformational effects of charismatic leadership', *Organisation Science*, 4, pp. 577–594.

Shapero, A. (1971). *An Action Programme for Entrepreneurs*. Austin, Texas: Multi-Disciplinary Research Inc.

Shea, J.E. (1980), 'Target your market before you create', *Manage*, April, pp. 16–19.

Shearman, C. and Burrell, G. (1988), 'New technology based firms and the emergence of new industries: some employment implications', *New Technology, Work and Employment*, 3, 2, pp. 87–99.

Shostack, G.L. (1977), 'Breaking free from product marketing', *Journal of Marketing*, 41, pp. 73–80.

Shrivastava, P. and Schneider, S. (1984), Organisational frames of reference', *Human Relations*, 37, pp. 795–807.

Shrivastava, P. (1983), 'A typology of organizational learning systems', *Journal of Management Studies*, 20, 1, pp. 7–28.

Shutt, J. and Whittington, R. (1987), 'Fragmentation strategies and the rise of small units: Cases from the North West', *Regional Studies*, 21, 1, pp. 13–23.

Siebert, W.S. and Addison, J. (1991), 'Internal labour markets: causes and consequences', *Oxford Review of Economic Policy*, 7, 1, pp. 1–17.

Slocum, W. L. (1974). *Occupational Careers*. Chicago: Aldine Publishing Company.

Small Business Research Trust (1990). *Quarterly Survey of Exporters*, vol. 1, No. 1.

Small and Medium Enterprise Agency (1986). *Outline of the Small and Medium Enterprise Policies of the Japanese Government*. Tokyo: the Ministry of International Trade and Industry in cooperation with the Japan Small Business Corporation.

Smith, N.R (1967). *The Entrepreneur and His Firm: The Relationship between Type of Man and Type of Company*. East Lansing: Michigan, Michigan State University Press.

Smith, N.R. and Miner, J.B. (1983), 'Type of entrepreneur, type of firm, and managerial motivation: implications for organisational life cycle theory', *Strategic Management Journal*, 4, 4, pp. 325–340.

Soeters, J.L. and Schwan, R. (1990), 'Towards an empirical assessment of internal labour market configurations', *International Journal of Human Resource Management*, 1, 3, pp. 271–287.

Sonnenfeld, J.A. (1989), 'Career system profiles and strategic staffing', in M.B. Arthur, D.T. Hall and B.S Lawrence (eds) *Handbook of Career Theory*, Cambridge/Port Chester/Melbourne/Sydney: Cambridge University Press.

Spender, J-C. (1991), 'Organisational Renewal: Innovation and the Organisational Knowledge-Base', unpublished paper, Graduate School of Management, Rutgers University.

Staehle, W.H. (1990), 'Human resource management and corporate strategy', in R. Pieper (ed.) *Human Resource Management: An International Comparison*, Berlin and New York: Walter de Gruyter.

Stahlman, M. (1992), '"Big Blue" sees red', *The Boston Globe*, December 20.

Stanworth, J. and Curran, J. (1973). *Management Motivation in the Smaller Business*. Epping: Gower.

Stanworth, M.J.K. and Curran, J. (1976), 'Growth in the small firm – an alternative view', *Journal of Management Studies*, 13, 2, pp. 95–110.

Stanworth, J. and Gray, C. (eds) (1991). *Bolton 20 Years On*. London: Chapman.

Stanworth, J., Stanworth, C., Granger, B. and Blyth, S. (1990), 'Who becomes an entrepreneur?', *International Small Business Journal*, 8, 1, pp. 11–22.

Starbuck, W.H. and Hedberg, B.L.T. (1977), 'Saving an organisation from a stagnating environment', in H. Thorelli (ed.) *Strategy + structure = performance*, Bloomington: Indiana University Press.

Starr, J.A. and MacMillan, I.C. (1991), 'Resource Parsimony and the 'Miser's Touch': New Venture Investment Strategies of Habitual Entrepreneurs', 11th Annual International Conference of the Strategic Management Society, Toronto, October.

Stevenson, H.H. (1983), 'A perspective on entrepreneurial management', working paper, Harvard Business School, reprinted in J. Kao, *Entrepreneurship, Creativity, and Organisation: Text, Cases, and Readings*, Englewood Cliffs, NJ: Prentice-Hall International.

Stevenson, H.H. and Gumpert, D.E (1985), 'The heart of entrepreneurship', *Harvard Business Review*, March–April, pp. 85–94.

Stevenson, H.H. and Jarillo, J.C. (1989), A paradigm of entrepreneurship: entrepreneurial management', Working Paper #89–040, Harvard Business School.

Stevenson, H.H. and Jarillo J.C. (1990), 'A paradigm of entrepreneurship: entrepreneurial management', *Strategic Management Journal*, 11(5), pp. 17–27.

Stevenson, H.H. and Sahlman, W.A. (1989), 'The entrepreneurial process', in P. Burns and J. Dewhurst (eds) *Small Business and Entrepreneurship*, Basingstoke and London: MacMillan.

Stewart, A. (1989). *Team Entrepreneurship*. Newbury Park: Sage.

Stoner, C.R. (1983), 'Planning in small manufacturing firms: a survey', *Journal of Small Business Management*, January, pp. 34–41.

Stoner, C.R. (1987), 'Distinctive competence and competitive advantage', *Journal of Small Business Management*, 25, April, pp. 33–39.

Storey, D. (1982). *Entrepreneurship and the New Firm*. Beckenham: Croom Helm.

Storey, D.J. (1985), 'The problems facing new firms', *Journal of Management Studies*, 22, pp. 237–345.

Storey, D.J. (1988), 'The role of small and medium-sized enterprises in European job creation: Key issues for policy and research', in M. Giaoutzi, P. Nijkamp and D.J. Storey (eds) *Small and Medium Size Enterprises and Regional Development*, London: Routledge.

Storey, D.J. (1991), 'The Managerial Labour Market in Fast Growth Small Firms', unpublished paper, University of Warwick.

Storey, D.J and Johnson, S. (1987). *Are Small Firms the Answer to Unemployment?*. London: The Employment Institute.

Storey, D., Keasey, K., Watson, R. and Wynarczyk, P. (1987). *The Performance of Small Firms*. London: Croom Helm.

Storper, M. and Scott, A.J. (1990), 'Work organisation and local labour markets in an era of flexible production', *International Labour Review*, 129, 5, pp. 573–591.

Stratos Group (1990). *Strategic Orientations of Small European Businesses*. Aldershot: Avebury.

Super D.E. (1992), 'Towards a comprehensive theory of career development, in D.H. Montross and C.J. Shinkman (eds) *Career Development: Theory and Practice*, Springfield, Ill.: Charles C. Thomas, pp. 35–64.

Sweeny, G.P.S. (1987). *Innovation, Entrepreneurs and Regional Development*. London: Francis Pinter.

Szarka, J. (1990), 'Networking and small firms', *International Small Business Journal*, 9, 2, pp. 10–22.

Thomas, R.J. (1989), 'Blue-collar careers: meaning and choice in a world of constraints', in M.B. Arthur, D. T. Hall and B.S. Lawrence (eds) *Handbook of Career Theory*, London and New York: Cambridge University Press, pp. 354–379.

Thorelli, H.B. (1986), 'Networks: between markets and hierarchies', *Strategic Management Journal*, 7, 1, pp. 37–51.

Timmons, J.A. (1990). *New Venture Creation: Entrepreneurship in the 1990s*. Homewood, Ill.: Irwin.

Trevor, M. and Christie, I. (1988). *Manufacturers and Suppliers in Britain and Japan: Competiveness and The Growth of Small Firms*. London: Policy Studies Institute.

Tushman, M.L., W.H. Newman, and E. Romanelli (1986), 'Convergence and upheaval: managing the unsteady pace of organisational evolution', *California Management Review*, 29, 1, pp. 29–44.

United Nations Centre on Transnational Corporations (1988). *Transnational Corporations in World Development: Trends and Prospects*. New York: United Nations.

Venkataraman, S., Van de Ven, A., Buckeye, J. and Hudson, R. (1990), 'Starting up in a turbulent environment: a process model of failure among firms with high customer dependence', *Journal of Business Venturing*, 5, 5, 277–295.

Villemez, W.J. and Bridges, W.P. (1988), 'When bigger is better: differences in the individual-level effect of firm and establishment size', *American Sociological Review*, 53, pp. 237–255.

von Mises, L. (1949). *Human Action*, 3rd edition. New Haven, Connecticut: Yale University Press.

Vyakarnam, S. and Jacobs, R. (1993). *Teamstart – Overcoming the Blockages to Small Business Growth*. Enterprise Research and Development, St John's Innovation Centre, Cambridge.

Wall Street Journal, The (1992), 'IBM shares fall 11% as firm says it will cut 25,000 jobs and may trim dividend', 16 December.

Walsh, J.P. and Ungson, G.R. (1991), 'Organisational memory', *Academy of Management Review*, 16, 1, pp. 57–91.

Watkins, D. (1982), 'Management development and the owner manager', in T. Webb, R. Quince and D. Watkins (Eds.) *Small Business Research*, Aldershot: Gower.

Weick, K.E. (1979). *The Social Psychology of Organizing*. Reading, Mass.: Addison-Wesley.

Weick, K.E. and Berlinger, L.R. (1989), 'Career improvisation in self-designing organizations', in M.B. Arthur, D.T. Hall and B.S. Lawrence (eds) *Handbook of Career Theory*, Cambridge and New York: Cambridge University Press, pp. 313–328.

Whyte, W.F. and Whyte, K.K. (1988). *Making Mondragon: The Growth and Dynamics of the Worker Cooperative Movement*. Ithaca, NY: ILR Press.

Williamson, O.E. (1975). *Markets and Hierarchies*. New York: Free Press.

Williamson, O.E. (1981), 'The economics of organisation: the transaction cost approach', *American Journal of Sociology*, 87, pp. 548–77.

Williamson, O.E. (1985). *The Economic Institutions of Capitalism*. New York: Free Press.

Williamson, O.E. (1990), 'The firm as a nexus of treaties: an introduction', in M. Aoki, B. Gustaffson and O.E. Williamson (eds) *The Firm as a Nexus of Treaties*, London: Sage.

Williamson, O.E. (1991), 'Strategizing, economizing and economic organization', *Strategic Management Journal*, 12(S), pp. 75–94.

Wilson, P. and P. Gorb (1983), 'How large and small firms can grow together', *Long Range Planning*, 16, pp. 19–27.

Woo, C.Y., Willard, G.E. and Beckstead, S.M. (1990), 'Spinoffs, what are the gains?', *Journal of Business Strategy*, 10, 1, pp. 29–32.

Woodcock, C. (1990), 'Know-whos with the know-how', *The Guardian*, 17 December.

Yin, R.K. (1984; 1989). *Case Study Research: Design and Methods*. Newbury Park, Calif.: Sage.

Zan, L. and Zambon, S. (1993), 'Strategy, change, and the strategic approach: making sense in process', in L. Zan, S. Zambon and A.M. Pettigrew (eds) *Perspectives on Strategic Change*, Boston/Dordrecht/London: Kluwer Academic Publishers, pp. 1–41.

Author index

Subject index

acquisition 63, 95
ad hocracies 122, 165
adaptation 80–1, 84–6, 201–2;
   behaviour factors 85–6; causes 96–8;
   collective learning 184, 185;
   consequences 98–101;
   environmental beneficence 86–8;
   flexible resource base 91–3;
   incremental opportunism 88–9;
   innovative 60; niche specialization
   90–1; and opportunity 82; related
   products 93; routines 198; service/
   product packages 89–90; testing
   markets and boundaries 93–6
adventurism, niche-based 88,
   89–90
Aerospace Engineering 235–6; control
   34, 62; flexibility 91–2; leadership
   48; ownership 26 (n6); planning
   routines 192–3; quality
   improvement 180; skill
   development 148; specialized skills
   32, 115–17
apprenticeships 115, 142
Architectural Services 239;
   competitiveness 194–5;
   development 100, 182–3;
   recruitment 125–6; skill
   development 145, 150–1

belief systems 47–8
Bread Products 235; market
   penetration 32, 86; training 155, 185;
   unskilled workers 123–4
Brook, Geoff 55–7, 72–5
business development teams 182–3,
   191–2
business ethics 47–8

Cable Co. 239; casualization 127; crisis
   62; finance 26 (n6); networks 42–3;
   planning 106 (n3)
careers: blue collar 139; free agent 139,
   143, 160, 164, 168; in small firms 16;
   stages 140–1, 145–6
case studies, sample firms 227–30;
   adaptation 97; aggregate individual
   learning 175–7; crisis 59, 68, 70–1;
   employment 25 (n3); niche markets
   7–8; profitability 36–7; strategic
   planning 106; teams 179–81; see also
   individual firms
casualization 126–31
chief executive officers 163–4
Clean Air Co. 237; crisis 62; finance
   87–8, 90; hybrid skills 134;
   legislation 87; selective teams 182
collective learning 178–84, 185, 189
competencies transfer 96
competition 31, 194–5, 214, 222
competitive advantage, resource-
   based 30, 104
Construction Co. 238; casualization
   127; crisis 62; subcontracting 39–41;
   teamwork 183
construction industry: career structure
   129, 162; casualization 126–31;
   networking 39–41; recruitment
   144–5; subcontracting 39–41
consultation, management 49
consumer services 209–10
continuous learning 144
contracting 5, 39, 207, 226; see also
   subcontracting
control 45–6, 61–4, 68–9, 107 (n4)
Control of Substances Hazardous to
   Health (COSHH) 87
Convention Bureau 232; flexible